THE POLITICS OF COMPASSION

Immigration and asylum policy

Ala Sirriyeh

BRISTOL
UNIVERSITY
PRESS

First published in Great Britain in 2018 by

Bristol University Press
University of Bristol
1-9 Old Park Hill
Bristol
BS2 8BB
UK
t: +44 (0)117 954 5940
www.bristoluniversitypress.co.uk

North America office:
Policy Press
c/o The University of Chicago Press
1427 East 60th Street
Chicago, IL 60637, USA
t: +1 773 702 7700
f: +1 773-702-9756
sales@press.uchicago.edu
www.press.uchicago.edu

© Bristol University Press 2018

British Library Cataloguing in Publication Data
A catalogue record for this book is available from the British Library

Library of Congress Cataloging-in-Publication Data
A catalog record for this book has been requested

ISBN 978-1-5292-0042-3 hardcover
ISBN 978-1-5292-0045-4 ePub
ISBN 978-1-5292-0046-1 Mobi
ISBN 978-1-5292-0043-0 ePdf

Cover design by Andrew Corbett
Front cover image: Mahmoud Salameh

For my lovely dad, Hussein Sirriyeh

(1946–2018)

GLOBAL MIGRATION AND SOCIAL CHANGE

This series showcases ground-breaking research that looks at the nexus between migration, citizenship and social change. It advances new scholarship in migration and refugee studies and fosters cross- and interdisciplinary dialogue in this field. The series includes research-based monographs and edited collections, informed by a range of qualitative and quantitative research methods.

Series Editors:

Nando Sigona, Institute of Research into Superdiversity, University of Birmingham, UK: n.sigona@bham.ac.uk
Alan Gamlen, School of Social Sciences, Monash University, Australia: alan.gamlen@monash.edu

Forthcoming titles:

Time, migration and forced immobility: Sub-Saharan African migrants in Morocco by Inka Stock (2018)
Home-Land: Romanian Roma, domestic spaces and the state by Rachel Humphris (2018)

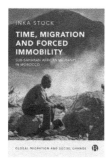
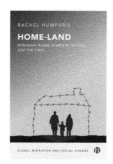

Contents

Acknowledgements   ix

Series Preface   xi

1   A Crisis of Compassion   1

2   The Emotional Politics of Immigration and Asylum   19

3   Emotion, Colonialism and Immigration Policy   37

4   The Intolerable Death of Alan Kurdi   51

5   Victims, Villains and Saviours   77

6   Withholding Compassion   97

7   Outrage, Responsibility and Accountability   117

8   Self-Care and Solidarity: The Undocumented   139
     Immigrant Youth Movement

9   Conclusion   161

References   169

Index   201

Acknowledgements

I began writing this book in 2015, in the summer before the tragic death of Alan Kurdi. I took some time out as I tried to process what the unprecedented outpouring of sentiments of compassion in response to his death meant. While (sadly) this did not lead me to substantially revise my analysis, it did have a strong impact on the way I have chosen to write and order my analysis and argument. Since then there have been so many seemingly 'game-changing' migration events (the election of Trump, the vote for Brexit, the closure of Manus Island detention centre, and so on), that it has been, to say the least, a challenging process writing this book.

I was very fortunate to have had such valuable guidance and support from the editorial team at Policy Press, especially Victoria Pittman and Shannon Kneis, during the editing process. Many thanks also to the anonymous reviewer who gave such helpful and encouraging feedback and suggestions on the final draft.

I am deeply grateful to all those people who took part in the interviews that I have drawn on in this book, particularly the undocumented activists in California who engaged in this research at such a challenging time in their lives.

I was very fortunate to receive funding from the Leverhulme Trust and from Santander Bank, which enabled me to conduct the research in California. I would also like to thank the Faculty of Humanities and Social Sciences at Keele University for funding me to travel to Australia for data collection for this study in 2016, and to the School of Social Science and Public Policy at Keele for granting me research leave for a semester during that same year, which gave me much needed writing time. While conducting fieldwork and writing this book in the US and Australia I also had the privilege of being hosted as a Visiting Scholar at the Institute for Culture and Society at Western Sydney University, and the Institute for the Study of Societal Issues at University of California, Berkeley. I am indebted to these institutes and the colleagues who facilitated my enjoyable and productive visits there.

There are many colleagues and friends who I would like to thank for the support they gave me through: suggestions and advice during fieldwork; reading chapters; providing very helpful and insightful critical engagements with the topics explored in the book; and by giving me encouragement, confidence boosts and comfort. I would particularly like to thank: Kim Adams, Andrew Dawson, Nadena Doherty, Esmee Hanna, Emma Head, Hannah Lewis, Katherine Ludwin, Nathan Manning, Lydia Martens, Ian Martin, Kirsteen Paton, Michelle Peterie, Shanthi Robertson, Amy Russell and Kate Smith. While writing this book I had the privilege of being hosted as an invited speaker and being given the opportunity to present and discuss some of the issues explored in this book at: the Sociology departments at the University of Warwick and the University of Newcastle; the Centre for Migration and Diaspora Studies at SOAS; Professor Pierrette Hondagneu-Sotelo's PhD migration studies class at the University of Southern California; the Institute for Culture and Society at the Western Sydney University; the Sydney Asia Pacific Migration Centre at the University of Sydney; and as part of a plenary at the ISA RC21 conference in 2017.

Most of all I am grateful, as always, to my lovely family. Thanks Elizabeth, Hussein, Matthew, Reema, Steve, Jesse and all the family pets for your love, warmth – both physical (Splash) and emotional, wonderful humour and somewhat delusional belief in my capabilities. Thanks Mum for the proof reading. This is the last time I promise!

Series Preface

The book you are holding, or reading on your screen, is the first in a new series with Bristol University Press, entitled *Global Migration and Social Change*. The series aims to open up new interdisciplinary terrain and to develop new scholarship in migration and refugee studies that is theoretically insightful and innovative, empirically rich, and policy engaged. We envisage commissioning at least 15 books over a period of 5 years, with the expectation that a higher proportion will emerge towards the end of this period, as the series gains momentum.

The idea for this new book series took shape in early 2016, as a refugee crisis – within a wider European crisis – was vividly revealing the intimate nexus between migration, citizenship and social change around the world. At that time, the EU's struggle to offer an answer to the arrival of a million forced migrants over a relatively short period of time ignited the interests of researchers from a wide range of disciplinary backgrounds.

Against that background, we envisaged several broad questions informing the series. How does the refugee crisis fit into the broader and longer term unfolding pattern of global migration? For example, how do the current flows to Europe interact with and alter flows of migrants and refugees in other regions? How are these interactions on the global scale mediated by the politics and policies emanating from Europe? Are the current population movements in and around Europe, and the crises of cooperation surrounding them, fundamentally changing broader global patterns of people on the move?

We set out to showcase research that looks beyond Europe to understand the continent's current crisis of cooperation within the broader dynamics of global migration, exile and social change writ large. We wanted to attract manuscripts that could reveal global trends and analyse the role of the European situation within them, and research findings that could explore how these wider trends figure within the migration goals and projects, and the upended everyday habits, of refugees and migrants themselves. A core aim of the series, as we initially conceived it, would be to analyze where these macro- and micro-patterns meet, in the interplay of migration and asylum politics, policies, and everyday practices and experiences.

Little did we know how much more urgent this agenda would become just a few months later. As we were developing the agenda above, the focus on the European situation still obscured the true worldwide extent of the crisis around migration, mobility and displacement. Hillary Clinton remained far in front of the Democratic primary pack and was the clear favourite to win the 2016 US presidential election. In the UK, the Remain campaign was still polling well ahead in the UK's referendum on EU membership. Meanwhile in Australia, the Prime Ministership had recently passed from immigration-hawk Tony Abbott to Malcolm Turnbull, known amongst other things for rising in parliament in 2005 to call for a more "compassionate and humane" asylum seeker policy. Despite the crisis in Europe, it seemed that much of the world had largely come to grips with what is sometimes called 'the human face of globalisation'.

Soon afterwards the world changed in two fundamental ways that deeply interested us and our new series. First, after a vicious Vote Leave campaign in which migrants were targeted as scapegoats for anti-EU sentiments in the UK, Britons voted narrowly to leave the European Union – a result that was unpredicted by almost everybody, including Prime Minister David Cameron who had called the referendum, who had campaigned to Remain, and whose political career came to an end the morning after. Second, Republican outsider Donald Trump had shocked the establishment by winning the US Presidency, after a campaign based on labelling migrants as "rapists" and "murderers", vowing to build a "Great Wall" across the US-Mexican Border, and calling for Muslim immigration to be banned. Immigrants and immigration bore the full brunt of a backlash against all forms of globalization. Migration had become central to the fates of powerful leaders, and to wider patterns of geopolitics.

Despite – or perhaps because of – the increasing urgency of the topic of global migration and social change, many of our initial aims remain central as we move forward with the series. As at the outset, we still aim to include research-based monographs and edited collections, informed by a range of qualitative and quantitative research methods. We are open to in-depth ethnographic/qualitative case studies, international comparative analyses, and everything between. We will also welcome contributions that address dynamics of migration, exile and social change at different scales (municipal, national, regional, global and so on), and which pay attention to different intersections of race, ethnicity, class, gender and age, and other key identities. We will commission work from both individual researchers and research teams. Because migration and refugee studies are almost by definition interdisciplinary and multidisciplinary fields of research, we welcome contributions that are unified in their thematic focus rather than in their disciplinary perspective.

It is fitting to open the new series with Ala Sirriyeh's fascinating book exploring the shifting politics of compassion for refugees and vulnerable migrants. The book builds a compelling portrait of the plight of refugees and other survival migrants seeking international protection and better life chances in today's interconnected world. What we hear every day from politicians and opinion leaders is talk of taller, stronger, more technologically advanced walls and fences. And this is only the tip of the iceberg, as Sirriyeh shows in the book. Immigration control and enforcement operates also in more subtle and insidious ways, far away from the physical borders of wealthier states, more and more often operating remotely or through proxy states. The overall picture that emerges globally is one of a hostile environment to people on the move. Not all migrants are constructed as 'unwanted' and 'undesirable', but the effects of the current climate are experienced to varying degrees by a growing number of migrants. So where can we locate the politics of compassion?

As Sirriyeh observes in her readable exploration of asylum and migration politics and policies in the UK, Australia and the US, there are moments of interruption to the dominant discourse on migration, there are openings, tiny fractures in which it is possible to imagine an alternative narrative and these are to do with emotions such as compassion. It is not surprising that politicians have come to fear such 'irrational' responses and actively try to shield themselves and their policies from emotions that can inform and transform moral judgements. And indeed, at the time of writing these words of introduction, the rumblings of something like 'compassion earthquakes' can be felt in all three of the countries discussed in Sirriyeh's book.

In the UK, in the face of mounting pressure from MPs and the wider public, the UK government was forced to apologize for the distress caused by the treatment of the so-called 'Windrush Generation' of post-war Jamaican 'subjects of the British Crown' recruited to fill labour shortages in the UK. Having failed to keep records on the immigration status of these Commonwealth-born, long-term British residents, the Home Office has accused them of residing in the UK without authorisation, denied them access to services and threatened them with deportation. This manifestly unjust treatment has led many observers and a growing section of the British public to openly criticize the UK government's 'hostile environment' policy towards undocumented migrants – a policy that was, until recently, considered the foundation of the Tory government's political success.

Across the Atlantic, hundreds of counties and municipalities have joined the 'sanctuary cities' movement which refuses to fully comply with US federal immigration law. The aim of the movement is to make irregular migrants less fearful of detention, deportation and separation from family members, and therefore more likely to make it easier for them to comply with laws like driver licensing, to report criminal offences, and to register for healthcare, education and other services. Despite Trump Administration efforts to crack down on sanctuary cities, for example by attempting (unsuccessfully) to implement a campaign promise to deny them federal funds, some 300 US jurisdictions have joined the movement to make US cities more compassionate places for migrants in spite of Trumpian anti-immigration policies.

Meanwhile, the Australian Labour Party, polling well ahead of the Liberal-led Coalition Government as the country enters the next federal election campaign, has released a draft national policy platform proposing to radically re-fashion the country's asylum-seeker policies along a more compassionate and 'humane' basis. If elected – as currently looks likely – the Party would review the status of the Home Affairs 'super-ministry' that is responsible for national security, immigration and border control agencies. Asylum seekers would no longer remain indefinitely detained, but would be released after a 90-day period of health, identity and security screening. LGBTI refugees and asylum-seekers would not be detained, processed or resettled in countries where they would experience legal or other discrimination, and an ALP-led government would make 'every humanly practical effort' to get children out of immigration detention centres.

If these trends are anything to go by, Sirriyeh's study of the politics of compassion marks the beginning of a pendulum swing against the anti-immigrant triumphs of 2016.

Nando Sigona and Alan Gamlen
Oxford and Melbourne, May 2018

A Crisis of Compassion

A compassionate refusal

Several years ago, I was put in touch with Grace,[1] a Nigerian woman whose asylum claim in the UK had been refused. She was being detained with her toddler in the notorious Yarl's Wood immigration detention centre where they faced imminent deportation from the UK. While she was detained I spoke with a member of staff in her local member of parliament's office to ask for support for her case. This person was not hostile, aggressive or unkind. They listened to me and they expressed some sympathy for Grace's circumstances, but then reflected that it would be better for her and her small child if they were deported rather than living in limbo and hardship in the UK as refused asylum seekers. This person suggested that in trying to help Grace and her child to remain in the UK, their allies were possibly doing them a disservice and causing them further harm and suffering.

There has been extensive discussion of the now all-too-familiar hostile attitudes expressed towards undesired migrants and refugees in many societies that receive them (Wazana, 2004; Anderson, 2013; Chavez, 2013; Jones et al, 2017). In this instance, however, I was struck by the way that deportation was justified not simply as an enforcement of immigration restrictions against an undeserving migrant, but also as an act of compassion and care. Through this logic, deportation was presented as a means of alleviating suffering – in effect, this was a 'compassionate' refusal.

Introduction

During the 1880s and onwards, following the exclusion of Chinese migrants during the gold rushes in California (United States [US]) and

Victoria (Australia), the US and self-governing colonies in Australia began legislating 'to regulate the entry of "undesirable immigrants"' (Bashford and McAdam, 2014:309). Although relatively late on the scene, Britain joined this legislative trend set by territories of its former Empire by introducing the Aliens Act 1905. It was passed in response to the arrival of Eastern European Jews in Britain who had escaped the pogroms in the Russian Empire (Solomos, 2003). Since this period at the turn of the 20th century, the discursive category of the 'undesirable' migrant has endured and become embedded at the heart of political debates and policy making on immigration, citizenship and national identity in the minority world.[2] As the term 'undesirable' suggests, these policies, which are designed to exclude, have often been justified through recourse to hostile and negative emotions such as fear, anxiety and hate. However, while sentiments of hostility have been a defining feature of immigration discourses, the emotional landscape and discourses of contemporary immigration controls and the resistance to these controls are more complex and nuanced.

In this book, it is maintained that in the context of the rise of a cultural and political script of humanitarianism (Berlant, 2004; Fassin, 2005; Ticktin, 2014) a discourse of compassion has also been present in political debates about 'undesired immigrants'. 'Compassion' has been called for and enacted by those who resist punitive immigration policies, but also by those who seek to enforce these policies. It is argued that the discourse of compassion has been used by both implementers and opponents of immigration policies, often building on the colonial origins of the use of this discourse in reference to racialised others. In doing so, these voices on both sides of the debate have grounded compassion within a relationship of power disparity, control and subjugation. However, there is also evidence of possibilities for alternative engagements with compassion that are grounded in solidarity, and which offer more promising modes of responding to and resisting suffering and social injustice.

This book explores the role of compassion and its relationship to other emotions in asylum and immigration policy discourses in Australia, the UK and the US, and examines how these manifest in compassionate refusals (justifying deterrence through compassion), compassionate resistance (resisting immigration controls), and resistance to compassion (excluding people from being recognised as deserving subjects of compassion). It reflects on the ways in which immigration policies have been expressed and justified in public debates in these states; it also considers the responses they elicit. Policy cases from the Anglophone states of Australia, the UK and the US are used as examples of the response of societies receiving immigrants and refugees in the minority world, but also to investigate the specific experiences of discourses on migration and compassion in the Anglo-colonial context.

#CompassionCrisis

In the summer of 2015, the world watched in horror as death washed ashore on Europe's southern borders. Migrants and refugees had been drowning in the Mediterranean Sea for years in their attempts to reach Europe, but in 2015 there was an unprecedented escalation in the numbers of people undertaking this journey. It was then that these tragedies came to prominence and played a central role in stimulating political and media interest in the region and across the globe. While numbers of people crossing the Mediterranean had remained constant on the deadly Central route (Libya to Italy), there had been a substantial rise in crossings on the Eastern route (Turkey to Greece); almost half of the people travelling on this route were refugees escaping the war in Syria (Crawley et al, 2016). Thus, while numbers of deaths per thousand were lower in 2015 than in 2014, greater numbers of people were making the journey and the numbers of dead continued to rise. This, at the time, made 2015 the deadliest year on record for deaths of migrants and refugees in the Mediterranean (IOM, 2016). It had been anticipated that the peak season for refugee and migrant sea crossings would end as summer moved into autumn and the conditions at sea became more treacherous. However, people continued to attempt the crossing and the number of dead continued to rise. By December 2015, 990,671 people had survived their journeys and arrived into Europe by land and sea routes; this was nearly five times the total for 2014 (IOM, 2015).

In this context, there was a proliferation of 'crisis' talk, with several different terms emerging to categorise and represent these events over the time of 'the crisis' – 'Mediterranean migrant crisis', 'European migrant crisis', 'refugee crisis' (De Genova and Tazzioli, 2016; Goodman et al, 2017). These different and evolving categories reflected the debates that ensued over the identities of the people making these journeys and how Europe should respond to these events. It was debated whether the very nature of the response was itself part of the crisis; that is a crisis in the fundamental values and policies of the European Union (EU) (a project which originated in the aftermath of the earlier genocide and mass displacement of peoples in the 1930s). The crisis discourse surrounding this movement of people coincided and intersected with crisis talk around the economy and austerity in Europe, particularly in its southern states, and the political project of the EU (Heller et al, 2016).

It has become well established that the governments, media and electorate in many societies receiving migrants and refugees are in favour of restrictive immigration and asylum policies. However, over the course of the summer of 2015, and most dramatically after the drowning of the three-year old child, Alan Kurdi, on a Turkish beach on 2 September, it seemed that perhaps this was changing as there were increasing invocations of compassion and a sense of disquiet and unease about Europe's responses to refugees. In addition to the usual critiques of a politics of hostility, scapegoating and exclusion, there was increased focus not just on the *presence* of inappropriate emotions, but on the *absence* of ones deemed more appropriate (compassion, care) in a civilised society. European governments (some more than others), the EU and other political actors were condemned for their lack of compassion for refugees (Amnesty International, 2015; Townsend, 2015; Head, 2016). To fill the compassion gap in government responses, there was an outpouring of expressions of compassion among the people of Europe who began to act directly to welcome refugees by mobilising through campaigns such as Refugees Welcome and engaging in other forms of volunteering and campaigning (Graham-Harrison and Davies, 2015; Anthony, 2016). A shift in the tone of media reporting was also notable during this period as 'migrants' became 'refugees' and hostility was, briefly, replaced with expressions of concern and care (European Journalism Observatory, 2015). Indeed, compassion became a buzzword of the crisis, reflected in the Twitter hashtag #CompassionCrisis. In response, there were some shifts in government policy, most notably seen in German Chancellor Angela Merkel opening the door to one million refugees who crossed over the border into Germany (Connolly, 2015; Agencies in Budapest and Vienna, 2015). Even in the UK, Prime Minister David Cameron, under pressure to respond, introduced an expansion to the Syrian Vulnerable Persons Resettlement Programme (SVPRP) in September 2015.[3] Such shifts, however, were eclipsed by a continuing overriding drive to keep these people out of Europe. This could be seen in the reluctance of many governments (the UK included) to receive what had been calculated as a 'fair share' of refugees arriving into Europe (BBC, 2015); the EU–Turkey deal through which refugees arriving by boat to Greece from Turkey were to be returned to Turkey (Crawley et al, 2016); the scaling back of rescue operations at sea (Follis, 2017; Stierl, 2017); and the (re)institution of borders within Europe, including the UK-funded border wall in Calais (Head, 2016; Travis and Chrisafis, 2016).

In Australia, there have been similar expressions of public dismay at an absence of compassion in government policy towards refugees, most notably around the use of offshore detention centres on the Pacific islands of Nauru and Manus Island (Papua New Guinea) to intern and warehouse people seeking asylum (Gleeson, 2016). In 2015, people came out on to the streets and online as part of the 'Let Them Stay' campaign, to protest plans to return 267 people (including 37 babies) to Nauru following medical treatment in Australia (Doherty, 2016a). It was the death of a child, Alan Kurdi, that was a catalyst for protests in Europe. In Australia, a baby girl known as 'Baby Asha' who was being treated hospital in Brisbane and 37 other babies facing deportation to Nauru became the faces of Let Them Stay. In August 2016, following the leak of the Nauru Files by *The Guardian* newspaper, there were further protests against offshore detention as thousands of people rallied in cities across the country. The Nauru Files had revealed widespread and endemic physical, sexual and psychological abuse and harm reported by staff working in the detention centre on the island, over half of the cases being against children (Farrell et al, 2016).

Despite the surge in numbers of refugees fleeing conflicts and violence in the Central American states of Honduras and Guatemala in recent years, there has been no equivalent public outcry at the deportations and pushbacks taking place at the US–Mexico and Mexico–Guatemala borders (Tuckman, 2015; Canizales, 2015). However, following the rise in immigrant deportations since the 1990s (Golash-Boza, 2012), there has been a growth in immigrant-led protests against detentions and deportations, amid a wider campaign for the recognition of the rights of undocumented immigrants (Patler, 2017). Within this broader campaign, since the early 2000s the undocumented youth movement has attempted to secure a pathway to citizenship for undocumented young people through their campaign for the DREAM (Development, Relief, and Education for Alien Minors) Act. The movement has seen some success, most notably in the introduction of the Deferred Action for Childhood Arrivals (DACA) administrative relief by President Obama in 2012, which granted a temporary, renewable deferral on the deportation of some eligible young people[4] (Obama, 2012). Compassion for the plight of innocent and deserving undocumented young 'Dreamers' held in limbo was a central theme in the campaign for the DREAM Act, and later for DACA when the DREAM Act failed to pass (Nicholls, 2013).

In denouncing the absence of compassion in the actions of governments, some people protesting government policies have argued that there is a crisis in the *heart* and the moral and political values that supposedly define these regions and their peoples – a crisis in Western civilisation. Engaging with the perceived crisis of the European heart, in June 2015 art activists from the Center for Political Beauty in Berlin announced their plans to exhume the bodies of some people who had died trying to reach Europe from the inhumane graves or storage in which they lay at Europe's external borders. The activists stated they would rebury them with dignity in Berlin, at the *heart* of Europe, explaining that the aim of this intervention was 'to tear down the walls surrounding Europe's sense of compassion' (Center for Political Beauty, 2015). As part of this action, Europe's civil society was invited to participate in a 'March of the Determined' in which they would accompany the dead to the Federal Chancery to create a graveyard in the forecourt dedicated to the 'Unknown Immigrants'. Here the German cabinet and visitors would have to literally walk over the dead bodies of migrants.

Their aim 'to tear down the walls surrounding Europe's sense of compassion' suggests not simply an absence of compassion, but that this emotion was in fact present, only dormant and buried under the weight of the cold rationality of European political bureaucracy, or confined behind the wall of hostile emotions and responses from the people of Europe that had been raised against those who attempted to reach her shores. There was a sense that Europe had lost its way and public commentators made references to the lessons that were supposed to have been learned in the aftermath of the Holocaust (Chu, 2015). However, the refugee crisis in Europe and the response to it was not a complete break with history, or an exceptional moment in time. The longer history of this crisis was present in the ideas and practices that were produced through European modernity and that formed its very foundations. Modern Europe has been walking on the dead bodies of the subaltern since its conception. Indeed, it was given birth through this violence. There was no golden age of compassion in Europe's relationship with its former colonial subjects, ready to be reawakened. Similarly, claims in Australia and the US that the treatment of refugees and undocumented migrants was out of character with the core principles, national character and values of those nations also rested on shaky foundations. In the case of these two settler colonial states, these claims overlooked their founding race regimes and migration histories. This book considers how the colonial and settler colonial histories and structures of the racial states of Australia, the UK and the US have shaped some of the contemporary immigration and asylum policies explored in this book. It considers how they have operated in the withholding of compassion, but also in the use of a discourse of compassion in repression, and how other emotions present in debates on immigration and asylum come into play in these contexts. The focus in this book is not on all migrants (some of whom travel freely and are among the most privileged people on the planet). Instead, it focuses on undocumented immigrants and refugees who have been at the centre of policy debates on immigration and asylum because they have been deemed as undesirable in the receiving nation-states. An overview of this population and the historical context is provided in greater detail in Chapter Three.

An outline of the argument

Hostility and compassion

This book examines the role of compassion in immigration and asylum policy discourses through exploring the ways in which policies are expressed, justified and responded to in public debates. In a context of increasingly restrictive and exclusionary immigration and asylum policies towards undesired migrants and refugees across the minority world, we are now acutely aware of, and used to, the blatant discourses of hostility engaged with by some politicians, media and other public commentators. There is a long history to these discourses, but at certain periods of time they have become more visible and pernicious. In each of the three nation-states there are localised political and social contexts, histories and significant events that have led to differentiated versions of this broad discourse of hostility. However, since the 1990s each of these states has seen the passing of immigration legislation that has imposed increasing restrictions on entry into, and settlement in, these societies (Solomos, 2003; Golash-Boza, 2012; Vickers and Isaac, 2012). There has been rapid growth in the use of detention and deportation to manage those who have been deemed to be unwanted in this new regime (Golash-Boza, 2012; Bosworth, 2014; Gleeson, 2016). Alongside these policy developments, media and public hostility has grown towards certain populations of migrants and refugees, although the precise relationships and direction of cause and effect between government, media and public attitudes are contested (Gilligan, 2015; Morales et al, 2015). In response to the perceived reduction of state sovereignty in the age of globalisation and the challenges this and neoliberal economics have delivered for some citizens, it has been argued that governments have used stronger immigration border controls to placate aggrieved citizens. They have scapegoated immigrants to demonstrate some sense of retaining state sovereignty (Bauman, 2004).

Those who advocate restricting and excluding immigrants and refugees have been described as mobilising emotional discourses of hate, fear and disgust towards them (Chavez, 2013; Tyler, 2013; Jones et al 2017). Meanwhile the actions of those who oppose such measures are characterised by emotions of grief, empathy and compassion (Stierl, 2017). However, the emotional politics of immigration and asylum is also complex and nuanced. It is unsurprising that, in an environment of increased border controls and restrictive reception conditions, academic literature examining the role of emotion in immigration and asylum policy has focused predominantly on 'negative' hostile emotions and on the exclusionary and repressive practices with which they are linked. In this book, it is argued that this predominant focus, while offering valuable and necessary insights, can obscure the more mundane or seemingly *humanising* emotions that are used to enforce and justify repression, and how these intersect with the negative emotions discussed. Meanwhile, with reference to Australia, the UK and the US, it can also overlook the Anglo-colonial legacies which they build on, particularly the racialised manifestations of these emotions. Nor, on a more optimistic note, does it assess how those attempting to counter and resist restrictive immigration and asylum policies and practices engage with humanising emotions, and the challenges and paradoxes that have emerged consequently. Often humanising emotions are simply called for as a necessary antidote, but not interrogated in any great depth.

In seeking to contribute to a more nuanced account of how emotions are engaged with in immigration and asylum policy discourse, this book therefore begins from a rather different starting point to much of the existing literature on emotion and immigration. Through exploring discourses of compassion in immigration and asylum policy, how and to whom compassion is professed or withheld from and on what terms, this book examines the role of these discourses in justifying and resisting policies and practices.

The immigration policies of nation-states, and the position of immigrants in these societies, can be understood through the Deleuzian metaphor of assemblage (Landolt and Goldring, 2016). This describes a social phenomenon assembled from different elements that operate at a multi-scaler level, including, for example, discourses, *emotions*, social actors, bureaucracies, histories, sectors, social and political events and relations of power. There are patterns in immigration policy, but also some fluidity as changes take place in one or more of the elements and the ways in which they are assembled with other elements in this policy assemblage. This means that a discourse of compassion can manifest in different ways and lead to different outcomes depending on how it is assembled with other elements. For example, manifestations and outcomes of a discourse of compassion may differ depending on which social actors deploy compassion (charities, voters, politicians or media); and it may differ with changes in their relations of power with other social actors.

There may also be fluctuations depending on whether a compassionate discourse fits, or conflicts, with the objectives and ethos of a particular sector (such as health, education, employers in an industry or the charity sector) and with their status and influence in society. Further differences may be a consequence of how the discourse sits and is understood within a particular narrative of national or regional history (such as a 'civilised' society, a 'nation of immigrants' [the US], 'the lucky country' [Australia], a welcoming society or one with a shameful history). It also depends on how a discourse of compassion is assembled with other discourses (strangers as a threat, the necessity of looking after 'our own' first) and other emotions that are present. For example, there may be a discourse of compassion towards some people who seek asylum in the UK that draws on the discursive frames, laws and policies that recognise them as genuine refugees, as vulnerable and as people to whom society has an ethical obligation to protect. This may depend on the social characteristics of the refugees (their nationality, age, gender, ethnicity, behaviour) and how this fits with understandings of who a 'genuine' refugee is. It will also depend on the range and strength of other emotions present in the debate and whether these are compatible or in tension with compassion; the role and ethos of institutions that refugees encounter; the power relationships between different interest and lobbying forces; the UK's historical legacy and identity as a state that receives refugees; and so on. Even if it is agreed on, a discourse of compassion may be used to lobby for different outcomes; this could be for the protection and resettlement of refugees in the UK, or, indeed, preventing refugees from embarking on sea crossings ostensibly to save them from drowning (and appease more hostile attitudes). The mode of engagement depends of course on how genuinely 'compassion' is felt, but also on how compassion is understood and the type of resolution that is envisaged as being a compassionate response.

Compassion as a basic social emotion

Philosophers regard compassion – 'a painful emotion directed at the serious suffering of another creature or creatures' (Nussbaum, 2013:142) – as a basic social emotion because it is 'a central bridge between the individual and the community and so it is conceived of as our species' way of hooking the interests of others to our own personal goods' (Nussbaum, 1996:28). Compassion should therefore be of key interest to sociologists who hold as their central concern the relationship between the private troubles of individuals and the public issues facing social groups and wider societies. Exploring the workings of compassion provides insights into how particular social groups are included or withheld from our circles of concern and care. Compassion as a moral sentiment guides us to judgements, but also actions. While sympathy for the suffering other is a key element, compassion moves beyond this by containing a directive to action to alleviate the suffering. This is reflected in the verb 'to compassion' which has fallen out of use (Garber, 2004). Historically there were two meanings of the term 'compassion': 1) indicating 'co-suffering' among equals, and 2) compassion shown at a distance to someone who is suffering from someone who is free from this suffering (Garber, 2004). The former fell out of use while the latter became the dominant definition and is more akin to contemporary definitions of 'pity' (Garber, 2004). The use of the latter definition has led to debate and divergent perspectives on who is deemed worthy of a compassionate response, what constitutes a compassionate response, and what outcome is envisioned through this action. This book draws on discussions in moral philosophy and the social sciences on suffering, rights and humanitarian interventions to argue that, with its imperative to action, compassion can be a powerful emotion of resistance, although as Gill (2016) argues, it is often used as a last resort. Yet, when there is distance and unequal power dynamics in the compassionate relationship, it risks producing several forms of refusal.

A politics of compassion has been shown to provide some resistance to oppressive and exclusionary immigration policies (for example, pressuring governments into pledging to resettle refugees, or to stop detaining children). However, such forms of resistance can be fragile, and sometimes placed at risk or undermined by the social distance in 'compassionate' relationships because the voices and needs of those directly affected become diminished while attention is focused on their 'saviours'. It is also argued that it is not only hostile emotions that are embedded in oppressive immigration policies, but that a politics of compassion has also been co-opted by governments to justify and enforce restrictive policies through violence.

Central to this argument is the analysis of compassion as a racialised emotion emanating out of coloniality. 'Coloniality of power' is a concept first introduced by the Peruvian sociologist Anibal Quijano (2000) in the late 1980s to refer to the structures of power and control produced during the emergence of colonialism and enduring into the present day. As Mignolo (2011:2) explains, it 'names the underlying logic of the foundation and unfolding of Western civilisation from the Renaissance to today of which historical colonialisms have been a constitutive, although downplayed dimension'. Chapter Three traces the roots of compassion as a discourse and political practice in earlier relationships with racialised 'Others' during colonialism, settler colonialism and later migration histories of the three nation-states discussed. The remainder of the book traces how structures of feelings from colonial and settler colonial histories have developed and endured into the present, and have been challenged and reinforced in current immigration policy debates.

In addition to grounding the discussion in the history of coloniality, the politics of compassion in immigration and asylum policy is also placed within the broader landscape of the rise of political cultural scripts such as 'humanitarian reason' (Fassin, 2005), 'liberal terror' (Evans, 2013) and 'compassionate conservativism' (Berlant, 2004) in contemporary politics. These scripts have engaged supposedly progressive humanising emotions that drive the moral principles that it is claimed are guiding governance, but this is often in pursuit of what many would regard as inhumane and repressive ends. These political cultural scripts also feature as part of a recent turn in political discourse from 'evidence-based policy' drawing on quantifiable, 'rational' (read as non-emotional) evidence, towards an engagement with, and attempt to govern, emotions (Forkert et al, 2016).

Meanwhile, in recent years there has also been a growing literature on resistance by migrants and their allies in response to restrictive immigration policies (Nyers and Rygiel, 2012; Marciniak and Tyler, 2014). Crises are not only about disruption and chaos, but can also be turning points that bring potential for transformation. This book is also concerned with these movements and moments of resistance, including points at which resistance has gone beyond the realm of activists, and captured wider public interest and action, such as the public response in Europe to refugees during the summer and autumn of 2015. There is an assessment of the possibilities and successes of such engagements with compassion to elicit change and resist restrictive immigration policies. As mentioned earlier, the book also explores some of the challenges for discourses of compassion in resistance and how there has been a co-optation and distortion of compassion and care. It investigates the nature of the crisis of compassion. Is it simply the absence of compassion in policy and practice or also the ways in which compassion has been defined, understood and mobilised, and the outcomes that have been produced through it?

It is argued that mobilising a version of compassion that is closer to that earlier definition described by Garber (2004) as co-suffering – grounded in *compassion with*, or solidarity – offers more promising prospects for resistance. Furthermore, it is maintained that there is a timeline to compassion and, while an urge to compassion can be a powerful (but not unproblematic) force, this initial intense feeling is a moment in time and must quickly shift into critical reflection, dialogue and action to avoid its capture in problematic power relations, but also to avoid compassion fatigue. This argument is set out in further detail in Chapter Two where the concept of compassion is outlined and discussed within a broader review of the role of emotions in social life and policy, and specifically in immigration and asylum policy debates.

Policy case studies

This book focuses on a selection of policy case studies which have featured centrally in recent immigration and asylum policy debates in Australia, the UK and the US. These case studies are used to illustrate and explore the prominent role of a discourse of compassion within these debates and the way in which emotions have been engaged with in this. The role of coloniality in the development and use of a discourse of compassion, and the Anglo cultural and historical formation of this discourse, is examined through the focus on these three states, which were established in different eras of the Anglo-colonial project.

Since the 1990s, immigration and asylum have become central policy issues, and often heated topics of debate, in each of these three nation-states. Across Australia, the UK and the US there has been debate over what the state's response should be to uninvited 'spontaneous' immigration, and there has been a preoccupation with the idea of state sovereignty and control. In the UK and Australia there has been a significant focus on people seeking asylum whose numbers increased in the 1990s and 2000s (McMaster, 2001; Hynes, 2011; Lewis et al 2015; McKay et al, 2017). Following the enlargement of the EU in the mid-2000s, attention in the UK increasingly turned to Central and Eastern European economic migrants whose numbers rose during this period (Lewis et al, 2015). However, asylum has also re-emerged as a central focus of public debate during the ongoing refugee crisis, and particularly since the summer of 2015.

In Australia, debates on asylum have predominantly centred on the fate of people travelling to Australia by boat without visas. In 2001, the Howard government introduced the policy the Pacific Solution (McKay et al, 2017). Under this policy, people arriving through this route were intercepted and removed to offshore detention centres on Manus Island and Nauru. These centres were briefly closed by the Labor government in the late 2000s, but, as boat arrivals began to increase once more, were re-opened in 2012 (Gleeson, 2016). In 2013, the Coalition government led by Tony Abbott, introduced Operation Sovereign Borders (OSB), a military-led border security operation. Under this policy, 'irregular maritime arrivals' were transferred to the offshore detention centres, with no prospect of resettlement in Australia; boats were intercepted and turned back out of Australian waters by OSB forces; and a communications campaign was launched to deter both those seeking to travel by boat and potential smugglers (Gleeson, 2016).

In the US, the focus of the debate on immigration policy has predominantly centred on undocumented immigrants, especially Latina/o immigrants, although there is also some overlap with asylum particularly since the 2014 spike in numbers of refugees arriving from Honduras, Guatemala and El Salvador (Canizales, 2015). There are approximately 11.7 million undocumented immigrants in the US (Terriquez, 2015). There has been an exponential rise in the detention and deportation of undocumented immigrants (and other non-citizens) since the 1990s (Golash-Boza, 2012). Meanwhile, following numerous failed attempts to pass immigration reform legislation at federal level during the 1990s and 2000s, there has been a flurry of state-level legislation attending to the rights and entitlements of immigrants; these have followed exclusionary or more progressive policy directions depending on local state politics (Ioanide, 2015; Schwiertz, 2016). Since the 1990s there has also been a growth in immigrant-led activism in the US in response to some of the more punitive policies that have emerged and the failure to enact immigration reform at federal level (Nicholls, 2013).

This book examines a selection of high profile policy case studies (located in these wider policy contexts) that have attracted significant debate in recent years and in which a discourse of compassion has been engaged. It is notable that children and young people have featured centrally in each of these case studies. It is argued that a politics of compassion in immigration and asylum policy has drawn on both the emotions of immigration and childhood, and the intersections of these in the notions of vulnerability, innocence and deservingness. The first case study is that of the UK (and wider European) response to the refugee crisis from 2014/15 onwards, focusing on the death of the three-year-old child, Alan Kurdi, in September 2015. It is argued that the response to his death was a key turning point in contemporary public discourse on asylum.

However, while the death of Alan was a significant (yet temporary) interruption to well established discourses of hostility, an intersection of the emotional regimes of childhood and immigration in the development of a politics of compassion has also been seen in other contexts. This is discussed through the second case study explored in this book which is the Australian policy of OSB. Introduced in 2013, the aim of OSB has been to 'stop the boats' and end people smuggling, ostensibly with a key aim of 'saving lives at sea'. OSB is considered alongside UK and EU responses to smuggling operations during the refugee crisis in Europe, and the Obama administration's attention to smuggling in their policy response to the increased numbers of unaccompanied children from Central America crossing the Mexico–US border in 2014.

Continuing the discussion on OSB, resistance to offshore detention (a central element of OSB) is then examined through a discussion of the 2016 'Let Them Stay' and 'Close The Camps'/'Bring Them Here' protests in Australia and Nauru. These protests coalesced around attempts by the government, in the winter and spring of 2016, to return children from Australia to offshore detention after they and their families had been transferred to Australia for medical treatment. Meanwhile, from March 2016 onwards on Nauru, detainees also held daily protests about the delays in the processing of their asylum applications and conditions in detention. These protests were reignited and garnered extensive international attention in August 2016 following leak of the 'Nauru Files' by *The Guardian* newspaper.

The final case study is the campaign for the DREAM Act, which would have provided a pathway to citizenship for eligible undocumented young people who had arrived in the US as children. The discussion centres on the emergence and development of the undocumented youth movement that campaigned for this act. It also examines the introduction of DACA by the Obama administration in 2012, following repeated failure to pass the DREAM Act. A debate about the fate of undocumented populations also featured centrally in the 2016 US presidential election, which is also discussed in Chapter Six.

Data and analysis

Political parties, state institutions, migrant and refugee rights organisations, other civil society organisations and the media engage in political debate to discuss, negotiate and contest how immigrants and refugees are categorised and understood, and the stories that are told about them: that is, how immigration and asylum are framed (Goffman, 1986). This book explores how discourses of compassion are engaged with in the debates on these immigration and asylum policies. The book examines how emotions feature and are drawn together in these discourses to set out and justify what are often divergent, if not opposing, political positions, policies and practices. The analytical approach taken in this book is influenced by discursive psychology (Potter and Wetherell, 1987), and thus the analysis is focused on what is *achieved* through discourse, rather than a cognitive approach that attempts to uncover what those speaking actually believe, which we cannot authoritatively know (Goodman and Burke, 2010). Therefore, the analysis examines the discursive devices that are used to make arguments with an action orientation, for example, to explain and justify particular actions, or to support or undermine positions and actors. This may be done by employing 'interpretive repertoires', that is recognisable descriptions and arguments that are found in the routines of everyday talk, often in the mode of familiar clichés or anecdotes (Seymour-Smith et al, 2002). There may also be an engagement with 'ideological dilemmas' as people try to negotiate competing ideologies, often in the form of competing interpretative repertoires (Goodman and Burke, 2010:335); this is a key feature of discourse on immigration and asylum. Finally, as identity is understood as a socially constructed process of becoming, the analysis also takes account of 'subject positions', that is how speakers (and writers) construct themselves and others in discourse.

McMahon (2016) has observed that a common limitation of discourse analysis on immigration is the lack of attention to why certain discourses become more prominent and powerful than others. Taking account of McMahon's (2016) critique, particularly given this book's focus on 'compassionate turns', the analysis of text and imagery is placed in context by examining the influence of discursive structures (common discourses and ideas that influence how immigration and asylum issues are interpreted) and institutional frameworks. This enables us to consider who is able to mobilise politically and have their voices heard and who faces barriers in doing so, but also how these can shift and the impacts of these shifts.

The book draws on a range of data including: government policy documents, speeches, press releases and campaign materials; newspaper articles; and campaign materials and actions used by those advocating for migrant and refugee rights. Chapter Four examines media reporting in the immediate aftermath of the death of Alan Kurdi. The data corpus drawn on in this chapter comprised 362 news articles from national UK newspapers that mentioned 'Aylan Kurdi' or 'Alan Kurdi' and were about migration or refugees. These articles were published between 2 and 30 September 2015 and were retrieved through NexisUK. These forms of data are supplemented with a small number of qualitative interviews with migrant and refugee rights campaigners, and ethnographic observations at protest rallies, to explore ways in which emotions have been engaged with by campaigners in resistance. Incorporating insights from people engaged in political movements can throw light on the way that compassion and other emotions are mobilised in practice, and also directly elicit perspectives that are present in public debate but less likely to be recorded in textual documents.

In 2015, I received a grant from Santander Bank to conduct pilot research and networking activities with organisers in California. I interviewed seven organisers in California who had worked with the undocumented youth movement, including undocumented young people and allies. The interviews focused on the emergence of the movement and the messaging it used. In 2017, I returned to California through a Leverhulme Research Fellowship to conduct a study titled, *Undocumented Young People, Political Activism and Citizenship in the US*. At the time of writing I was partway through the fellowship, having completed the first stage of fieldwork in Los Angeles and Orange County. In this book, I draw on the analysis of data from the 17 interviews that I conducted with young activists as well as an undocumented parent activist and an ally activist in Los Angeles and Orange County who had been involved with the movement before and/or since the introduction of DACA. These young people were born in Argentina, Colombia, Mexico, South Korea, the Philippines, and Thailand, and had lived in the US since they were children. The study has also included 44 hours of participant observation and I discuss ethnographic observations from two protest rallies in Los Angeles.

While on research leave in Australia in 2016 I interviewed eight refugee rights activists and campaigners from Sydney and Melbourne. I also observed a protest outside a Department of Immigration office and a rally organised in response to *The Guardian's* leak of the Nauru files. In the UK, I conducted five telephone interviews with migrant and refugee rights campaigners working at national and regional (Yorkshire) organisations.

Outline of chapters

Chapter Two examines social science approaches to the study of emotion and makes the case for why social scientists should consider emotion in their analysis of the social and political world. It is maintained that decision-making, whether considered 'rational' or 'irrational', 'good' or 'bad', draws on cognitive and emotional reason (Burkitt, 2014), but that these also intersect. Emotions move people and are the outcomes of being moved. Emotional reason leads to certain kinds of decisions being made. Rather than attempting to peel away emotion from discussions of immigration and asylum, in this book emotions are regarded as central to how these policies are made, justified and operate. They are also a vital feature of modes of resistance. The chapter also makes the case for extending our attention beyond hostile emotions in immigration debates, to explore the role of 'humanising' emotions such as compassion. It examines differing definitions of compassion and subsequent critiques of it in relation to the question of social justice, and ways in which it might be recovered or adapted. Chapter Three provides an overview of the colonial and immigration histories of the nation-states featured in this book. In doing so it examines the historical roots of contemporary policy discourses and feeling rules (Hochschild, 1979).

The analysis of the policy case studies begins in Chapter Four with a discussion of resistance and the phenomenon of bearing witness, the role of compassion within this phenomenon and the tasks and perils that are involved. It then examines the case of the iconic visual testimony of the death of Alan Kurdi in 2015, to explore how this acted as a catalyst for the mobilisation of compassion in critiques of the UK government's (and European governments' more broadly) restrictive policies and lack of action in response to the refugee crisis. This discussion continues with an analysis of the photographs of Alan, newspaper articles reporting on his death, parliamentary speeches and interviews with campaigners to examine why the photographs were recognised as a 'compelling' message and how responses drew on the discourse of compassion. In addition, the analysis highlights some of the 'perils' of witness bearing that arose.

Chapter Five examines the 'war on smugglers' to explore how governments have co-opted discourses of compassion to enact violent and punitive policies in the name of 'compassion' for 'deserving' migrants and refugees. In this process, seemingly contradictory emotions of hostility and care have been made compatible through connecting compassion to the emotion of outrage.

Chapter Six examines the turn to 'vulnerability' in UK asylum policy and the recent resurgence of populist politics, focusing on Donald Trump's presidential election campaign in 2016. In doing so this chapter examines how compassionate refusals also take place when governments mobilise a discourse of compassion to reinforce a divide between 'deserving' and 'undeserving' migrants and refugees, and therefore *withhold* compassion from those unable to enact the conditions necessary for recognition as a worthy subject of compassion.

Chapter Seven reflects on protests against Australia's use of offshore detention to examine how refugee and ally activists have challenged these violent and repressive policies and reclaimed a politics of outrage to identify and hold governments accountable for policies which cause and exacerbate the suffering and harm experienced by refugees. The chapter examines the challenges of holding governments to account in a context where testimonies of suffering have been obscured and denied through the physical separation and regime of secrecy created through offshore detention. The discussion attends to ways in which activists have sought to bridge this physical and social distance through their bodily testimonies and physical protests.

Chapter Eight draws on recent research with undocumented young activists in California to consider some of the challenges raised by a politics of compassion. In examining the emergence and development of the undocumented youth movement it explores how compassion defined as proximate solidarity and co-suffering (rather than pity felt at a distance) can respond to some of the challenges outlined in earlier chapters and play an important role in enabling witness bearing and the building of a more inclusive and enduring resistance.

Notes

[1] This is a pseudonym.
[2] In this book, the term minority world is used to refer to wealthy states receiving migrants, in what is commonly referred to using the term 'Global North'. This is because Australia shares features with these states, but is in the southern hemisphere. Majority world is used to refer to states in the Global South where most of the world's population live.
[3] Hansard HC Deb. cols. 23-24, 7 September 2015.
[4] This programme was rescinded by the Trump administration on 5 September 2017 (Sessions, 2017).

2

The Emotional Politics of Immigration and Asylum

Introduction

Most people seek asylum in nation-states that neighbour their own. Consequently 80% of the global refugee population are in the majority world (UNHCR, 2015a). Undocumented immigrants contribute approximately US$11.8 billion in state and local taxes in the US (Ewing, 2015). Academics, journalists and non-governmental organisations (NGOs) regularly provide 'hard' facts like these on the experiences and impacts of immigration and asylum. Their evidence has made a clear case for loosening up immigration controls and implementing a more humane approach to refugee and migrant settlement. Yet there is little evidence that this has produced a substantial shift in government policies or in public opinion. In 2016, a UN summit of heads of state and government on large movements of refugees and migrants was held in New York (UN, 2016). It was billed as 'a watershed moment to strengthen governance of international migration and a unique opportunity for creating a more responsible, predictable system for responding to large movements of refugees and migrants' (UN, 2016); it produced little concrete action. The main outcome was an abstract declaration that refugee camps should be an exception, refugee children should have a right to education, and that the welfare of refugees is a global responsibility. Yet, as this was declared, construction began on yet another border wall, this time in Calais (France) to prevent migrants and refugees in camps there from traveling on to the UK (Travis and Chrisafis, 2016). Meanwhile, refugees continued to languish in camps on the edges of Europe, and in Australia's offshore detention centres.

Research-based evidence alone has not pushed governments into action or transformed public opinion. Furthermore, it has been argued, especially in the aftermath of the Brexit vote in the UK and the election of Donald Trump in the US in 2016, that we have entered a 'post-truth' world where 'facts' have lost their status and credibility (Davis, 2016) and where feelings trump facts (Ioanide, 2015). This chapter begins with a review of the role of emotions in social and public life, and how this has been understood in sociology and the social sciences and philosophy more broadly. There is a focus on how the relationship between emotion and reason has been theorised and how emotion is defined in this book. The role of emotions in immigration and asylum policy is then explored with attention to the interest in hostile emotions in research on immigration and asylum. Leading on from this, the core concept for this book, the emotion of compassion, is defined and explored. The discussion charts the rise of this emotion in contemporary political discourse, and the opportunities and challenges this produces for immigration and asylum policy.

A case is made for the importance of engaging with emotions in social science analysis of immigration and asylum policy discourses. It is argued that it is important to consider the role of 'humanising' emotions in the support and contestation of restrictive immigration policies. Declarations of compassion and care by politicians have not simply been disingenuous (although they may well be disingenuous). In its logic, the model and structure of compassion that has been evoked and engaged with by politicians and other actors has implied and often inevitably led to restrictive outcomes. In contrast, the pursuit and implementation of alternative models of compassion that are grounded in solidarity, rather than hierarchical power relations, offer more promising prospects for social justice.

Emotion and social relations

The affective turn

In recent years, it has been claimed that there has been an 'affective turn' in the social sciences as emotion and affect have become a focus of research inquiry (6 et al, 2007). This is linked to the 'discursive turn' in the 1980s which saw a growth in interest in language, meaning and discourse. However, Hoggett and Thompson (2012) have observed that this interest in emotion is not entirely new, but rather a re-emergence following the neglect of emotion in the post-Second World War period when positivism dominated the social sciences. They remind us that there is a long history of reflection on the role of emotion in social and public life. Ancient Greek philosophers wrote about emotions in politics and public life and recognised the links between emotion, cognition and judgement. Meanwhile, at the turn of the 16th century, Machiavelli also explored the role of love and fear in the exercise of power (see also Clarke et al, 2006).

Engaging with emotions in contemporary social science research has a lineage in continental philosophy from Nietzsche to the postmodernists, but also in psychoanalysis beginning with Freud through to Lacan and contemporary psychoanalysis (Hoggett and Thompson, 2012). Furthermore, there has been a longstanding interest and engagement with emotion in feminist thought (Ahmed, 2014). In psychology and neuroscience, there have been important developments in identifying different 'types' of emotions (including categorising these as basic or secondary emotions) (Burkitt, 2014). Among other social science disciplines, sociologists and social geographers have given the greatest attention to the role of emotions, critiquing predominantly biological understandings of emotion. They have shown the ways in which emotions are produced in social and cultural life, through our social relations (Wetherell, 2012; Burkitt, 2014) and through place (Davidson et al, 2005). Finally, despite a dominance of mind–body dualism in political science approaches to understanding reason and rational action in political life, there has also been growing attention paid in this discipline to the role of emotions in political behaviour (Marcus, 2002).

In this book, emotions are understood as being produced in and through social and cultural life. They are not purely biological, or produced and contained internally within the person's brain and body. Instead, they are social and relational, produced in patterns of relationships that the embodied individual engages in over time in the social world (Burkitt, 2014). As Ahmed (2014: 208) writes, 'emotions are a matter of how we come into contact with objects and others'. They are a product of culture and can vary across place and time. This is both influenced by and produces local 'feeling rules' which set normative expectations of how we should feel in particular contexts and circumstances, and towards particular people (Hochschild, 1979).

Emotion and reason

A perennial question in debates on emotion has been on the nature of the relationship between emotion and reason and whether emotions are a help, hindrance or even danger in public and social life (6 et al, 2007, Hoggett and Thompson, 2012). In this book, it is maintained that decision-making, whether considered 'rational' or 'irrational', 'good' or 'bad', draws on an intersection of both cognitive and emotional reason (Burkitt, 2014). There is a cognitive element of emotion; one can learn to feel compassion, or not (Spellman, 1997). Emotional reason leads to certain kinds of decisions being made; the 17th century philosophers of the passions, Descartes, Locke and Spinoza, described how 'a judgement of something can be a matter of how we are affected by that thing' (Ahmed 2014: 208). Something may be judged as good if it affects us in a positive way or bad if it affects us negatively. The emotions evident in public debates on immigration and asylum are a response to the ways in which people are embedded in relationships with other people, but also in important social and political events and circumstances.

The concept of 'affect' has been used to provide nuanced accounts of the role and relationship between experiential states and cognitive reasoning in feeling (see Wetherell, 2012; Ahmed, 2014; Burkitt, 2014). 'Affect' has been described by Massumi (1987: xvii) as a 'prepersonal intensity corresponding to the passage from one experiential state of the body to another'. It refers to the embodied and less conscious form of feeling (Hoggett and Thompson, 2012; Ahmed, 2014). Emotion has been defined in contrast as the more conscious form of feelings, as experiential states are understood, mediated and signified through language (Hoggett and Thompson, 2012). However, it is problematic to imply such a clear distinction between the conscious and unconscious (Davidson et al, 2005; Burkitt, 2014; Jones and Jackson, 2014). As Burkitt (2014) asserts, while studies of affect contain some valuable insights, feelings are an element of consciousness and the 'embodied capacity to be affected by other bodies, human or non-human' does not 'take us beyond emotion, language and consciousness in its various forms' (Burkitt, 2014:14). Consequently, Wetherell's (2012) concept of 'affective practice' is perhaps rather more helpful than a clear division between affect and emotion. 'Affective practice' reminds us that emotion and affect as 'embodied meaning-making' is something we *do* rather than a force that we are subject to (Burkitt, 2014:14). In this book, 'emotion' is used to refer to this more entangled phenomenon of emotion and affect. It is concerned with what emotions *do* in immigration and asylum policy debates. The relationship between emotions and political action and resistance is examined with a focus on 'the kinds of relations that affective practices make, enact, disrupt or reinforce' (Wetherell, 2012:17).

Emotions and immigration policy

Political emotions

If emotions can drive judgements and therefore actions, what is the role of emotions in politics and, specifically, the politics of immigration and asylum policy? Martha Nussbaum (2013:2) defines political emotions as those emotions that are to do with political principles or public culture and 'take as their object the nation, the nation's goals, its institutions and leaders, its geography and one's fellow citizens'. There has been increasing recognition in academic literature of the role of emotion in politics and social policy, with attention being given to how populations are governed through emotion and how people's emotions are governed (Richards, 2007). Emotions are integral to judgement making and, therefore, can drive and mobilise political action (Warner, 2015). Emotions can also become embedded in cultures and institutions where affective patterns are produced and reproduced (Hoggett and Thompson, 2012; Warner, 2015).

Immigration has persistently retained a centre-stage position in contemporary political debates in Australia, the UK and the US. Whether addressing questions of loss, belonging, fears of an immigration 'invasion' or resistance to perceived injustices in immigration policies, debates on immigration and asylum policy are infused with strong emotions, reflect polarised standpoints and are closely tied to discussions of identity, belonging and citizenship, and race and racism.

While public attitudes and behaviours have always to some extent been guided by emotions, Richards (2007:30) argues that emotions in civic culture have become more visible and prominent in recent years; he refers to this process as 'emotionalisation'. He observes that there are differing perspectives as to whether this is desirable or not, with some people questioning how genuine these emotions are and whether this undermines rational thought. Nevertheless, a new style of leadership is based on a 'growing concern for the emotional dimensions of the public and its opinions and of the political issues that confront us' (Richards, 2007:5). Increasingly political leaders are expected to engage in emotional governance by calming our fears or directing our passions.

Some social scientists have argued that the presence of emotions in public life is problematic because they are independent of, and undermine, rationality (6 et al, 2007). Political commentators often lament that voters are ill-informed and 'more moved either by habit or by momentary passion than by thoughtful reason' (Marcus 2002:2). In this scenario politics is seen to become more about the drama of framing and manipulating issues to 'elicit the desired emotional response rather than reasoned debate'

(Marcus, 2002:2). This perspective on voter behaviour is evident in the despair and disbelief levelled at those who voted for Brexit and those who support President Trump (Cohen, 2017). However, proponents of an alternative thesis, such as Marcus, argue that emotions operate with reason in a more functional way. Following Hulme, he asserts that the goals that we rationally pursue are those that appeal to us because of the emotional satisfaction that we derive from them. Meanwhile, the ability to pursue a goal also depends on being able to sustain the emotions that support its pursuit (Barbalet, 1998; 6 et al, 2007).

Emotions give the pursuit of national and political goals 'new vigour and depth, but they can also derail that pursuit, intruding or reinforcing divisions, hierarchies and forms of neglect or obtuseness' (Nussbaum, 2013:2). Therefore, emotions should be considered because they can be helpful or problematic depending on the *purpose* for which they are engaged, the *way* in which they are engaged with and the *impacts* they have. Nussbaum (2013) acknowledges that people may be convinced and moved by political principles and arguments. However, she (2013:10) asserts that emotions must also be engaged with to ensure the stability of support over time because 'the human mind is quirky and particularistic, more easily able to conceive in strong attachment if these high principles are connected to a particular set of perceptions, memories and symbols that have deep roots in the personality and in people's sense of their own history'. She argues that all major emotions are eudemonistic, meaning that we appraise that world from our own viewpoint and evolving conceptions of a worthwhile life. Although we may believe that other people's lives have value, the ones who move us deeply and who we grieve for the most are in some way connected to our own flourishing, goals and projects; they are in our 'circle of concern'. This book examines how people are placed within and outside of such 'circles of concern' in immigration and asylum policy discourse.

Hostile emotions and immigration

Rather than attempting to peel away emotion from discussions of immigration and asylum, in this book emotions are seen as central to how these policies are made, justified and operate. They are also a vital feature of modes of resistance. Understanding the workings of emotional reasoning in immigration and asylum policy is important for understanding why we have the policies we do, how these come about, and what kinds of policies may be beneficial and for whom. Emotion has often been presented as a factor that has complicated and hindered sensible discussions of immigration and asylum because it has distorted accounts of these phenomena and their impacts. It has been treated as a layer that needs to be peeled away to get to the truth. As discussed in the introduction to this chapter, critiques of policies and attitudes have often challenged irrational fear or hostility about immigration and asylum by (importantly) challenging myths and presenting counter-facts about the benefits that immigration can bring to societies receiving migrants (Dustmann and Frattini, 2013; Ousey and Kubrin, 2018).

However, despite the availability of a mass of evidence documenting the benefits brought by immigration, there has yet to be a substantial and sustained shift in public opinion or government policies in favour of easing restrictions.[1] Polls indicate that since the 1960s, public opinion internationally has consistently remained largely in favour of restricting immigration (Scheffer, 2011). Recent research from the UK has shown that there is little evidence to suggest that the government uses research evidence on immigration to inform policy development; instead it focuses on the management of public feelings (Jones et al, 2017). In *The Emotional Politics of Race*, Ioanide (2015) argues that 'feelings trump facts' in talk about race, and explores how the emotional politics of race has led people to hold on to views even when these are refuted by empirical data. Ioanide's thesis that 'feelings trump facts' can also be applied to immigration and asylum, which cannot be divorced from discussions of race and racism. Therefore, it is important to explore how emotions are engaged with to justify certain policies or outcomes as desirable or not. The book examines how emotions are used to define, express, and justify certain actions as 'reasonable' and 'unreasonable'. It also examines the relationship between emotion and morality, exploring how emotions guide and form people's sense of morality in immigration debates.

Significant attention has been paid to attitudes to immigration. These studies have focused predominantly on measuring and explaining levels of hostility to immigration among the public and media, and on the development of restrictive government policies; often they examine the relationships between public attitudes, media coverage and policies (Davidov and Meuleman, 2012; Morales et al, 2015; Laney et al, 2016). There has been discussion in sociology and geography about the role of emotions in migration. This has explored a range of emotions engaged with in the day-to-day experience of migration. These studies have examined how migrants or more established populations have managed and responded to migrant journeys and settlement (McKay et al, 2011; Bloch, 2014; Jones and Jackson, 2014).

However, when emotions are examined in immigration policy (usually within cultural studies rather than mainstream migration policy literature), attention has predominantly been given to how repression is driven by, and justified through, negative hostile emotions (Bleiker et al, 2013; Chavez, 2013; Tyler, 2013; Ahmed, 2014; Hogan and Haltinner, 2015). The focus on 'negative' emotions reflects broader interest within cultural studies on fear and panic (6 et al, 2007) and, particularly in the recent context of austerity politics, shame and stigma (Skeggs, 1997; Jenson and Tyler, 2015). However, in contrast, there has been relatively less engagement with the role of humanising emotions in immigration policy discourses in ways that look beyond these emotions as simply countering negative emotions.[2]

There have often been calls for negative emotions in immigration and asylum policy to be replaced by a compassionate response. This has been treated as a self-explanatory solution with limited interrogation of what compassion in these contexts might mean. It is perhaps assumed that, if it is genuine, then compassion is instinctively felt, known and acted on. Indeed, Arendt (1977) argued that because genuine compassion is so instinctive, a stance is already taken from the outset and so compassion cannot be a political emotion because there is nothing to debate. However, there are different understandings of what compassionate responses and outcomes should look like. These ideas about compassion can be learned and nurtured, or challenged and changed. This is significant because, as Waite et al (2014) state, compassion has an action element to it. As a moral sentiment, compassion guides and develops our moral judgement and behaviour. It directs our attention to the suffering of others, which we seek to alleviate. Affect drives the values that direct our actions (Fassin, 2005); empathy precedes a sense of good. Alongside anger, compassion is perhaps *the* key moral sentiment driving political struggles and campaigns. However, although compassion is often associated with progressive politics, compassion has been engaged with in varying ways and for very different purposes in public life, including, for example, to justify racism, military action and neoliberal economic policies (Woodward, 2004; Clarke et al, 2006; Ahmed, 2014; Evans and Giroux, 2014). These agendas and actions are based on differing interpretations of compassion. Therefore, in this book it is argued that it is necessary to debate what compassion means and the kinds of policies and practices that are justified through a discourse of compassion. These have important implications for the relationship between compassion and (in)justice; implications of which are explored in this book.

Compassion and the politics of compassion

Tough love

'I'm sorry I'm quite emotional about these…19-year-old…my aspiration for my daughter was boundless. And here I'm sitting with a 19-year-old girl who had written off her life and had no aspiration and no self-worth' (Iain Duncan Smith, British Conservative MP and former Work and Pensions Secretary, quoted in Martinson, 2016). In an article in *The Guardian* newspaper, Martinson recounts his interview with the teary former British Work and Pensions Secretary. Iain Duncan Smith expressed pain at the suffering of a young woman he had met who was living in poverty. This appears inconceivable given that under the remit of austerity politics Duncan Smith resided over the most severe cuts and reforms to the UK welfare system since its inception. As Martinson reminds us, this was not the first time that the MP had become emotional in public. As Conservative Party Leader in 2002, Duncan Smith had appeared visibly distressed at the poverty he witnessed on the Easterhouse estate in Glasgow, Scotland. He is also not the only politician on the political right who has been prone to incongruous outbursts of sentimentality. In the Australian federal election campaign of 2016, the Liberal Party candidate Malcolm Turnbull was said to have bared his soul when he cried as he spoke to the media about his father's struggles as a single parent raising him after his mother left when he was nine years old (Hunter, 2016).

In the context of the emotionalisation of public life, there is an increasing expectation that politicians display sentimentality in their public interactions; they must show that they are touched by witnessing suffering and that they are caring and compassionate 'real' people, as opposed to cold and detached career politicians. Although such displays are viewed cynically when they appear to be inauthentic or opportune, politicians are often critiqued as out of touch, uncaring and too distant if they are reserved (Merrick, 2017). Meanwhile, on an international stage, demonstrations of care and compassion can be regarded as a form of 'soft power' as seen in the case of the Canadian Prime Minister Justin Trudeau who, during 2015 and 2016, received widespread praise and admiration compared other world leaders for his apparently more caring response towards refugees (Austen, 2017).

Woodward (2004:60) has declared that 'we are living in a cultural moment in which a new economy of the emotions is emerging'. She argues that cultural scripts for the emotions have become more flexible and mixed; there is now an expectation that leaders are both strong and sensitive. Politicians who are unable to adapt to this new political cultural script may find that they falter. Woodward (2004) recalls one such example. In 1992 at a US presidential election rally, the Republican candidate, George HW Bush was asked by a member of the public to speak about how the national debt had affected him. He appeared perplexed and struggled to answer. In contrast, his rival, the Democrat candidate Bill Clinton, responded by stepping forward with his arms open, saying that he personally knew people who had lost their jobs and were suffering, implying that he knew about and felt their pain. The lesson had been learned by George W Bush who, in the 1998 presidential campaign, framed his policies through the philosophy of 'compassionate conservatism'. The ideology of 'compassionate conservativism' was also used by Duncan Smith to articulate his concern for people living in poverty in the UK, and his explanation of the causes and solutions to their predicament. Drawing on a rhetoric of tough love, strength and independence, Woodward (2004) argues that compassionate conservatism represents the public masculinisation of the emotion of compassion.

The discourse of compassionate conservatism has been used to promote policies and practices that many would contend are entirely uncompassionate; yet these have still been claimed as compassionate through appealing to a particular logic and moral framing of this emotion (Berlant, 2004). There are divergent ideas among those who engage with a discourse of compassion about who are worthy subjects of compassion and the kinds of justice that are secured through its mobilisation. The following section explains how such divergent understandings can emerge, yet all may lay claim to being driven by compassion.

Defining compassion

Compassion is one of the 'humanising emotions' (compassion, empathy, sentimentality, love) (Berlant, 2004:5). It comprises two core elements: 'empathy with the *suffering of others* together with an active *desire* to alleviate another's suffering' (Waite et al, 2014:327). This involves *feeling* and *understanding* someone's experience as constituting suffering. This emotion explicitly impels people to a course of action that they believe will alleviate someone's suffering (Woodward, 2004). Although there may be some agreement on the overarching definition of compassion, the politics of compassion in immigration policy, and in social policy more broadly, demonstrates divergent mobilisations of this concept. The varying discourses of compassion reflect different understandings of who the 'deserving' sufferer is we should feel empathy for. They are also based on differing interpretations of our relationship and obligation to them, and of the most appropriate course of action to alleviate suffering.

Most contemporary Western philosophical understandings of compassion have resonated with Aristotle's concept of 'pity', which he outlined in *Rhetoric*. Nussbaum (1996) has observed that this is more akin to the contemporary term 'compassion' than more condescending connotations of the term 'pity' today. Aristotle described pity (or compassion) as:

> 'a painful emotion directed at another person's misfortune or suffering (Rhet. 1385bl3ff). It requires and rests on three beliefs: that the suffering is serious rather than trivial; that the suffering was not caused primarily by the person's own culpable actions; and that the pitier's own possibilities are similar to those of the sufferer.' (Nussbaum, 1996:31)

Nussbaum's (2001:321) theorisation of compassion draws on the Aristotelian definition, but her explication of the third criteria for compassion is more expansive in her assertion that it is a *'eudaimonistic judgment'* that 'this person, or creature, is a significant element in my scheme of goals and projects, an end whose good is to be promoted' rather than a narrower sense that this could or has happened to us. She posits that we are more likely to feel deep emotions in relation to people or events which 'we are somehow connected to through our imagining of a valuable life', that is if they are in our 'circle of concern' (Nussbaum, 2013:11).

The basis of this eudaimonistic judgement may differ according to the degree of social distance or proximity perceived to exist between the person suffering and the person who feels compassion. In her discussion of the etymology of compassion, Garber (2004) explains that between the 14th and 17th centuries the term compassion had two meanings that centred on this degree of social distance. The first was derived from the Latin word *com* meaning 'together' and *patri* meaning 'fellow feeling' and was used to describe a sense of *'suffering together with one another,* or "fellow feeling"' (Garber, 2004:20). There was a high degree of proximity between the sufferer and the person responding. The other's pain was felt as their own. The second use of the term was to describe an emotion felt at a distance from a spectator towards a sufferer, rather than between equals (Garber, 2004). It was 'shown towards a person in distress by one who is free from it, who is, in this respect, his superior' (Garber, 2004:20). While the first interpretation fell out of use, the second interpretation remained. Arendt (1977) also identified two divergent understandings of 'compassion' – 'compassion' and 'pity'. She was critical of the distortion of 'compassion' into the more condescending 'pity' that is characterised by a power disparity whereby people speak and act on behalf of others and may even benefit through the feelings of satisfaction and praise that they receive for their sense of 'compassion' for others. She argued that genuine compassion could only be felt in the context of co-suffering where someone was stricken by the other's pain. Since a complete stance is taken, there should be nothing to debate, and therefore she argued that there was no place for political debate in the public realm about compassion (Arendt, 1977; Spellman, 1997).

This question of social distance, the relationship between this and contested interpretations of compassion, and the consequences of this for social (in)justice, have formed central themes in debates on the role of compassion in political life. Reflecting on the Aristotelian criteria for compassion, Nussbaum (1996) observes that compassion is a form of reasoning. The vocabulary of compassion makes links between values and effects, qualifies the issues involved, and defines and justifies the reasoning behind choices made (Fassin, 2012). There are divergent interpretations about what constitutes worthy suffering and what appropriate responses might be. While compassion has been mobilised in resistance and solidarity, the reasoning of compassion has also been used to justify withholding this sentiment or mobilising it in ways that have reinforced relationships of inequality and injustice or produced new iterations of these.

Levinas (1979) discussed the significance of the 'face to face' encounter (not necessarily a literal physical encounter) with a person who is suffering and who addresses us directly, observing the power of proximity to suffering and direct engagement to induce a response. In these encounters, witnesses are struck by the serious suffering of others. These encounters take us out of our pre-social self-centred state and induce an impulse to recognise suffering and feel a duty to help. In the contemporary globalised and mediated world, we are more likely than ever to encounter even geographically distant suffering (Sontag, 2003). As is discussed in Chapter Five, there have been efforts in immigration bureaucracies to obscure suffering from view and to prevent such direct encounters. Yet, as Stan Cohen explored in *States of Denial*, even if people are confronted with scenes of suffering, denial is still a feature of contemporary societies. In seeking to explain how denial occurs, is justified, and is legitimated, Cohen (2001) suggests that there are three possibilities as to what is being denied. These are: 'literal denial' (claiming that something did not happen or is not true); 'interpretive denial' (claiming that what has happened is not what it appears to be) and finally 'implicatory denial' (denying or minimising the moral implications of what has happened). He (2001:9) argues that denial includes, '*cognition* (not acknowledging the facts), *emotion* (not feeling, not being disturbed), *morality* (not recognizing wrongness or responsibility) and *action* (not taking active steps in response to knowledge)'.

While, it is difficult to maintain literal denial in the highly mediated world in which we now live, interpretive denial is frequently engaged. Hoggett (2006) has observed that the 'no fault of their own' Aristotelian condition of compassion requires an unrealistic idealised version of humanity. Such abstract and idealised notions of humanity are more likely to be fostered when people's circumstances are viewed from a social distance and without a direct encounter and knowledge of what it is like to live as the other person. Hoggett (2006:146) is highly critical of the 'idealisation of the suffering other', which constructs an essentially passive object of compassion who must live up to this vision of innocent victimhood. He and others have shown how neoliberal social policies have been framed around the notion of 'deserving' and 'undeserving' populations (Anderson, 2013). An increasingly narrower perimeter has been drawn around the deserving categories with an emphasis on individual responsibility and choice (Anderson, 2013; Tyler, 2013). There are so many ways in which a person could be judged as being at fault. Ironically, despite emphasis on personal responsibility and choice, once someone does exert their agency and become a subject who makes decisions about their lives, they are more likely to be mistrusted and judged as being at fault, especially if judged as making the 'wrong' choices (Nunn and Tepe-Belfrage, 2017). In Chapters Five and Six, it is argued that through this logic people are not only blamed for their own circumstances, but are also seen as being a threat to others, including established populations in societies receiving migrants who have, in turn, been identified as the rightful subjects of compassion. As Waite et al (2014) suggest, in this scenario refugees and other migrants are understood as having the capacity to cause hurt.

Even if it is agreed that someone is suffering and deserving of compassion, when compassion effectively tips into a socially distant relationship of pity, there may be implicatory denial. Boltanski (1999:3) has observed that a politics of pity is often centred on a 'spectacle of suffering' which moves from action to observation, without a sense of responsibility to act.

This gap between observation and action can also be understood within the frame of the 'post-emotional'. Mestrovic (1997) has argued that a move to observation and inaction is a feature of the 'post-emotional' era as emotions have become increasingly shallow, bite sized, superficial and fleeting. Instead of anger we feel indignation, and instead of compassion we feel pity. Fleeting and unanchored from an enduring social relationship, pity (rather than compassion) does not induce a feeling of responsibility and sense of a duty to act. This difficulty of sustaining a truly compassionate response, or 'compassion fatigue' as it has commonly been termed, has been commented on extensively and is one of the largest fields of literature on compassion. Compassion fatigue describes 'desensitization and emotional burnout, as a phenomenon associated with pervasive communication about social problems' (Kinnick, 1996:687). Originating in psychology and psychotherapy, it has also been engaged with in disciplines such as development studies, nursing and social work (see Kinnick, 1996; Moeller, 1999; Jenkins and Warren, 2012). Hoggett (2006) suggests that compassion fatigue occurs in part because what is being felt is not compassion, but rather the fleeting emotion of pity that depends on the idealised notion of the innocent suffering other. Based on an unrealistic expectation of the ideal other, pity is difficult to sustain when expectations and reality diverge, and it builds a fragile and socially distant relationship which is easier to discard. Those who attempt to alleviate suffering can feel impatience and disillusionment if people experiencing suffering do not respond in the manner anticipated. Taken out of historical context and a recognition of relationships of interdependence, compassion can be seen as a generous gift rather than a duty; it is something done out of care and benevolence rather than justice and recognition. But, as the Aristotelian criteria for compassion indicate, this is a conditional gift and the conditions can be hard to meet, leading to the withdrawal of compassion.

In addition to the challenge of inaction, the move to observation can recentre the spotlight on to the observer's experience, leading to the appropriation of pain whereby the feelings of the observer become the focus and their pain becomes the object of sadness (Ahmed, 2014). Even where action is taken, there can be a tendency to admire and celebrate those who display this compassion; for example, this was seen in news stories centred on heroic volunteers rescuing refugees during the refugee crisis (Tufft, 2015; Smith, 2016). There is an absence of a sense of obligation in compassion. Although compassion can be a catalyst for action, the lack of obligation can also inhibit action. The threads that bind lives together are obscured through this celebration of benevolence, and expressing condolences becomes about expressions of kindness and generosity rather than responsibility. There are no demands to which a duty is owed.

It is argued in later chapters that, in the context of immigration and asylum policy, this is problematic when considering the hollowing out or even the flouting of national and international rights frameworks and conventions. Fassin (2012) has shown how in France, following the undermining of the credibility of the 'threatened body' and the 'working body', the suffering body (recognised briefly through a clause in the 1998 Conditions of Entry and Residence of Foreigners legislation) became the only way for many precarious migrants and asylum seekers to gain leave to remain. Even in cases where asylum was granted, this became an act of generosity to a suffering victim rather than the fulfilment of a political debt to a rights-bearing person. Thus, 'a display of sympathy replaced the recognition of a right' (Fassin, 2012:376). In this refashioning of compassion as a gift rather than a duty there is a denial of the legacy and ongoing practices of colonialism, neo-colonialism and racial neoliberalism, and their relationship to contemporary asylum and immigration politics; this has been discussed in 'postcolonial asylum literature' (Farrier, 2011; Fernando, 2017). Ahmed (2014:22) writes that, 'the West takes and then gives, *and in the moment of giving repeats as well as conceals the taking*'. The 'gifts' of others and prior relations of indebtedness to them are forgotten, while the generosity of the West and the Western subject is celebrated as an inherent part of that individual, national or regional character.

Inaction or the limited scope and terms of action is problematic. However, it is argued in Chapter Five that compassion has also been used to explain and justify actions that on the face of it are about the person who is suffering, but in practice benefit the interests of those voicing compassion and have little to do with social justice. Such critiques have levelled against the use of humanitarianism as justification for military intervention. Evans (2013) terms these interventions 'liberal terror', in which violence is justified through the proclaimed aim of saving lives, or protecting human rights, or 'our way of life'. Perugini and Gordon (2015:3) write that, in this logic, 'violence and human rights are not necessarily antithetical. Violence protects human rights from the violence that violates human rights'. Violence is presented as not just serving domination, but as performing an emancipatory function.

Policies justified through compassion can also lead to seemingly contradictory practices and outcomes in domestic politics. Berlant (2004) observes that compassion is usually associated with an expansion of action, such as expanding the welfare state to offer more assistance to disadvantaged populations. However, in the ideology of 'compassionate conservatism' the subject of compassion is the 'hard-working citizen' (not necessarily the most disadvantaged). They are argued to have done everything right, yet still they suffer through paying too much tax to support others who made the 'wrong' choices, or through state interference which undermines their independence and dignity. Therefore, instead of an expansion of action, compassion is used to justify the shrinkage of the state. Rather than seeking to respond to historical and structural damage that caused the poverty and exclusion of some social groups, justice is envisaged in a more individual than collective sense. This can be seen in the increased use recently of the language of 'working families' or 'working people' ('class' conveniently missing in this phrasing) or the 'tax payer' (Walsh, 2017), which obscures the politics and structures of class and race.

Although hostility and compassion are seemingly polarised emotional responses, through the concept of 'compassionate refusal' this book explores how at times they are two sides of the same coin. The sentiment of compassion can intersect with hostility to repress and exclude some migrants and refugees from full membership in societies of arrival and settlement and, through doing this, they can also be used to (re)configure the identities of societies receiving migrants in the context of colonialism and settler colonialism.

Compassion as solidarity

It is proposed that a notion of compassion based on proximity and solidarity rather than distance and pity is more conducive to the realisation of social justice. In contrast to the idealisation inherent in socially distant relationships, a relationship of compassion structured along the model of solidarity accepts the full humanness and complexity of the sufferer and, as such, is a more enduring and genuine commitment (Hoggett, 2006). 'Solidarity' is understood as 'standing together' – because of pragmatic shared interests and/or because of shared values, not based on a hierarchical relationship, but rather one of equality (Dawson and Verweij, 2012). In either sense, there is an understanding of our lives as connected and interdependent. This notion of compassion as solidarity connects to the feminist ethics of care which recognise that humans are interdependent rather than autonomous (Tronto, 1995; Sevenhuijsen, 1998). We all need care and we all give care. This approach addresses those who are suffering as subjects rather than objects and is based on a more nuanced and less idealised notion of the human.

Despite challenges associated with relationships of compassion, as Ahmed (2014:29) writes, there is a 'sociality of pain'. Pain may be solitary, but it is not private. Rather than rejecting compassion in politics, there must be a recognition of the sociality of pain, the need for response and for witness bearing. We seek witnesses to our pain to recognise it and grant it the status of an event, bringing it into being as a known event (Laub, 1992; Ahmed, 2014). This is understood in the phenomena of witness bearing, which goes beyond a recognition of suffering.

Witness bearing in its dual meaning as proof of the event, and testimony about an event, involves both listener and sufferer constructing the known event (Laub, 1992). It involves actively listening to what people say about what is happening, why it is happening to them and what they want to be done. People bearing witness may not be able to alleviate suffering directly, but they can acknowledge and respond to it, enabling the people suffering to also respond and maintain their subjective agency. Through their recognition and amplification of the testimony of people who are suffering, witness bearers can also encourage the wider community to respond. Public recognition of pain and invocations of compassion can therefore be an important means of directing resources to the relief of suffering.

In her analysis of Harriet Jacobs' *Incidents in the Life of a Slave Girl,* Spellman (1997) has explained how such a model of compassion might operate. Linda Brent, writing under the pseudonym Harriet Jacobs, understood that compassion is something that can be learned, moulded and directed to an appropriate response that furthers social justice. Instead of seeking co-suffering from the northern white Christian women she addressed, Brent sought an informed compassion on her terms by carefully guiding readers through an understanding of the suffering that enslaved people experienced. Rather than relying solely on harrowing stories of brutality and suffering that told a story of innocent victimhood, she also allowed space for the voice and subjecthood of those people to enter the story, even when this complicated easier and less contentious notions of the 'innocent' victim. She spoke of the impossible 'choices' she had faced as an enslaved woman experiencing sexual abuse, and the moral dilemmas and agony she experienced. In doing so, she interpellated a complex and full human-being who was, nevertheless, still worthy of compassion. She was also clear that the appropriate compassionate response was not to simply give oneself over to sentimentality, but to combine compassion with outrage so that compassionate action was directed in care and solidarity towards the enslaved woman, but also in outrage towards the slave masters.

Compassion implies a social relation between those who suffer and those who witness this suffering (Berlant, 2004). Yet the nature of this relationship and its implications have been contested through divergent interpretations of what constitutes compassion and the nature of justice that is envisioned through this framework. This remainder of this book examines these divergent interpretations in the context of immigration and asylum policy debates, and the implications these have for social justice.

Notes

1   Although there have been some shifts in attitudes and policies towards specific migrant groups at particular times.

2   There are some exceptions to this. For example, in *The Cultural Politics of Emotion* Ahmed (2014) examines the discourse of love in far-right activism. Meanwhile, in *Nothing Personal?* Gill (2016) has a chapter on how activists and charities mobilise compassion as a means of challenging distance and indifference to suffering in the immigration bureaucracy.

3

Emotion, Colonialism and Immigration Policy

Introduction

This chapter reviews key discourses present in the colonial and immigration histories of Australia, the UK and the US, the states from which case studies are drawn from in this book. Later chapters examine how debates in contemporary immigration and asylum policy cases discussed in this book have engaged with the histories and discourses that emerged during these periods. Immigration policy has been a central pillar of nation building and debates on identity in each of the states (Vickers and Isaac, 2012). While settler colonial societies must inevitably link colonialism and immigration in telling the stories of their nation-state, in the UK these histories have, to an extent, become detached; colonialism as the story of what happened 'over there' is under-acknowledged in the ways in which it has a direct connection to 20th and 21st century immigration in the UK (Bhambra, 2017).

Colonial and immigration histories have not only shaped perceptions of who the alien outsider is, but also the identities of these states and 'their' peoples. Racialised hierarchies developed and were maintained alongside a sense of *imperilled* and fragile privilege. Pride was felt at the perceived superiority of white Europeans (and descendants) and their position as the 'chosen ones' guiding others towards civilisation. Yet, there was an enduring narrative that these advantages and privileged status needed to be protected from dangerous others who sought to destroy or usurp. There was also a narrative of danger that asserted that this privilege and status could be jeopardised from within by the actions of white Europeans themselves; their lack of humanitarianism and their uncivil conduct risked tarnishing their moral standing and status.

Compassion is a social emotion concerned with the relationship between self and other. It addresses questions of proximity, distance and relationships of power. In considering contemporary relationships between 'new strangers' forged in the context of immigration, it is important to reflect on how these have been shaped by the emotional legacy and patterns imprinted from those earlier encounters (Ahmed, 2014). In understanding the origins and development of the politics of compassion in contemporary immigration policy, and the power, utility and attachment to this discourse, we need to reach back into the foundational stories of the states. Some of the discourses such as 'compassionate' control and refusal, discussed later in the book, bear some similarity to discourses of compassion that emerged in the colonial eras. Meanwhile, the current hostilities of immigration regimes towards those deemed to be 'undesirable migrants' are the latest iteration of long histories of immigrant exclusions that stretch back into the late 19th century.

Colonialism and the 'civilising process'

Early colonialism

Australia, the US and the UK are threaded together through a history of British colonialism. The first British colonies outside Europe were established in the Caribbean in the second half of the 16th century, and in North America in the early 17th century. This period also marked Britain's entry into the slave trade as British ships began transporting enslaved African people to work on plantations in the colonies. Britain came to dominate the slave trade, transporting more slaves than any other nation; between 1760 and 1779, 391,200 enslaved people were traded by the British (Oldfield, 2008). The colonies played a vital role in the rapid growth of the British economy, while also serving as an arena for testing out and developing central ideas emerging out of the Enlightenment.

British colonialism is often narrated as an event that happened 'over there' on the other side of the world, and thus has been accompanied by some sense of perplexity and outrage when colonial and former colonial subjects have the temerity to appear on the threshold of the 'motherland' (Bhambra, 2016). Although, compared with Australia and the US, the UK does not have an equivalent colonial 'founding of the nation' public narrative, the modern British nation-state was constituted, and its identity made, through colonialism. Colonialism was a vehicle through which ideas about racial others were developed and their otherness interpellated. This was a fundamental aspect of Western modernity and played a central role in the development of British (and more broadly European) identity and understandings of British nationhood, character and boundaries of belonging (McClintock, 1995). Colonialism was central to both self-definition and the defining of 'dangerous others'.

Towards the end of the 16th century, British colonialism began to be interwoven with the ideas and conditions of modernity, including Enlightenment philosophy, the emergence of capitalism, and the Reformation (Vickers and Isaac, 2012). These ideas informed notions of morality, justice and what it is to be human; they also guided and justified understandings of the structure of societies and social relations. Colonialism was central to this process: as Lowe (2015:16) writes, 'it is the pronounced asymmetry of the colonial divisions of humanity that is the signature feature of liberal modes of distinction that privilege particular subjects and societies as rational, civilised and human, and treat others as labouring, replaceable or disposable contexts that constitute that humanity'. Drawing on the narrative of progress, civilisation was understood as a scale with white Europeans placed at the top and 'savage tribes' at the bottom. By the 18th century, a 'planetary consciousness' (McClintock, 1995) had developed which drew the whole world into a universal standard of cultural value developed by Europeans, with a single global history understood from their privileged position.

Justifications for establishing settlements and colonies were based on a perceived distinction between different human populations. In the early colonial period, it was claimed that religious motivation drove the colonisation of America to deliver people from their state of savagery (Arneil, 1996). This was grounded in the notion of 'Manifest Destiny' – a belief in the natural superiority of white people and their divinely ordained mission to claim territory and civilise the heathens (Hogan and Haltinner, 2015). While seeking to bring the indigenous 'heathen' out of the dark and into the fold of the Christian family, their perceived 'savagery' and lack of civilisation was simultaneously used to justify the theft of their land (Arneil, 1996).

Later in the 18th century when James Cook and the naturalist Joseph Banks mapped the east coast of Australia, they too reported on the 'uncivilised' nature of indigenous people, remarking that they had no social organisation (O'Brien, 2015). Considering this assessment, and not facing competition from other colonial powers as they had in the Americas, the British decided that 'instead of legal entitlement and a treaty, they would give "friendship" and "kindness"' (O'Brien, 2015:11). Rather than recognising their humanity and attendant rights, they were offered paternalistic and disingenuous sentiments of compassion and care that were bound to the violent and repressive practices of colonialism.

While the political and economic motivations of early British colonialism in the US and the Caribbean were thinly disguised through reference to the civilising mission, a discourse of compassion became more developed and nuanced in colonial practices and rule during Britain's 'second empire'. This is evidenced in the settlement of Australia, and the debate on the abolition of slavery in the Caribbean and the US.

The second empire and 'benevolent colonialism'

The British colonisation of Australia took place in the late 18th and early 19th centuries during the second wave of empire. This coincided with the emergence of the slavery abolition movement (Davis, 2014), reforms and changing social policy discourses towards the working class in Britain (Twells, 2009), and the development of 'bio-racism' (Field and Field, 2014). These factors shaped understandings about people's capacity for civilisation and 'compassionate humanitarianism'. There were debates about where populations lay on a perceived scale of civilisation, bound to conceptualisations of race. It was contested whether positions on the scale were static, or if there was capacity for change and development. The static view was envisioned in the development of taxonomies of races (Field and Field, 2014). The belief that there was capacity for development was evinced by Scottish Enlightenment thinkers who perceived societies as moving through stages of development from the savage to the civilised; this also mapped onto Christian understandings of the Christian and the heathen (Twells, 2009).

The 'civilising mission' and the narrative of 'Imperial Progress' shifted to the forefront of colonial discourse in this second wave of empire and became central features of how colonialism was marketed at home and in the colonies (McClintock, 1995); populations in the British colonies were given the non-refundable 'gift of empire' (Ahmed, 2014). Colonialism, and the oppressions and violations that it wrought, were established and enforced through atrocious violence and brutality. Yet, they were also instituted and justified through a discourse of compassion and benevolence; this was portrayed as 'tough love' and guidance from white Europeans who were further advanced along the scale of civilisation.

At the outset of British colonialism in Australia, the loss of the American colonies was imminent, the violence of the forced displacement of indigenous peoples in the Americas was being questioned, and the slavery abolition movement was on the rise. It was this context that 'reinvigorated the literature of the "good empire"' and preference was expressed for 'benevolent colonialism' as a route to a more peaceful (and unobstructed) occupation (O'Brien, 2015:11).

Captain Cook, at the time and in his memorialisation, has been celebrated for his 'Christian humanity' (O'Brien, 2015:11). The establishment of the first penal settlements in 1788 was brutal and difficult to cloak in a narrative of benevolence. Therefore, a founding narrative based on Cook's earlier arrival enabled the presentation of a benevolent first chapter in Australian colonial history (Thomas, 2006). Nineteenth century narratives of the voyage of Cook's ship, the Endeavour, were heavily abridged, with accounts of violence doctored. Thomas (2006) observes that, while supporting the 'benevolent colonialism' narrative, the story of Cook's humanity has also been used to challenge the brutal treatment of Aboriginal people by presenting this as out of step with early European responses to indigenous peoples. In Chapter Four, it is shown that a more recent iteration of this argument can be seen in pro-refugee campaigns which make reference to national narratives of Australian 'fair go' values, civility and tolerance.

This discourse of 'benevolent colonialism' had parallels with the civilising mission in the philanthropy movement that the Victorian middle class embarked on 'at home' with the British working class, initially drawing inspiration from American missionaries (Twells, 2009). Benevolence was viewed as 'a central characteristic of a reformed, Christian middle-class manliness which prided itself on its sensitivity, morality and guidance to others' (Twells, 2009:53), although gentle and caring compassion was also gendered as a key feminine trait in American abolitionist discourse (Lasser, 2011).

According to the middle class British reformers of the 19th century, material aid was seen as irresponsible, encouraging idleness, sin, waste, luxury and discontent (O'Brien, 2015). Instead, it was argued that philanthropy should attend to inducing moral reform. This was grounded in the Enlightenment belief in human capacity for improvement as well as the Methodist belief that people are sinners, but capable of redemption. The interventions into indigenous peoples' lives in the colonies were shaped by the ideas and practices circulating around the 'problems' of white populations at home (O'Brien, 2015). Ideas about moral reform were reflected in the regulation of Aboriginal people who were punished for 'immoral conduct' (unauthorised sexual conduct) and minor infractions such as 'untidiness', which were criminalised (Vickers and Isaac, 2012). The removal of Aboriginal children into institutions, where they would learn domestic trades, was modelled on a similar practice of placing 'neglected' white children in Australia into such institutions (Kidd, 1997). The notion that children could and should be saved was also apparent in missionary publications from this era which portrayed the 'savagery' of their culture embodied in the supposed practices of their parents (O'Brien, 2015).

However, the brutality and violence of colonialism was also challenged through appeals to empathy for the other, and through expressing concern about the European's soul, sin and civility; the abolition movement is perhaps the best example of this. In resistance to slavery and campaigns for abolition in this era, there were concerns around agency, voice and solidarity – concerns that exist today in migrant and refugee rights campaigns. Some gendered discourses of compassion had limitations since they implied that compassion could be apolitical and divorced from meaningful action that challenged the causes of suffering, a critique also levelled at contemporary expressions of compassion to refugees. Lasser (2011) remarks on the highly gendered terms under which US women abolitionists entered the debate. A culture of sentimentality was present in the interventions of women abolitionists on both sides of the Atlantic. However, while in Britain women engaged in debates on political economy, abolitionist women in the US outlined their position purely through a frame of moral sympathy, evoking women's supposedly greater capacities for emotion (Lasser, 2011). In formulating their appeals in the language of compassion, grounded in a religious understanding of morality, these women could speak without stepping out of acceptable gendered roles and into the 'male' *political* world.

It is in this 19th-century era of British colonialism, and in debates about the British slave trade, and abolition in the Americas and the Caribbean, that we can see an early iteration of both compassionate resistance and the compassionate refusal discourses that are discussed in later chapters in this book.

Building the fortress: immigration policies from the 1890s to 2000s

The remainder of the chapter provides an overview of the emergence and development of exclusionary immigration policies from the 19th to the 21st centuries, and the links made between race and immigration in these periods.

Race and the 'undesirable immigrant'

In both the 'old' world and settler colonial nation-states in the 'new' world, the turn of the 20th century saw the emergence of restrictionist immigration legislation and policies. These identified and sought to respond to the problem of the 'undesirable immigrant' who was presented as a cultural, social and, in some cases, economic threat. As peasantry were dispossessed of their land in Ireland (Britain's first colony), many sought work opportunities in Britain where the Industrial Revolution was underway (Virdee, 2014). By the 1861 peak in Irish immigration, the Irish-born population in England and Wales numbered 601,634 (Solomos, 2003). While the Irish faced considerable racism, the legislative and policy response to their immigration was radically different to the response to the much smaller population of Jewish migrants who arrived at the turn of the 20th century, escaping pogroms in Eastern Europe (Solomos, 2003). In disturbingly familiar echoes of contemporary discourses on immigration, Jewish immigrants were blamed for unemployment, disease, strains on housing and social unrest. This led to the Aliens Act 1905, setting a precedent for subsequent immigration policies (Hayter, 2004). Under the 1905 Act, 'aliens' could be refused permission to enter the UK if they did not have means to obtain sanitary living conditions. They could be expelled if they received poor relief within a year of entry, were 'guilty' of vagrancy, or found to be living in unsanitary conditions (Solomos, 2003).

Similar sentiments about the risks posed by undesired migrants were being expressed in the US and Australia, although as settler colonial nation-states constituted through immigration, the story of immigration in these states also differed from the UK. As Vickers and Isaac (2012:105) write, in settler societies, 'the story of nation building by the dominant white population is simultaneously a story of recruiting suitable immigrants and settling them on lands from which indigenous peoples have been dispossessed, while other European settler groups are being assimilated'. White democratisation took place earlier in settler societies than in Britain: in the US, white men gained suffrage by the 1830s. As democracies with white electoral majorities and endemic racism, nationalism in the US and Australia was based on white solidarity, and immigration policies were from the outset based on racist exclusion (Vickers and Isaac, 2012; Fitzgerald and Cook-Martin, 2014).

The US was conceived as a nation of *white* immigrants. Congress passed nationality (1790) and immigration (1803) laws that prevented Africans and Asians from becoming citizens (Fitzgerald and Cook-Martin, 2014). In this new democracy, the exclusion of part of the population from democratic participation was justified on grounds that Africans and Asians lacked personhood and were incapable of self-government, so were unfit for democracy (Fitzgerald and Cook-Martin, 2014), building on theories about civilisation discussed earlier in this chapter. The Chinese Exclusion Act 1882 was introduced in response to immigration from China during the goldrush. It became the first piece of legislation restricting immigration from a particular country, leading to a ban on almost all immigration from China (Martin, 2014). There were similar concerns about Chinese immigration in the Australian colonies in the late 19th century and restrictive legislation was also enacted there to limit it. Retaining strong British cultural ties and geographically isolated from Europe, fears of an invasion from the north from this period onwards remained an enduring feature of Australian immigration discourse, despite changes in policy over time and a lifting of restrictions on Asian immigration (Hogan and Haltinner, 2015).

By the 20th century, anti-immigrant sentiment came to dominate US politics. Proponents of immigration restrictions argued that not only Asian immigrants, but also Southern and Eastern Europeans (often Catholic and Jewish), were a threat to US culture and values, lacked the ability to self-govern and were difficult to assimilate into American life (Martin, 2014). The Johnson-Reed Act 1924 established national-origin quotas for migrants from Europe, which were designed to keep out 'undesirable' Southern and Eastern Europeans. As in the UK at that time, concerns were also expressed about race, criminality and hygiene (Tirman, 2015). Meanwhile, all Australian colonies had a White Australia policy by the 1890s, which became a central element of the federal Immigration Restriction Act 1901, in the year when Australia was established as a federal nation-state. In contrast to much of the spontaneous and individually organised migration to the US, Australian immigration policy was highly planned and managed from the outset. This planning was evident from the early forced migration and settlement of convicts in Australia, through to the financial assistance scheme provided by the Australian government to selected migrants in later years (until 1982) to fund their travel and resettlement (Jupp, 2007). This perhaps goes some way to explaining contemporary concerns with 'spontaneous migration', routes of entry and playing by the rules.

International disapproval of race-based policies in the wake of the Holocaust was one factor precipitating the removal of race as grounds for immigration determination in the US and Australia (Vickers and Isaac, 2012). In the US, the Immigration and Nationality Act 1965 'prohibited preferences or discrimination in the issuance of immigrant visas based on "race, sex, nationality, place of birth, or place of residence", with specified exceptions' (Fitzgerald and Cook-Martin, 2014:120). Meanwhile, in Australia, international pressure combined with domestic economic interests to push for an opening of the borders to non-British immigrants (Jupp, 2007). The White Australia policy was dismantled gradually between the late 1940s and early 1970s and officially rescinded in 1972 by the Whitlam-led Labor government (Jupp, 2007).

Yet, just as immigration and race were becoming officially delinked in Australia and the US, in the UK in the 1960s and early 1970s a series of immigration acts were passed[1] which effectively (although not explicitly) linked nationality and immigration status to race. This was in response to concerns from the public and some politicians about the supposed social discord that would ensue from 'coloured' immigration. As the UK sought to rebuild after the war, it faced the loss of Empire while receiving migrants who were pursuing employment opportunities in the post-war economy. Beginning in the late 1940s, an increasingly narrow legal definition emerged of who was British in this new context and world order, and tiered statuses and entitlements were established; this linking of immigration status to entitlements has since become a familiar feature of British social policy. Finally, after promising in the election of 1970 that there would be no further large-scale permanent migration to the UK, the Conservative government passed the Immigration Act 1971. This distinguished between citizens of Britain and its colonies on patrial lines, taking away rights of black citizens of the Commonwealth to automatically settle in the UK (Solomos, 2003).

'Deserving' and 'undeserving' immigrants and the criminalisation of migration

Tirman (2015) states that two central pillars of the US national narrative are that it is a nation of immigrants and a nation of laws. There is a preoccupation with whether and how people have entered 'illegally'. A similar claim could be made about the UK or Australia where mode of entry and the notion of 'illegality' have become increasingly dominant in public debates. However, laws are not neutral. Certain groups have been scapegoated and made 'illegal' through the creation of laws and shifts in their enforcement (Cacho, 2012; Ioanide, 2015; Tirman, 2015).

While early 20th century concerns around immigration in the US primarily centred on Asian and Southern European immigrants, from the 1980s the debate shifted to Latinx, and specifically Mexican, immigrants. Mexicans comprise more than a quarter of legal permanent residents and half of undocumented immigrants in the US (Golash-Boza, 2012). There is a long history of Mexican immigration to the US as people crossed the border to work seasonally in agriculture or to fill other labour shortages. During the 1970s and 1980s, the need for Mexican labour did not match the number of visas issued and undocumented immigration rose to unprecedented levels, leading to public pressure to introduce controls (Golash-Boza, 2012). The Immigration Reform and Control Act 1986 legalised 2.7 million undocumented immigrants. However, it also heightened border enforcement and introduced sanctions for employers who employed undocumented immigrants (Golash-Boza, 2012).

The Immigration and Nationality Act 1990 expanded the grounds for deporting those engaged in criminal activities, which increased the number of deportable immigrants. The Illegal Immigration Reform and Immigrant Responsibility Act 1996 then eliminated judicial review of some deportation orders and introduced mandatory detention for many non-citizens, including asylum applicants (Golash-Boza, 2012; Nicholls, 2013). In the post-9/11 era, immigration policy became increasingly subject to securitisation. As Golash-Boza (2012:142) observes, 'the War on Terror has translated into a War on Immigrants. That's because of the fusion of national security with immigration law enforcement and the consequent allocation of funds to enforce immigration policy'.

Debates on Latinx immigration have centred on concerns about 'illegality' and criminality (Stumpf, 2006). Given that Latinx are the fastest-growing ethnic population in the US, there have also been fears among white populations about the loss of cultural identity (Chavez, 2013; Tirman, 2015). Despite evidence that immigrants commit less crime than native-born populations and pay taxes, myths have been propagated in the media and by anti-immigrant groups that portray undocumented migrants (particularly Mexicans) as criminals, and as 'invaders' who want a Reconquista of the southwest of the US (Tirman, 2015; Ousey and Kubrin, 2018). They are shown as a drain on public services, while simultaneously taking jobs from US citizens (Chavez, 2013). The frequent use of the term 'illegals' in public debates on undocumented immigration, not least in the presidential election in 2016, dehumanised this population by criminalising not only their behaviour, but also their very personhood; they themselves were defined as 'illegal' (Cacho, 2012).

There have been numerous failed attempts to introduce substantial immigration reform since the Illegal Immigration Reform and Immigrant Responsibility Act 1996. These have included enforcement only, and enforcement and legalisation bills (Martin 2014). Due to failure to pass federal legislation, laws and resolutions relating to immigration (considered a federal issue) have subsequently been introduced and passed at state level (Ioanide, 2015). By the end of 2011, state legislatures had passed 306 laws and resolutions which restricted or excluded undocumented immigrants in 45 states (Tirman, 2015; Schwiertz, 2016). Following the 2016 presidential election, there has been a renewed flurry of state-level legislation as states have sought to roll out, or resist, the policies of the

Trump administration which have faced legislative hurdles at federal level (Johnston and Simon, 2017; Ulloa, 2017).

In Australia, there has also been significant attention to the supposed 'illegality' of some would-be immigrants and refugees. This has primarily been directed towards 'boat people'; this vernacular term has been used to describe immigrants (usually people seeking asylum) who arrive by boat without visas. The first refugees to arrive in Australia by boat came in 1976, following the establishment of the Communist regimes in Vietnam, Cambodia and Laos and the subsequent Indochinese refugee crisis. Over the next year around 2,000 people seeking asylum arrived via this route (Gleeson, 2016). Although there were concerns about the unregulated flow, Australia took part in facilitating the resettlement of these people in Australia and elsewhere in the region (Gleeson, 2016). However, when arrivals via this route increased again in 1989, border controls began to be instituted. In 1992, the Keating government introduced mandatory detention for unauthorised immigrants arriving in Australia, including asylum seekers arriving by boat (Laney et al, 2016).

In 2001, the Howard government introduced offshore detention (McKay et al, 2017). Under this policy, boats were intercepted at sea and passengers shipped to offshore detention centres on the Pacific islands of Nauru and Manus Island (Papua New Guinea) (Peterie, 2017). The policy was introduced in the aftermath of what became known as the Tampa Affair, which took place in the run up to the 2001 federal elections (Laney et al, 2016). On 24 August, the Norwegian freighter, the MV Tampa, rescued 438 mainly Afghan asylum seekers from a sinking vessel that had set sail from Indonesia. The Australian government refused to permit the Captain to enter Australian waters, stating that Indonesia (which had not ratified the 1951 Convention on Refugees) was responsible. When the Tampa entered Australian waters without permission and anchored off the coast of Christmas Island, the Australian military intervened and boarded the ship. Border protection laws were adjusted retroactively so that Christmas Island was excluded from the Australian immigration zone and the Tampa passengers were not deemed to have landed in Australia. The Australian government paid its impoverished former colonies of Papua New Guinea and Nauru to detain people from the Tampa until their asylum claims were processed (Vickers and Isaac, 2012). It was in this period that Prime Minister Howard issued his infamous statement that, 'We will decide who comes into this country and the circumstances in which they come' (Martin, 2015:314). As mentioned earlier, this is a sentiment that stretches back to Australia's history of planned immigration and settlement (Martin, 2015). This focus on control has endured since then, as illustrated by Tony Abbott's statement in the 2013 election (which he went on to win) that, 'This is our country and we determine who comes here' (Martin, 2015:314). A month after the Tampa Affair, on 7 October 2001, the 'children overboard incident' took place. The HMAS Adelaide intercepted an Indonesian fishing vessel with 187 Iraqi asylum seekers on board. In what were later proven to be false allegations, it was claimed by the government that children had been thrown overboard by their parents (Perera, 2013). This was used to discredit their humanity, evidencing the uncivilised nature and savagery of these people who did not love their children (Perera, 2013), and, thus, their incompatibility with Australian values. This echoed colonial assertions that children should be saved from their savage cultures and parents. Taking place in the run up to the election, political advantage was maximised to garner public support for a restrictive asylum regime.

Kevin Rudd's Labor government ended the 'Pacific Solution' policy in February 2008 (Maley, 2008). This was announced as part of Rudd's 2007 election pledge in which he promised a more 'compassionate Australia' that would also deliver a better deal for indigenous people, homeless people and low paid workers (Schubert, 2007). This demise of offshore detention was short lived. As the numbers of refugees arriving by sea increased again, offshore detention was reintroduced by the Labor government in 2012. In 2013, following his re-election, the Liberal Prime Minister, Tony Abbott, renewed his party's commitment to offshore detention, which formed a central pillar of the new military-led Operation Sovereign Borders. The operation comprises mandatory and indefinite detention for unauthorised people who arrive by boat to Australia, boat turnbacks, and temporary protection visas (Gleeson, 2016).

In the UK, asylum also became a central topic of debate in the 1990s and 2000s as the numbers of people applying for asylum there rose, reaching a peak of 84,132 applicants in 2002 (Bloch and Schuster, 2002; Blinder, 2016). Over the 1990s, 2000s and 2010s there was a proliferation of immigration and asylum legislation beginning with the Asylum and Immigration Appeals Act 1993. Since then 10 more immigration and border acts have been passed, including most recently, at the time of writing, the Immigration Acts of 2014 and 2016. Each new piece of legislation has introduced further conditions and restrictions on asylum seekers and migrants[2] (Hynes, 2011; Lewis et al, 2015). It has been argued that the central premise behind this catalogue of immigration legislation and policies was to create a distinction between 'deserving' refugees and 'undeserving' asylum seekers (Sales, 2002; Hayter, 2004). In breaking down the generic category of 'refugee' into 'refugees' who have had their asylum claims accepted, and 'asylum seekers' who have applied for asylum and are waiting for their case to be resolved, the government continued to claim that the UK welcomes and supports 'genuine' refugees, while simultaneously enacting harsh conditions for asylum seekers who had yet to prove their deserving status. A common mantra that the UK has a 'proud history of welcoming refugees' is often proclaimed at the beginning of government statements and documents, which then proceed to set out further restrictions (Sirriyeh, 2014). This claim is used to pre-empt criticism that the UK is averse to receiving refugees and neglects its ethical responsibilities. However, although the UK has a long history of receiving refugees, this has often been through gritted teeth, and the state also has a long history of refusing and excluding refugees (London, 2000; Hayter, 2004; Trilling, 2016).

Immigration detention (introduced in the Immigration Act 1971) was rarely used before the 1990s, but over the course of the 1990s and 2000s its use expanded rapidly as part of the broader criminalisation and securitisation of asylum and immigration (Bosworth, 2014; Lewis et al, 2015). The UK now has the largest detention estate in Europe with between 2,000 and 3,500 people detained at any one time, approximately 45% of whom are asylum seekers (Migration Observatory, 2017).

The mid-2000s also saw a shift from a focus on restricting asylum to restrictions on immigration more broadly (Lewis et al, 2015), and an increased blurring of immigration categories in public debates. In this period, migrants from the eight Eastern European EU accession countries who joined the EU in 2004, and Bulgaria and Romania in 2007, attained rights to work and settle in the UK. Despite evidence that these migrants made a net fiscal contribution (Dustmann and Frattini, 2013), there was a public and political backlash with fears expressed about competition for jobs with British workers, strains on public services and the often voiced, but less tangible, sense of a 'loss of control'. This culminated in the vote for Brexit in the June 2016 referendum on Britain's continuing membership of the EU.

Conclusion

Since their inception, the emotional regimes of immigration policy have centred on anxieties and fears about immigration, and have been constructed around attempts to identify and exclude the undesirable migrant. It has become an established social norm that the governments, and populations they govern, should feel concerned about immigration and fearful about its consequences. While such responses have fluctuated in their intensity during different periods, they have been an enduring and dominant feature of political discourse.

However, they are not the only emotions on display, nor are such responses applied in equal measure to all immigrants. While the social category of 'undesired' migrant endures, at times there have been shifts as particular populations fall into or are, to some degree, cleansed and released from the hostile gaze which turns its focus on another group. Meanwhile, governments have also expressed celebratory sentiments about immigration. The precise nature of these vary from state to state according to the way in which immigration is configured in the national story. However, there is a sense of celebration that centres as its subject not just the immigrants, but the society which receives and incorporates them. Since the late 20th century, celebratory discourses about immigration have become a central tool in demonstrating the realisation of the modern, civilised and successful nation-state and peoples. The remaining chapters in this book explore how governments maintain and weave together these seemingly contradictory responses to immigration, and how this is challenged through mobilisations of compassion. Each chapter explores a different element of the feeling and framing rules of compassion discussed in Chapter Two, to examine how these enable resistance to exclusionary immigration policies, but also how various forms of compassionate refusal emerge. This begins with a discussion of the visual testimony of the death of Alan Kurdi, to examine compassion as a catalyst for resistance.

Notes

[1] See the Commonwealth Immigration Act 1962, the Commonwealth Immigration Act 1968, and the Immigration Act 1971.

[2] There is insufficient scope to discuss these in depth here. See Hynes (2011).

4

The Intolerable Death
of Alan Kurdi

Introduction

In the early hours of 2 September 2015, the photo-journalist, Nilüfer Demir, arrived at a beach in Bodrum to photograph refugees embarking on treacherous journeys in rubber dinghies across the Aegean Sea from Turkey to Greece. As the morning light broke she spotted the small drowned figure of three-year-old Alan Kurdi washed up on the shore. Alan had died along with 11 other Syrian refugees, including his mother (Rehan) and five-year-old brother (Galip), who had set off in the same boat. Demir took a series of photographs of Alan who was wearing a red t-shirt, blue shorts and trainers. Some depicted him alone lying face down on the beach as the water lapped against his face. Others showed him being carried by a Turkish police officer. The photographs were initially posted by journalists on Turkish social media and then rapidly shared across the world accompanied by the hashtag #KiyiyaVuranInsanlik (humanity washed ashore) (D'Orazio, 2015). They went on to become iconic images of the refugee crisis and were a catalyst for an unprecedented outpouring of sentiments of compassion among media, the public and politicians.

Since the late 19th century it has been claimed that some immigrants and refugees are 'undesirable', and that their arrival should evoke hostility in receiving societies because of the supposed threats that they pose to citizens and their way of life. However, although such responses have remained an enduring and dominant feature of political and public discourse, these are not the only emotions present in contemporary debates on immigration and asylum. The current and following chapters examine how a discourse of 'compassion' has been incorporated into political and public debates on immigration and asylum policy. The discussion begins in this chapter with the case of the iconic visual testimony of the death of Alan Kurdi in 2015, which was (prematurely) heralded as a turning point in public attitudes to refugees in Europe. After discussing the role of testimony and the phenomenon of witness bearing, the response to the tragic death of the child is examined to explore how compassion was mobilised in critiques of the restrictive policies and lack of action by the UK during the refugee crisis. Drawing on a discourse analysis of UK national newspaper articles that reported on Alan's death between 2 and 30 September 2015, the chapter examines why the photographs were recognised as a compelling message and how responses engaged with a discourse of compassion. The final section of the chapter draws on an analysis of speeches in the UK parliament on the refugee crisis to consider the debates on proposals to resettle refugees in the UK, particularly children, in the aftermath of Alan's death.

Emotion and resistance

There is a growing literature on protest and resistance by migrants and allies which explores their production of counter-narratives of identity, belonging, legality and social justice (McNevin, 2011; Nyers and Rygiel, 2012; Marciniak and Tyler, 2014). Studies have examined how counter-narratives have contested exclusions through demonstrating how people fit into the category of the 'good' immigrant: through seeking to shift understandings of what this category is, or by rejecting such categorisation altogether. Yet, despite acknowledging that hostile emotions drive restrictionist policies, discussion of how activists engage with emotions in efforts to disrupt and rewrite these feeling and framing rules has been more limited.

Emotions play a central role in guiding attitudes and decision-making, and are a key feature of contemporary political and public discourse. As George, a campaigner from a leading refugee rights organisation in Australia interviewed for this research, said, simply presenting factual-based arguments alone in immigration debates is not enough since, 'fact is not going to win. Fear trumps fact always'. Therefore, campaigning must also engage with emotions. Pro-migrant and refugee campaigns frequently seek to invoke compassion, which is often perceived as the antidote emotion to hostility. Compassion, an emotion that connects individuals with one another and hooks the interests of others to our own, is potentially useful for resistance, but is not without perils.

The following chapters examine how campaigners have engaged with compassion through exploring how this emotion features in the testimonial discourse and evidence engaged with in the process of bearing witness. Woolley (2016:8) explains that testimony has become 'the prevailing narrative mode for refugee experience' and for some campaign organisations is a 'cornerstone of a process of bearing witness to oppression, torture and marginalization'. Campaigns have used testimonies to personalise and thus humanise people's stories in their effort to generate compassion for refugees and other immigrants who are marginalised.

In the case of Alan Kurdi, the invocation of compassion through testimonial evidence interrupted and problematised hostile political discourse towards immigrants and refugees. It even succeeded in mobilising a temporary shift in public attitudes, media reporting and government policy. As seen in the response to the death of Alan and other cases explored in this book, children and young people have often been the primary focus of compassion. It is argued that this is because of the way the stories of these children and young people were encountered and narrated, engaging an audience through the emotional regimes of childhood and national identity. These narratives mapped onto the criteria for compassion outlined by Nussbaum (2013) (see Chapter Two), and interrupted the hostile emotional regime of asylum and immigration. However, compassion has also been problematic when the model of compassion engaged with has engendered exclusions and inhibited the response-ability of migrants and refugees giving testimony.

Bearing witness

Kurasawa (2009) perceives that 'in response to distant suffering, global civil society is being consumed by a generalised witnessing fever that converts public spaces into veritable machines for the production of testimonial discourses and evidence'. Bearing witness as part of the response to human rights violations has been sanctioned and institutionalised through international criminal tribunals and truth commissions, and the use of testimonies by humanitarian organisations and activist groups in awareness and fundraising campaigns (Kurasawa, 2009; Kilby and Rowland, 2014). With the proliferation of contradictory information and evidence and a denigration of the credibility and status of experts, being convinced is often a matter of hearing the most convincing narrative from the most convincing messenger who persuades us through a melding of logic *and* pathos. As the 2016 vote for Brexit and election of President Trump attest to, 'facts' are increasingly disbelieved or, even if accepted, are not sufficient if they do not sit comfortably with an emotional narrative that is felt and invested in by those who feel hostility or ambivalence towards immigrants and refugees. Therefore, a key task for campaigners is to challenge hostile emotional narratives on immigration and asylum and offer a persuasive alternative emotional narrative in their place. Kelly Oliver (2015:473) reflects on the dual meaning of witnessing which can refer to '*eyewitness* testimony based on first-hand knowledge', or '*bearing witness* to something beyond recognition that can't be seen'. Witnessing takes us beyond eyewitnessing and recognition to 'the affective and imaginative dimensions of experience' (Oliver, 2015:473). Seeing requires not only recognition, but also imagination and pathos.

In discussing the ethico-political labour of bearing witness, Kurasawa (2009) observes that bearing witness is a dialogical process. Within it, primary witnesses (victims and survivors of atrocities) and secondary witnesses (those who witnessed these atrocities, but did not experience them), such as journalists, NGO staff and international observers, 'reconstitute and transmit their first-hand experiences of catastrophe in order to initiate struggles against silence, incomprehension, indifference, forgetting and return; they write messages, place them in bottles and send them out to sea' (Kurasawa, 2009:96). However, bearing witness depends on these messages reaching land, being read, understood and responded to accordingly, by addressees who in doing so become testimonial audiences. Testimonial practices aim to raise an awareness and understanding of suffering and, in doing so, elicit compassion, induce a feeling of moral responsibility and, therefore, a desire and action to alleviate that suffering. Kurasawa (2009) draws attention to the perils that can jeopardise the process: the message may not be sent or may not reach its intended audience; it may be incomprehensible to the audience; and, even if comprehended, it may not elicit empathy. Finally, the message may be distorted over time and may not help to alleviate this suffering or avert future suffering.

Some groups have a better chance than others of navigating these perils successfully because they have greater access to material and symbolic resources that enable them to influence and gain support from audiences who make judgements on what is a compelling message. Whitlock (2007) has argued that while some life narratives enter the 'transit lane' and are heard by wider audiences, others become 'trapped' in the immediate communities that experienced the suffering. She (2007:74) observes that this is often due to 'whose lives count and under what circumstances' and that to 'accrue value and jurisdiction testimony needs fortune, history and national history on its side' (Whitlock, 2007:79). Due to these challenges, testifiers are sometimes unable to present their experiences in the terms they would prefer, as these would not appeal to the addressees (Wright, 2009). This is problematic if testifiers are required to repress, or alter, aspects of their identities and experiences, or if the process of bearing witness becomes more about the feelings and needs of the addressee than the person who is testifying.

Humanity washed ashore

The death of Alan Kurdi

Speaking with *Vice News* two days after Alan's death Demir said, 'I am happy that the world finally cares and is mourning the dead children. I hope that my picture can contribute to changing the way we look at immigration in Europe' (Kupeli, 2015). In the initial aftermath of the publication of the photographs it seemed as if her hope had materialised. The photographs were a catalyst for an unprecedented outpouring of sentiments of compassion among the media, the public and politicians. In Western Europe the tone of media coverage and public debate on refugees altered overnight (European Journalism Observatory, 2015; Goodman et al, 2017); this was the case even among those British newspapers known for negative reporting on immigration and asylum (Philo et al, 2013). For example, referring to the fate of 'tragic Aylan Kurdi', the *Sun* newspaper launched a 'For Aylan' campaign to raise funds for the charity Save the Children for its work with refugee children.

Mortensen and Trenz (2016:344) described the spontaneity and immediacy of the emergence of a social media public response to the images of Alan, referring to this as an example of the formation of 'impromptu publics' online. Boltanski (1999) has used the concept of 'moral spectatorship' to describe such scenarios where audiences are confronted with suffering at a distance through the media. Instead of encountering suffering as an individual spectator, the openness and interaction on social media supports the constitution of 'publics of shared concerns' (Mortenson and Trenz, 2016:345). People respond to the suffering which they are directly confronted with, but due to the public nature of social media, they can also scrutinise the responses of other spectators and be scrutinised by them. Support for action can be mobilised online by sharing feelings and responding to each other's feelings to raise alarm or call for action.

The outpouring of sentiments of compassion following Alan's death also translated into debate and action in the offline world. In the UK, there was a substantial rise in public donations to charities working with refugees and enquires about volunteering (Merrill, 2015). Campaigners interviewed in the UK for this study spoke of the immediate response their organisations saw. One campaigner, Jane, said,

> The picture of Alan moved a lot of people. That picture spoke more than a thousand words [...] I know our website went up from a couple of hundred hits a week to over 5,000 the following week. People were searching the internet for 'this is more than I can bear. What can I do.'

Due to the UK's geographical location and the limited humanitarian resettlement opportunities provided by the UK government, this iteration of the refugee 'crisis' did not actually reached the UK, although people have experienced serious suffering in the asylum process there (Sigona, 2016). During the third quarter of 2015, 11,870 people applied for asylum in the UK (Eurostat, 2015). In contrast, 108,305 people applied for asylum in Germany, more than any other European state (Eurostat, 2015). Even before Alan's death there had been a widespread response of welcome among the German public with many offering housing and other forms of support (Harding, 2015). At the end of August 2015, Chancellor Merkel announced that Germany would grant asylum to Syrian refugees arriving in the country. A few days after the publication of Alan's image, hundreds of German citizens turned out to cheer refugees arriving at the train station in Munich from Hungary and Austria (Connolly, 2015). Conor, another UK-based campaigner interviewed for this study, suggested that the circulation of Alan's photographs, the example set by Germany, and a sense of impatience with the lack of action from the British government, prompted the British public to take direct action.

> It helped to galvanise a sense of what is possible. If German people can do it, we should be able to do something similar. They've opened up hostels, or started English lessons; there was a sense of the possible. People like us are helping so there is an element of permission. So that was a huge part of it too. People saying, "refugees welcome in Germany", and people saying, "refugees welcome here [UK]" as well.

In addition to donating to existing charities, people established grassroots campaigns and aid groups. As Mayblin (2015) has observed, these focused on the plight of refugees in Greece and Calais, but less attention was given to hardships faced by people in the UK asylum system.

Refugees welcome?

In January 2014, the UK's Coalition government launched the Syrian Vulnerable Persons Resettlement Programme (SVPRP), in response to lobbying from charities and politicians across political parties (May, 2014) (discussed further in Chapter Six). No fixed quota was established, and by September 2015 only 239 refugees had been resettled under the scheme (Gower and Cromarty, 2016). Given the limited humanitarian resettlement offered thus far, pressure mounted on the UK government both from civil society and within the political establishment to act further to alleviate the suffering of refugees. On 2 September, the *Independent* newspaper (2015) launched a petition titled 'Refugees Welcome', calling on the British government to resettle more refugees. This was published alongside Demir's photograph of Alan's body. By the following day the petition had been signed by 100,000 people (Withnall, 2015). A series of rallies under the banner of 'Refugees Welcome' were organised (Graham-Harrison and Davies, 2015). A national 'Refugees Welcome' movement was established by Citizens UK which campaigned for increased refugee resettlement in the UK and aimed to provide a welcoming response to those refugees who arrived.[1] As pressure mounted, on 7 September, Prime Minister David Cameron announced an expansion of the SVPRP in response to 'the heartbreaking images' of Alan.[2] The government committed to resettling 20,000 Syrian refugees through the SVPRP over the course of that parliament.

Emotions are ambivalent and unpredictable, and so attempts by governments to engage public emotions can have unpredictable results (Burkitt, 2005). Politicians must be quick to sense shifts in public sentiment and adjust their messaging accordingly (Gilligan, 2016), especially since these shifts can be rapid and fluid as 'impromtu publics' suddenly emerge (Mortensen and Trenz, 2016). Hostile or ambivalent feelings that had framed dominant political discourse on asylum and immigration for so long, no longer made sense when applied to the image and moment of Alan's death. Therefore, expressions or actions from politicians or public commentators that drew on hostile emotions were now interpreted by many members of the public, the media and other commentators as disgusting, inappropriate and therefore shameful. This was a demonstration of the power of the emotional regime of childhood to disrupt, or at least problematise, the hostile emotional regime of asylum and immigration. This perhaps explains why children, especially young children, are often the face of refugee and migrant rights campaigns that draw on a discourse of compassion.

The outpouring of sentiments of compassion among the British public became, in itself, a news story in the British press (Addley and Gani, 2015). This shift in media reporting initially appeared as a rupture in the feeling rules that had dominated immigration and asylum policy discourse in the UK for such a long time. However, although coverage in UK and other Western European newspapers became more sympathetic towards refugees and migrants immediately after the publication of Alan's photographs, by the end of September 2015 it had reverted to a more negative stance (European Journalism Observatory, 2015). Two months later, on 13 November 2015, terrorist attacks took place in Paris and a Syrian passport was found at the scene. A few weeks later, on New Year's Eve, a number of women were sexually assaulted in a public square in Cologne in Germany. In both cases it was alleged that people[3] who had entered Europe in the refugee flows were among the perpetrators (Traynor, 2015a; Mortimer, 2016). There were subsequent reports of a wane in public enthusiasm for resettling refugees in the UK, while media reports associated 'migrants' with security risks (Nail, 2016). Still, volunteers and donations continued to make their way to refugees and migrants in Calais and Greece.

Meanwhile, concern for the suffering of child refugees shifted focus to the plight of unaccompanied refugee children who had already reached Europe. In January 2016, Europol claimed that 10,000 unaccompanied minors had gone missing in Europe (Townsend, 2016) (although this figure has been queried) (Sigona and Humphries, 2017). This led to further pressure from campaigners and parliament's International Development Committee (IDC) on the government to resettle some of these children in the UK (IDC, 2016). The government initially refused to do so, stating that children and families would only be resettled directly from camps in the Middle East so as not to incentivise children to make risky journeys to Europe (Brokenshire, 2016). However, an amendment to the Immigration Bill 2016, proposed by Lord Dubs in February 2016,[4] provided for the resettlement of some unaccompanied young people who had arrived in France, Greece and Italy. The amendment was eventually passed on 4 May 2016. The original proposal was for 3,000 children to be resettled through this programme, but no quota was established in the final version of the amendment. The first young people accepted through this programme finally began arriving in the UK in October 2016 (Lusher, 2016). However, less than a year later in February 2017, it was announced that the programme would end, after just 200 children had been brought to the UK.[5]

Visual testimony

Speaking of the response to Alan's death, Josie (an Australian anti-detention campaigner interviewed for this study) commented that a challenge in campaigning against Australia's offshore detention of refugees was the lack of visual images in public circulation (see also Perera [2013] and Gleeson [2016] about restrictions on media access). She compared this to news footage in the early 2000s showing boats arriving in Australia carrying asylum seekers on board:

> When the boats were still coming. You could see it every night of the week on the telly. It was a very visual thing. People drowning in sight of Christmas Island. There aren't any visuals really, unlike Alan Kurdi. No one can take photos on Nauru legally.

According to Evans (2017:3) the way in which we narrate images is 'crucial to the authentication and disqualification of the meaning of lives'. Studies on audience interactions with visual material used in the media highlight the power of visuals to arouse emotion, including fear and disgust, but also empathy (Joffe, 2008). Discussing the representation of refugees, Hoijer (2004:520) claims that 'compassion depends on visuals'.

On social media and in newspaper articles, people described the emotional experience of engaging with the photographs of Alan Kurdi, often stating that they had cried when they saw them. A common metaphor used in the press coverage reviewed for this study was that of physical damage to the heart (which was 'breaking', 'aching', 'screaming' and being 'wrenched') and so damaging their feeling of emotional well-being (Hall and Macfarlan, 2015). These images seemed to penetrate, enter and jolt the physical body. Commenting in *The Guardian*, Jonathan Freedland (2015) observed that while we knew hundreds of thousands of people were dying in Syria, 'it seems, we needed to see those little shoes and bare legs to absorb the knowledge, to let it *penetrate our heads and hearts*' [italics added].

Twelve people died on that ill-fated journey out of Bodrum, but it was the young child who was photographed and memorialised. Grief for a tragic young death was the central narrative in the news reports in the immediate aftermath. The political aesthetics of immigration and childhood can be drawn on to explore why these images evoked a response of compassion. Engaging with the work of Jacques Rancière, Evans (2017:1) argues that the photographs resonated with the notion of the 'intolerable'. He defines the intolerable as that which 'disrupt[s] the aesthetic field of perception' and causes 'a fundamental rupture or breakthrough in how we come to see the world' (Evans, 2017:1). 'Too difficult to bear, yet impossible to ignore', the images of Alan were intolerable (Evans, 2017:2). In this chapter it is argued that the images were encountered and narrated in a way that engaged with the emotional regimes of childhood and national identity, in doing so mapping on to the criteria for compassion outlined by Nussbaum (2013). The testimony was compelling to audiences because it was experienced as intolerable through its simultaneous familiarity, yet extraordinary horror. The flexibility of this visual testimony enabled the story of Alan and the refugee crisis to be told in ways that were understood through pre-existing narratives that were familiar to and invested in by these audiences. However, this flexibility also enabled a limited and problematic notion of compassion that succumbed to exclusions and a limited scope of responsiveness.

'Tragic Aylan'

It has been argued that 'refugee' identity has become increasingly discredited (Fassin, 2012). This is in contrast with the social identity of the child which has endured as *the* moral touchstone (Sirriyeh, 2014). In this book it is suggested that rather than stark discreditation, the terms on which the moral category of 'genuine' refugee is recognised have become increasingly narrow and conditional. Meanwhile, the contemporary conceptualisation of the 'genuine' refugee as an innocent and vulnerable person (see Chapter Six), as opposed to earlier notions of the heroic political exile, overlaps with the sentimental image of childhood that developed in the West during the Victorian era (Jenks, 1996). In the Victorian period, the 'ideal' child was understood as fragile, untouched by the evils and corruptions of the world, dependent on the guidance of others and, therefore, innocent (Piper, 1999). Thus, while in the past children struggled to be recognised as refugees because of their perceived lack of political engagement, this reinterpretation of the refugee identity means that young child refugees are now *the* image of the deserving refugee. Speaking about anti-detention campaigns in Australia, John (an Australian campaigner) observed that, 'In our leaflets that we hand out we use a lot of "children in detention are suffering"'.

It helped that Alan was a very *young* child. Following his death, British news media shifted inconsistently between using the terms 'migrant' and 'refugee' to describe the same groups of people on the move to and across Europe, including other passengers on Alan's boat. However, Alan, was always identified through the sympathetic moral category 'refugee' which was attached to his fragile and innocent child identity (Goodman et al, 2017); he was a '*young* Syrian refugee' [italics added] (Hall and Macfarlan, 2015). Refugee and migrant rights campaigners in the UK have emphasised that migrant and refugee children should be treated as 'children first' in accordance with their rights enshrined in the UN Convention on the Rights of the Child 1989. Yet, it can be difficult to convince people when the children in question do not fit the 'ideal' and sentimentalised image of childhood. This was seen in the case of unaccompanied children admitted to the UK from Calais under the Dubs Amendment in 2016. In October 2016, prompted by media images of teenage boys arriving in the UK, Conservative MP, David Davies, suggested that they did not appear to be 'genuine children' and hoped that British 'hospitality' was not being abused (Weaver, 2016). Davies suggested that their teeth should be examined to determine their ages. As literature on the reception of unaccompanied minors attests to, this is the latest incident in a long-running culture of disbelief around the age claims of teenage refugees (Crawley, 2007; Wade et al, 2012). On the cusp of adulthood, refugee young people lose the protective cloak of child 'vulnerability'. Ambivalence around the 'innocence' of older children explains the tendency in humanitarian aid campaigns and sympathetic media reports to use images of very young children (Manzo, 2008).

Demir's photographs of Alan are now discussed together with an extract from an article by Alison Phillips published in the *Mirror* newspaper, to explore how the emotional regime of young childhood was engaged with in news reporting on Alan's death and helped to invoke compassion.

Extract One: *Mirror*, 8 September 2015 by Alison Phillips

Headline: [1] After Aylan Al-Kurdi's tragedy we must let the refugees in and learn from them; [2] Many other children have died trying to escape Syria but these vivid images of the drowned boy remind us of our own children.

[3] This week another child will most likely wash up on a Mediterranean beach.
  [4] Last week it was little Aylan Kurdi whose sleeping-for-ever baby body was carried from Bodrum beach where, by rights, three-year-olds should be building sandcastles, collecting pebbles and licking ice creams. [5] But in our gone-wrong world five-year-olds now die on holiday beaches as their

> parents flee for a new life. [6] [...] The reality we've ignored
> for the past three years is hundreds of children are dying on
> that trip every year. Most go unphotographed, unnamed and
> unnoticed [...] [7] But we saw Aylan more vividly. We saw
> his little brown shoes and denim shorts and the soft baby skin
> of his face lying in the surf.

As in all news reports of his death, the central narrative of the story was
the tragedy of *young* death (4, 5). His young age was emphasised through
adjectives used to describe his body and clothes. Phillips referred to these
as 'little' (4, 7); other articles used terms such as 'tiny' or 'small' (Stanton
et al, 2015). Approaching the story through the sensory practices and
knowledge of a parent, Phillips described Alan's 'baby body' and imagined
his 'baby soft skin'; his was a newly formed and untainted body (4, 7).
As a young child, he had a recognisable human face that people could
imagine a relationship with and responsibility for; yet, as a human being
in the making (Qvortrup, 2007) he was still considered formless in terms
of his wider social group identity, so could be understood primarily
through the discourse of childhood. He had not yet taken on board the
full and complex characteristics of refugee adults that have been tainted
in political discourse on refugees.

As well as embodied in his physical form, his fragility was marked
through his lack of agency. The photographs depicted the small child
on his own in public. He was a tragic victim at the site of the terrible
event. The image of the individual suffering child was familiar because
its composition was reminiscent of other iconic images of children in
conflict and humanitarian disasters, such as that of Phan Thi Kim Phuc
(the 'Napalm girl') in Vietnam (Hariman and Lucaites, 2010) and Sharbat
Gula (the Afghan Girl) (Newman, 2002). This close-up shot of the lone
autonomous child 'cast adrift' and suffering in a hazardous environment
waiting to be saved is a common composition in aid appeals (Manzo,
2008:642). However, the images of Alan were also distinct from these.
While campaign images usually depict children looking straight back at
the viewer, Alan's face was turned away and unresponsive; there was a lack
of address and direct appeal from him. This lack of agency and action can
be seen in the language used in news reporting on his death. Some articles
published family photographs of him in the past in his home where he
was shown animated, laughing and playing. However, once out in public
and in danger he was passive and still; Phillips wrote that he was 'drowned'
(2) 'sleeping forever' (4) and 'carried' (4). He could be portrayed as a
paradigmatic innocent subject because of his social identity as a vulnerable,
passive and abandoned child. He did not demand anything from us, unlike

other refugees who were pictured having succeeded in crossing into Europe, or gathered at border crossings asking to be let through.

In much of the reporting, Alan was referred to as 'tragic Aylan'. In Phillips' article, and other news reporting and commentary, a contrast was made between these tragic circumstances and what a 'proper' childhood should be. In some articles, the story of Alan and Galip's deaths was published alongside a family photograph of them (Alan wearing the same red t-shirt) in happier times, laughing as they clutched a teddy bear; this was a childhood lost. The materiality of childhood was drawn on to connect Alan's childhood to familiar markers of childhood that were known and understood by the readers. His 'little brown shoes' were commented on (7). Meanwhile, his fate was contrasted with what a childhood experience on the beach should be like – 'building sandcastles, collecting pebbles and licking ice creams' (4). Leisure activities associated with a happy childhood were brought into sharp contrast with the tragic end to childhood that Alan and Galip had been dealt, 'dying on holiday beaches' (5). Death was even more horrific and shocking because it was out of place in this familiar and usually happy setting.

Since the Victorian era, charity campaigns have focused on the plight of 'children without a childhood' (Piper, 1999:36; Nunn, 2004) and the notion of 'child saving', whereby they are rescued and restored to proper childhood (O'Dell, 2007). Children in Victorian charity images were portrayed as physically frail, vulnerable, and without a voice (Piper, 1999). Children on the move in the public world of adults needed to be returned to the private and still world of the domestic and family sphere to be cared for. These sentiments also appeared in British colonial contexts. In Australia, missionaries reported their struggles in trying to 'help' Aboriginal children, who were mobile and would not stay in settlements (Kidd, 1997). In the UK, concern over child mobility focused on street children whose independence placed them at risk of harm, but also potentially made them harmful to others, reflecting the binary conceptualisation of children as either victims or threats (Brown, 2014). Young refugee children, such as Alan, mobile and thus out of place, are today's children without a childhood. Their fragility and dependence on others places them at risk of serious suffering or harm, and in need of protection from corruption and harm from adults. If their family or guardians are unavailable or unsuitable then this role falls on the wider community positioned as 'the universal parent' (Warner, 2015:7).

In the photographs where Alan was not alone, he was shown in the arms of a rescuer (the Turkish police officer), who was a stranger rather than his parents. We encountered him and were held in that moment with the child in the surf. We did not see where he came from, who he was with or where he was going. Shown as if he was alone in this tightly focused single scene, the image was cleansed of any complicating association with adult refugees or migrants and the wider political context. The primary narrative was that of the lone and suffering child. As Manzo (2008:636) observes, 'tropes of *innocence, dependence* and *protection,* have a far longer lineage in colonial ideology (including the child-centrism of missionary iconography) and development theory'. The civilising mission itself was based on 'the discursive relationship between an individual developed subject and a non-developed object', which 'implicitly contains a parent–child metaphor' (Manzo, 2008:636). Children in colonised populations were children and so considered to be relatively innocent and untarnished, with the potential to become civilised. Yet, raised in 'savage' cultures they were at risk of harm from their cultural environments and families, and so could also become harmful and threatening. Through understandings of the life course and civilisation based on linear and racialised notions of development (see Chapter Three), the colonial child precariously traversed these two moral frames of child and racialised Other at the borderlines of conditional inclusion. This could be said for the refugee or migrant child today.

Close-up shots of lone, autonomous and (sometimes) anonymous children obscure the distinguishing features of their experience, the adults in their lives, and cultures and environments. This enables the testimony to be more easily responded to by audiences in the West, while it risks undermining a more complex and authentic testimony of a child's particular experience. This could be anyone's child, even our child, as Phillips reflected on at the beginning of her article (2).

Circles of concern

People may recognise that other people have intrinsic value as human beings, and acknowledge that they have experienced serious and undeserved suffering. However, these plights do not all trigger the same emotional response or intensity of feeling. Nor do they trigger the same responses in everyone, since this also depends on people's individual biographical trajectories and how this disposes them to differing emotional entanglements, even as they encounter the same events and people (Burkitt, 2014). Nussbaum (2013) argues that emotions are eudaimonistic; that is, they appraise the world through an evolving conception of what is necessary for human flourishing or a worthwhile life from the viewpoint of the person who feels the emotion. People are more likely to feel strong emotions if people or events are in their 'circle of concern'.

It was not simply the narrative of childhood that generated a response of compassion in Alan's case, but how this was woven into imaginings of a 'valuable life'. This enabled Alan, and by extension some other refugees, to be drawn into people's circle of concern. Two overriding stories emerged. First, the photographs prompted audiences to reflect on their own familial experiences, and thus imagine themselves and their families into the story of Alan and his parents. Second, the story of his death became part of a story about national and European identity and the UK's supposed record as a role model nation on the 'right side' of history.

In their shoes

Eudaimonistic judgement is more expansive than Aristotle's judgement of similar possibilities (the sense that 'this could happen to us'). However, Nussbaum (2013:320) accepts that imagining that we have similar possibilities can be a tool that supports our 'eudaimonistic imagination' and so can be 'an epistemological aid to forming the eudaimonistic judgement'. One explanation for the response of compassion to Alan's death is that people were able to imagine similar possibilities for themselves and their loved ones. They connected the event of his death through the narrative of the family, including the emotional regime of the family, to their own lives. Without more extensive empirical and biographical data from members of the public who viewed and responded to the images, the following discussion does not seek to make claims about how this intersected with other factors and played out in the context of people's individual biographies. However, through reviewing emerging literature and commentary on social media postings about Alan, and analysis of the British press coverage of his death, it is argued that the 'if I were in their shoes' story was a key narrative that emerged in public debate and was a way in which the lives of those suffering in the refugee crisis became connected to those of British (and European) populations in the public imaginary.

A common theme in the press coverage and social media responses was how Alan's photographs prompted people to reflect on how they would feel if he was their child and to imagine the parental grief. This response is now explored through a discussion of an opinion column piece published in the *Sun* (Anon, 2015), a tabloid newspaper known for its anti-immigration reporting (Philo et al, 2013). This article is examined within a wider discussion of responses on social media to the photographs.

Extract Two: *Sun* 5 September 2015 by Anon

Headline: [1] Aylan's photo has changed everything
[2] For months we've worried about migrants massing at the borders. For years we've watched as millions were made refugees by conflicts raging out of control. [3] But none of the images we've been bombarded with has hit home with anything like the impact as that one haunting picture of Aylan Kurdi. [4] It's like all the casualties we saw only ever registered in our heads without ever truly troubling our hearts. [5] Well this week Aylan changed all that. [...] [6] We're used to seeing pictures of war and death and misery but this was different. This didn't look "foreign" or faraway. It didn't feel unconnected or "other". [7] The figure here of that little boy, dressed in clothes like ours, dead on a beach just like the ones we've all holidayed on, felt so close to our lives and our world. [8] A shiver went through me when I saw it. For an instant I had that panic all parents will know, that imaginary moment we all dread of seeing our own flesh and blood lying helpless and lifeless [...] [9] What Aylan's father must be going through I dread to imagine.

It was suggested that before Alan's photographs, images of migrants and refugees were only responded to cognitively without 'truly troubling our hearts' (4). This recognised that judgement is based on cognition and emotion, and so was partial when people drew only on cognition. Yet the author observed that people were 'worried' about 'migrants' (2) and, therefore, it is more a change of heart that they seemed to note. People had been worried about migrants 'massing at the borders' (2) (on ominous threat); British and European populations felt vulnerable, threatened and overwhelmed; they were 'bombarded' with images.

The author then described their response to Alan's image. Unlike the 'massing' 'migrants' or 'refugees', Alan was named and his individual story was told (3, 5). Compassion, especially when understood as co-suffering, is a response to a *particular* case of suffering; it emanates out of the particular relationship between the person who is suffering and the person feeling compassion (Arendt, 1977). This creates a challenge for translation into a wider social and political response, since politics aspires to generality (Boltanski, 1999). Boltanski (1999) suggests that where this paradox is negotiated successfully, testimonies often tell a story that is 'hyper-singularised through an accumulation of the details of suffering and, at the same time, under-qualified: it is he but could be someone else'; this means that 'although singular they are none the less exemplary'. Alan's death came to symbolise the suffering of Syrian children and refugee children more generally. However, while the hyper-singularisation meant that he could be any *refugee* child, the under-qualified details also enabled his story to be understood through cultural narratives of 'the European child', who was presented as 'our' child. In the two media extracts discussed so far, it can be seen that approaching the narrative through the death of the child enabled some extension of compassion to others who were suffering. The *Sun* article focused on describing the grief felt for Alan's death, yet since childhood was understood based on the child's relationship with his carers, compassion was extended to his grieving father (9). Phillips' article (Extract One) extended the compassionate response outwards from Alan through linking him not just to his family, but to other children fleeing conflict, and from there to all refugees fleeing conflict.

Images of children drowned in the Mediterranean were in the public domain before Alan's death. While it is difficult to determine conclusively why some images are circulated more widely than others, we can consider what was distinctive about Alan's images and how this was picked up on in public discourse. Unlike the bodies of other children, including his five-year-old brother, Alan's body was not distorted by death. The author of the *Sun* article observed that people were used to seeing shocking images of 'war', 'death' and 'misery' (6), but Alan's image was different precisely because of the ordinariness of it; it 'didn't look "foreign" or faraway. It didn't feel unconnected or "other"' (6). Although audiences knew a tragic event had occurred, the author explained how they and others responded to the ordinary aspects of life they could identify with and understand from their own life experience. The implication was also that the fate of others matters more to us if they are near and similar rather than faraway and dissimilar. In the commentary and images on Twitter, Alan was frequently likened to a sleeping child'; people remarked that his posture was like that of their own children when they slept. Meanwhile, familiarity was also conveyed through the clothes he wore; the *Sun* author observed that he was 'dressed in clothes like ours' (7). Reporting in *The Guardian*, Greenslade (2015) remarked, 'Here was the body of a little boy from the east dressed for the west – in trainers and red T-shirt'. Procter and Yamada-Rice (2015) found that, his 'little shoes' were often remarked on in tweets as people imagined how someone had put his shoes on that morning. Someone had dressed him with care, and he was dressed as a European child would be, as 'our' child might be; indeed, #CouldBeMyChild, was a popular hashtag used to comment on the photographs (El-Enany, 2016). Reflecting on the use of these terms and observations, there appears to be a coded reference to ethnicity.

Finally, like Phillips, the *Sun* author also observed that the child on the beach was reminiscent of holiday photographs, except we knew something was horribly wrong (7, 8) (Evans, 2017). The images simultaneously evoked both distance and proximity leading to this moment being understood and felt as intolerable. Alan's photographs enabled people in the UK and around the world to imagine that ordinary and familiar 'ideal' childhood, while simultaneously witnessing its horrific loss – all in one image – making it intolerable. Through the #CouldBeMyChild hashtag, parents reflected on this through posting images of their own happy and animated children playing on the beach as examples of what childhood should be like, in contrast to Alan's still and lifeless body. Even the extraordinariness of the images could be translated and related to as familiar through placing them in the spectrum of parental fears. There was a physically felt emotional jolt as the lives of the *Sun* author and Alan's father became connected in a circle of concern. The image of Alan's body induced 'a shiver' through the author's body as they 'had that panic all parents will know' which is the fear their child has been harmed.

Alan's parents were absent from Demir's photographs. Their displacement gave audiences the freedom to imagine the parents' feelings and actions by placing themselves hypothetically in that position as a parent. Children's lives are commonly understood in terms of their relationships to adults and position in familial relationships (Proctor and Yamada-Rice, 2015). Reflecting on the horror of Alan's death, the *Sun* article was written from the point of view of a parent. Having described the horrific image of Alan's death, the author imagined what Alan's father felt (9). Two days after Alan's death, on 4 September, the news stories reviewed for this study centred around the images of Alan's grieving father burying his family (Stanton et al, 2015).

In newspaper coverage of the photographs and the public response, parents reflected on their everyday practices with their children and described their embodied response of pain and compassion as they looked at the pictures, held and even smelt their own children (Addley and Gani, 2015). There was also some sympathetic response in the media to the position of other desperate refugee *parents* which became connected to the tragic tale of Alan and his family. For example, nearly two weeks later on 13 September, the *Daily Mail* reported on the deaths of refugees in a shipwreck off the Greek island of Lesbos (Burrows, 2015). A key protagonist in the story, who carried his baby out of the water, was identified not only as a refugee, but as a 'father' doing all he could to save his baby in 'heartbreaking scenes'. Collectively images of refugee fathers at the time represented a more sympathetic view of masculinity which, as Allsop (2015) has identified, is a departure from the 'militarised masculinities' commonly deployed in representations of refugees and migrants.

However, although social distance is often perceived as a barrier to compassion, imagined proximity can also be problematic. It can mean that audiences do not listen for the particularities of the story told by the person giving testimony; instead listening for what they already know and recognise (Oliver, 2015). Therefore, rather than witnessing another person's story and life, it is the audience who are centred in the testimony. This is a concern highlighted in critiques of 'experiential-based' campaigns. Since charities and campaign organisations have identified empathy as the antidote to fear and hostility, there has been a proliferation of experiential campaigns designed to engender empathy among participants. For example, in Australia, the 'Ration Challenge' was organised as a Refugee Week event in 2016 (Canas, 2016). Participants were invited to eat like a refugee for a week because, as the campaign suggested, "the way to a refugee's heart is through your stomach" (Canas, 2016) (see also Gill, 2016). Such experiential exercises may have a powerful impact and be done with the best of intentions, yet there is a risk that if audiences need to *feel* it to *believe* it, they appropriate the pain felt by others and undermine the voice and legitimacy of those who testify to their suffering. Canas (2016, from RISE, a refugee and ex-detainee led organisation in Australia) has argued there is a danger that 'essentially such campaigns perpetuate a toxic, pervasive dynamic in which the suffering experienced by the 'foreign' body, needs to be translated, validated and legitimised through the white body'. Witnessing is dialogical and centres on recognition, which is undermined when those directly experiencing suffering are de-centred in testimony. Meanwhile, the proximity that is felt is temporary and partial. While audiences may have felt a sense of connection to Alan's story because they understood what it was to love and care for their own children, they did not know what it was like to live the life of Alan's family.

Focusing on the discourse of parenthood and loss may invoke compassion, but this can be fleeting and quickly turn to blame if the parent is perceived as being at fault for not acting in the way we imagine we would in their circumstances. Within a culture of 'child saving' people often also look for someone to blame. This response was seen in the days after Alan's death, when some newspapers published rumours that his father was one of the people smugglers who organised the fatal journey (Hodges, 2015; Stanton, 2015; Sykes, 2015). While Alan's death was still reported as tragic, his father was now referred to as the 'migrant' (not refugee) father who was a 'PEOPLE SMUGGLER'; this characterisation was emphasised in bold in an article in the *Express* newspaper (Sykes,

2015). There was no longer a mention of the conflict the family fled, or of the limited availability of legal routes into Europe. In echoes of colonial narratives, it was the 'savage' parent instead who was portrayed as the greatest threat to the welfare of their children, while the benevolent European peoples were their potential saviours.

Telling a national story

The saviour narrative has been central to the eudaimonistic judgement. Whitlock (2007) has argued that testimonies are more likely to be heard and well-received by Western audiences when they have national history and civic virtue on their side. A compassionate response towards Alan, and by extension some other refugees, could be incorporated within the celebratory narrative British hospitality and humanitarianism.

Discourses of national identity have often been used to indicate that refugees are a threat and/or a burden to societies receiving refugees (Anderson, 2013; Sirriyeh, 2014). However, as Every and Agoustinos (2008) and Gale (2005) found, writing in the Australian context, discourses on national identity have been used in the Australian parliament and media to support both anti *and* pro-asylum positions. These positions have drawn on a narrative that celebrates Australia as a humanitarian and multicultural nation. Every and Agoustinos (2008) observe that both pro and anti-asylum standpoints have referred to Australia's supposed history of 'generosity' and commitment to the egalitarian notion of a 'fair go'. Similar claims to generosity and a proud history of welcoming refugees have been referenced in the British government's justifications for what are often restrictive policies (Greening, 2015; May, 2015a, 2015b).

In the UK, as in Australia and the US, a discourse of hostility towards certain immigrants sits alongside a celebratory discourse on immigration that centres as its subject not just immigrants, but the societies which have received them. While Australia and the US are portrayed as 'nations of immigrants' (Every and Agoustinos, 2008; Lauret, 2016), in the UK certain immigrants are presented as having successfully *joined* the nation; they have been welcomed or at least 'tolerated' by established populations due to contributions they have made. Since the late 20th century these celebratory discourses have become a central tool in demonstrating the realisation of the modern, civilised and successful nation-state and peoples. They have enabled governments to proclaim their hospitality, generosity and civility, and the 'multicultural' qualities of these states, thus acquiring legitimacy and soft power on the international and domestic scenes (Lentin and Titley, 2011). Alsultany (2007) has used the term 'diversity patriotism' to describe these celebratory accounts of diversity as a foundation for feelings of national unity and pride in the nation.

In the UK, as in Australia, pro-asylum campaigners used the supposed generosity and proud humanitarian history of the nation to warn of the potential shame and loss of status if the UK failed to live up to this historical precedent. A compassionate response not only fitted in a celebratory national narrative of welcome and hospitality, but was also understood as necessary for undoing shame caused by the British government's inadequate response thus far to the refugee crisis, and avoiding further shame. Shame is an intensely painful emotion signalling some fundamental deficiency as a human being (Kaufman, 1992). It is experienced because we perceive others hold, or will hold, us in contempt (Ben-Ze'ev, 2000). As well as being induced by feeling 'done to', people feel shame because of the way in which they have acted or not acted (Treacher, 2007). The failure to respond compassionately to refugees was felt as shameful because of the condemnation this inaction received and the unfavourable comparisons made between the UK's response and those of other nation-states, such as Germany (Harding, 2015). The government's unhospitable actions were also felt as shameful when measured against the values and national character promoted in the celebratory narrative of British hospitality and humanitarianism. Shame can enable us to be 'cognisant of our relationships and obligations to others' (Treacher, 2007:239-40). Yet, there is also a paradox here, because to expose and acknowledge the conditions that brought about shame is in itself shaming (Rose, 2003). Therefore, shame, in its essence, is difficult for people to confront and while it may direct some people towards meeting their social obligations, others respond through denial (Cohen, 2001). This was seen in some responses to appeals for compassion in the wake of Alan's death; it was claimed that the UK did not have the resources to help, they had already done their fair share to help, not all refugees were genuine, and taking in refugees encouraged perilous journeys (Greening, 2015; HL, 2015).

In the months following the publication of the photographs, refugee rights campaigners asserted that a compassionate response to refugees (especially children) was in keeping with a British history and culture of care and welcome towards refugees. This continued a long-established narrative used in pro-refugee campaigns, which frequently reference Britain's record of welcoming refugees at various times in history, including the Kindertransports of the Second World War (Cooper, 2015). The following analysis examines how the UK's experience and role in the Second World War became the predominant focus for such narratives in the aftermath of the Alan Kurdi photographs.

As mentioned earlier, on 2 September 2015, the *Independent* (2015) published the photograph of Alan lying face down in the surf and a petition, which they asked readers to sign. The petition called on European governments to suspend the Dublin Regulation that requires people to seek asylum in the first safe country they reach, citing pressures the Regulation had placed on Greece and Italy due to their geographical location. Instead, the *Independent* declared its support for the EU quota system, and called for the UK to take its 'fair share' of people. This position was justified by drawing on national and regional history, status and duty.

The petition began by making links between Alan's death and European and British history by reminding readers that his death coincided with the anniversary of the start of the Second World War which, like the conflict Alan was fleeing, led to mass displacement and death. The petition text stated that while Europe was now at peace, the continent was once more hosting people who were 'innocent' victims of conflict. In this way conflict and the fate of strangers was made proximate through being woven into the story of Europe. These new strangers were suffering in, or on the border of, European territory and were therefore under 'our' jurisdiction and responsibility. European governments were judged to have failed in their response to the crisis. As observed in Chapter One, this line of critique had already been established in the months preceding Alan's death. While the *Independent's* petition levelled criticism at European governments in general, David Cameron's refusal to accept quotas was singled out, considered in terms of the UK's reputation on the international scene, and compared with other state responses. Germany's Chancellor Merkel was declared to be unimpressed. News stories at the time often referred to the German response to refugees and compared this with the UK. For example, on 3 September 2015 an article in *The Guardian* titled *Refugees welcome? How UK and Germany compare on migration?* compared the two countries across various indicators (including press coverage, political responses and public responses) (Harding, 2015). While the *Independent's* petition shamed the government for its lack of action, the public could rescue refugees, but also the nation, from shame. By signing the petition, the British public could work to recover the UK's precarious national narrative of humanitarianism and compassion. Despite the government's shameful (in)actions, pride was expressed in the compassionate response of the British public who could restore the narrative of the compassionate and humanitarian nation. A key theme in news reporting from this period was the story of volunteers who responded to the crisis (Henley et al, 2015; Tickle, 2015). We learned of how British people took leave from their jobs, studies and families and travelled to Calais or Greece with donations or to volunteer (Prowse, 2015).

Following pressure on the government to resettle more refugees, the SVPRP was expanded. In his statement to the House of Commons on 7 September 2015[6] announcing this expansion, Prime Minister Cameron also engaged with this narrative of the hospitable and moral nation to defend against assertions that the UK had not responded appropriately to the crisis. He collectivised the emotional responses of the British people detailed in the press reports discussed earlier, and repeated the metaphor frequently used in those reports; he declared 'the whole country has been deeply moved by the *heartbreaking* images' [italics added]. In collectivising this feeling, it become a national emotional response insinuating that 'the nation has a feeling (the nation is the subject of feeling)' (Ahmed, 2014:13). In doing so he acknowledged that the nation as a collective whole must respond. However, while the press and campaigners lamented the shame of a failure to live up to these responsibilities, Cameron instead declared pride in Britain's response; he stated, 'It is absolutely right that Britain should fulfil its moral responsibility to help the refugees, just as we have done so proudly throughout our history'. He presented the expansion of the SVPRP as an adaptation to changing circumstances and a *continuation* of the country's 'extraordinary compassion always standing up for our values and helping those in need', and living up to its responsibilities. Again, the nation became a subject of feeling; it was compassionate, and this was a source of pride, something which they could 'show the world', implying that the UK's international reputation remained intact.

As the refugee crises heightened, reference continued to be made to the UK's history of welcoming refugees and to mass displacement during the Second World War. People volunteering in camps across Europe, NGOs, as well as MPs and others on fact finding delegations, reported on the dire conditions people were living in. Concerns were now expressed in particular about the safety and welfare of unaccompanied refugee children in Europe. As mentioned earlier, in a speech to the House of Lords on 9 February 2016, Lord Dubs[7] proposed an amendment to the Immigration Bill to resettle 3,000 of these children and young people in the UK. In proposing the amendment, Lord Dubs referred to the UK's history of providing sanctuary to refugee children in the Second World War through the Kindertransport programme, through which he himself had arrived in the UK. In his speech he attempted to invoke compassion for the fate of these children through appealing to both the emotions of pride and shame. He did this through referencing an interpretation of national history that proclaimed the UK as an exemplar nation-state that had always welcomed refugees, and by drawing on the narrative of 'child saving'.

Cameron's speech pointed to the UK's track record of hospitality and compassion towards refugees. In contrast, Lord Dubs began his speech by declaring that government action was out of sync with the 'mood of the country' because people felt more could be done. He highlighted the concern the public felt for children and described the figure of the vulnerable, innocent child at risk of serious harm. He contrasted the miserable conditions in the camps with the celebrated sophistication and humanitarianism of Europe, highlighting the discrepancy between the celebrated character, values and status of the region and the shameful proof that it had fallen short of these professed standards. At the outset of his speech Lord Dubs referred to his own personal connection to this cause. He had arrived in the UK as an unaccompanied child during the Second World War. He returned to that era when he reminded the House of the legacy of British hospitality towards child refugees. He drew attention to the parallels in the plight of past and current refugee children through observing how former Kindertransport children had themselves made this link. They had expressed concern that today's refugee children are in 'dire straights', just as they had once been, and so should have the same opportunity for sanctuary. Meanwhile, through mentioning the gratitude Kindertransport children felt towards the UK, a connection was made to the discourse of futurity and childhood (Jenks, 1996). In doing so, Dubs implicitly directed the audience to consider who these new refugee children might go on to become and what they might do in return for a nation-state who gave them sanctuary.

In observing the gratitude of the Kindertransport children, Dubs highlighted this as a proud moment in British history. He contrasted the UK's morally righteous response with other countries who had refused to assist at that time. The UK was presented as having been a moral leader in that era, setting an example to other nation-states. While seeking support through such appeals to national pride, Dubs quoted statements made by MPs in support of providing refuge to Jewish children in 1938-39, but also an MP who he would not name, who had been reprimanded for his negative statements on this matter. The withholding of the name and the mention of the reprimand signalled the risk of similar shaming that could befall those opposing the Dubs' amendment. Through these remarks and references to refugee children's future, there was a veiled caution about the longevity of shame, which was not only felt in the present, but could endure when people and states are remembered for being on the wrong side of history.

While this persuasive narrative, and the mobilisation of pride and shame, appealed to the eudaimonistic judgement needed for compassion, the Kindertransport experience was taken out of context of wider history during which the UK has not acted nobly or with generosity and compassion. Meanwhile, there was also a selective narration of the response to refugees in the Second World War. While photographs and newsreel footage of unaccompanied Jewish children arriving on the Kindertransports remind us of the sanctuary offered to these children, the fate of the children's parents left behind in Nazi Europe is absent from this national experience and memory (London, 2000). Britain is remembered in retrospect as welcoming the 'genuine' refugees of the Second World War, yet there was ambivalence. They were not always seen as 'genuine' and were treated with hostility among some of the press. Meanwhile it was Jewish charities not the government who footed the bill for the provision of sanctuary to these children (London, 2000).

Conclusion

The iconic photographs of the death of Alan Kurdi have come to symbolise a perceived turning point in the emotional script of refugee reception in Europe. Gill (2016) acknowledges that pursuing compassion as a tactic of resistance has sometimes yielded positive results in asylum campaigns. However, he suggests that compassion as an activist strategy should be approached with extreme caution because it does not lead to systemic change and reconfigurations of power. It can also reinforce divisions between the notion of deserving and undeserving immigrants and refugees. Bearing in mind the critiques of compassion discussed in Chapter Two, it could also be added that a sense of an ethical responsibility can be negated when compassionate acts are framed as generous ahistorical gifts rather than duties towards rights-bearing subjects.

As outlined in Chapter One, in this book considerable scepticism is also expressed about how compassion has been mobilised in political discourse. Indeed, this chapter has highlighted some of the limitations of compassion as a force for resistance, which is expanded on in the following chapters. However, while attempts to invoke compassion have often been used as a last resort in campaigns of resistance, the case of Alan Kurdi shows that they can also be understood as first steps; as moments in time, compassionate turns can serve as much-needed interruptions to hostile discourses, but a stimulus for further actions and not an end in themselves.

Notes

1 www.refugees-welcome.org.uk
2 Hansard HC Deb. cols. 23-24 7 September 2015.
3 Only three of the 58 men arrested for the Cologne attacks were refugees (Mortimer, 2016).
4 Hansard HL Deb col. GC125 9 February 2016.
5 Hansard HC Deb.Vol. 621 col. 637 9 February 17.
6 Hansard HC Deb. cols. 23-24 7 September 2015.
7 Hansard HL Deb col. GC125 9 February 2016.

Victims, Villains
and Saviours

Introduction

Alan Kurdi's death unleashed an outpouring of expressions of compassion and calls for increased aid for refugees travelling to Europe. However, the sabre rattling soon began in parts of the British press and in Westminster (Greenslade, 2015). Two days after Alan's death, the *Sun* newspaper published an article under the headline 'Bomb IS so Aylan didn't die in vain'. The article included an extended appeal from former soldier turned Conservative MP, Johnny Mercer, who called on David Cameron to extend the military action from Iraq into Syria to combat Islamic State (IS) (Newton Dunn, 2015). The article was published alongside one of Demir's photographs of Alan, and a photograph of a jubilant smiling IS fighter waving an IS flag. Mercer implored readers to 'please remember how you felt on Thursday morning when you saw that dead boy'. The implication was that if people relived, and thus re-embodied, those feelings of horror and sadness they had felt, this would be a catalyst to propel them forward along the emotional journey into feelings of outrage and would mobilise their will to act against those identified as responsible for Alan's death, that is IS. The sense here is that people can determine the morally right course of action through listening to and reconnecting with their feelings – through 'trusting their gut'. This does not require, and in fact actively discourages, nuance or more complex argument and debate (Berlant, 2005). On 3 December 2015, British MPs voted in favour of air strikes, which began immediately.[1]

While compassion has been used to mobilise resistance to restrictive government refugee policies, this chapter explores how governments have also proclaimed compassion for 'deserving' migrants and refugees to justify the enactment of violent and punitive policies. Seemingly contradictory emotions of hostility and care have been made compatible through connecting compassion to the emotion of outrage, a practice commonly associated with activism (Clarke et al, 2006). It is posited that although hostile emotions have featured centrally within restrictive and exclusionary immigration and border enforcement, invocations of compassion have increasingly played a significant role and fused together with more familiar hostile emotions.

The role of people smugglers became a central feature of policy discourse during the refugee crisis on the borders of Europe, as the scaling back of rescue missions at sea, enforcement actions directed against smugglers, and the UK's reluctance to take in people arriving by sea were presented as part of a battle against 'trafficking' and 'modern slavery' (Anderson and De Noronha, 2015). However, the war against people smugglers formed a central tenant of Australia's 'Pacific Solution', which was first introduced in 2001 and justified through the repeated mantra that it 'saved lives at sea' (McKay et al, 2017). Although in the US a humanitarian justification for tackling people smugglers and preventing irregular migration has been much more muted, in 2014 it was a prominent discourse in the Obama administration's response to the significant rise in the number of Central American unaccompanied children and families crossing the Mexico–US border. Through these case studies, this chapter explores the emergence of the figure of the people smuggler as a racialised and gendered villain in contemporary border enforcement narratives and as a target for outrage driven by 'compassion'.

Compassionate violence

The enactment of policies framed by governments as 'compassionate' has caused further suffering for people who have been recognised as valid subjects of compassion. Research on international humanitarianism, and domestic social policy, has revealed how care and control have often been firmly wedded together in government policy in ways that produce punitive and exclusionary outcomes (Harrison and Sanders, 2014; Ticktin, 2014). Analysis from academics, NGOs and journalists has repeatedly indicated that the most effective way to prevent migrants and refugees experiencing further harm is to expand the availability of legal routes of travel (UNHCR, 2015b; Crawley et al, 2016; Kingsley, 2016). People travel irregularly, use the services of smugglers and risk their lives on dangerous routes *because* increasingly restrictive border enforcement has prevented access to safer legal routes of entry. Nevertheless, governments have asserted that border enforcement measures have been implemented, in part, for humanitarian ends. A commitment to border enforcement is maintained not simply through dismissing the humanitarian critiques levelled against governments, but rather through appropriating and rearticulating this humanitarian discourse in an alternative narrative that fits with enforcement priorities in the 'military–humanitarian nexus' (Pallister-Wilkins, 2015).

Meanwhile, supporters of increased border enforcement have linked the emotion of compassion to the emotion of outrage. Through this connection, outrage has not been directed towards government policies and actions that cause or amplify suffering. Instead, outrage has been expressed towards the vilified figures of the 'callous people smuggler' and the 'migrant queue jumper', drawing on the legacy of colonial discourse about threatening and dangerous Southern men (Spivak, 1988). In addition, some NGOs have been presented as enabling the wrongful deeds of the smuggler and queue jumper. Through this narrative, governments have attempted to cleanse themselves of responsibility and shame for wrongdoing, which has been projected instead on to these discredited third parties. In instigating a 'war' on smugglers and asserting this is to protect the most vulnerable, governments have drawn together the seemingly contradictory emotions of compassion and hostility as professed drivers of their policies in a military–humanitarian nexus. This can be beneficial as they seek to appeal to heterogenous political interests and emotions present in contemporary immigration and asylum policy debates.

Critical analysis has highlighted the problematic relationship between humanitarianism and violence whereby Western governments have used claims of 'humanitarianism' as a justification for military intervention (Perugini and Gordon, 2015). While this is now a familiar aspect of Western states' foreign policies, this rhetoric, and the emotions that it draws on, are also visible in contemporary immigration and border control policies. Governments have prioritised enhanced border enforcement as the primary response to refugees and irregular migrants who attempt to enter their territories. Increased border enforcement has been justified through a discourse of securitisation and militarisation that draws on emotions of fear, anxiety and hate (Gale, 2004; Charteris-Black, 2006; Chebel D'Appollonia, 2015), and has had exclusionary and violent effects (Perkowski, 2016). However, in the EU and Australia, such measures have also been articulated through a discourse of humanitarianism (Pallister-Wilkins, 2015; McKay et al, 2017; Peterie, 2017) which has incorporated rather than replaced the security discourse (Pallister-Wilkins, 2015; Perkowski, 2016). Perkowski (2016:331) observes that the deaths of thousands of refugees and migrants in the Mediterranean Sea were framed as 'humanitarian crises', which linked 'discourses and practices of humanitarianism, security and human rights in the governance of the Mediterranean'.

These rationales and modes of governance appear contradictory but are entwined (Franko Aas and Gundhus, 2015). Bridget Anderson (Anderson and De Noronha, 2015) has described this policy as 'violent humanitarianism', which has been presented as a battle against 'trafficking' and 'modern slavery'. In this battle, sentiments of compassion are expressed for weak and vulnerable victims of 'callous' people smugglers, towards whom feelings of outrage are directed (Home Office, 2015a). The high-profile focus on people smugglers in immigration and refugee policy discourse has a long running history in Australia (Wazana, 2004) and formed a central tenant of the 'Pacific Solution', reinvigorated through Operation Sovereign Borders (OSB) from 2013 onwards. In contrast, in the US, the discourse of humanitarianism in border enforcement has been significantly more muted. However, it was mobilised in the Obama administration's 'Danger Awareness' anti-smuggling information campaign which was launched in 2014 in response to the significant rise in Central American young people crossing the Mexico–US border that summer. There are parallels in the characterisation of smugglers and victims in this campaign and in the overseas public information campaigns (OPICs) used in Australia's Pacific Solution, which are examined in this chapter.

This remainder of this chapter outlines how violent humanitarianism has been justified through the development of three archetype and neo-colonial characters through whom the emotions in this narrative are produced and played out. These map on to Costas Douzinas' (2007:69) description of the different elements of humanity – the 'three masks of the human' – which he has elucidated in his critique of the human rights regime as a new form of Western imperialism and civilising mission. He describes the development of three key characters in this regime: 'the suffering victim, the atrocious evil-doer and the moral rescuer'. He argues that the human rights regime combines the suffering victim and the evil-doer abroad in to the double-sided 'Other of the West'; 'the subhuman and the inhuman rolled into one' (Douzinas, 2007:70). Pity for the victims and aversion to the savages who harm them make the Western rescuer appear 'civilised'. In this chapter, it is argued that three 'masks of the human' are visible and disaggregated across the archetype characters developed through the border enforcement narrative. In this narrative, the 'masks' are epitomised by: the 'suffering refugee' (suffering victim); the villainous 'people smuggler' and 'migrant queue jumper' (atrocious evil-doers); and the saviour governments (moral rescuers). This chapter draws on government OPICs, press releases and policy documents to examine the development of the two villainous characters of the 'people smuggler' and the 'migrant queue jumper'. It explores how a discourse of compassion for 'genuine' victims has been used to direct disapproval and outrage against smugglers and migrant 'queue jumpers'.

Saving lives at sea

Targeting the other 'boat people'

Attention has been given to the racialised and gendered characterisation of undesired migrants and refugees as threats to receiving societies (Griffiths, 2015; Farris, 2017; Scheibelhofer, 2017). However, these are not the only Othered figures in contemporary border enforcement narratives. Even when *some* migrants and refugees are cleansed from this characterisation, this discursive category remains and is rearticulated through the figure of the smuggler.

People smuggling has become the ideological lynchpin for Australia's policy of mandatory offshore detention for 'irregular maritime arrivals' (IMAs) (Peterie, 2017). There is a long-standing focus on smugglers in public debates on asylum policy in Australia (Suhnan et al, 2012). In their defence of border enforcement policies since the 2000s, Australian prime ministers have regularly referred to the villainous people smugglers who facilitate the journeys of migrants and refugees. In 2009, the Labor Prime Minister, Kevin Rudd, called people smugglers 'the absolute scum of the earth' (Grewcock, 2013), while in 2015 the former Liberal Prime Minister, Tony Abbott, declared people smuggling to be an 'evil trade' (Hurst, 2015). Meanwhile, the use of offshore detention in the Pacific islands of Nauru and Manus since 2001 has been presented as 'saving lives at sea' and undermining the people smuggling trade. Framed as a battle against modern slavery and criminal 'trafficking' networks, the Australian government is represented as a saviour nation-state providing regional moral leadership. Australia, alongside Indonesia, is a co-chair of the Bali Process on People Smuggling, Trafficking in Persons and Related Transnational Crime. In March 2016, the Australian government launched its *International Strategy to Combat Human Trafficking and Slavery* at the sixth meeting of the Bali Process. According to the press release from Peter Dutton (2016a) (Minister for Immigration and Border Protection), the strategy outlined 'the Government's agenda to strengthen Australia's role as a regional leader in combatting trafficking and slavery'.

In Europe too, policy responses to the refugee crisis were dominated by the rhetoric of war on people smugglers. The UK response to the

Syrian refugee crisis primarily focused on providing humanitarian aid in the Middle East. The UN High Commissioner for Refugees (UNHCR) requested states to expand their existing resettlement programmes and increase the intake of Syrian refugees. However, the UK declined to take part, claiming that such efforts would be tokenistic as they provided places to a fraction of people affected. While he was Minister for Immigration, James Brokenshire (HL, 2015), argued that establishing such routes might also act as propaganda and 'get misinterpreted and manipulated by the traffickers and therefore lead to greater exploitation'.

In March 2015, the European Commission launched its plan and priorities for a *New Comprehensive European Agenda on Migration* which centred on 'fighting irregular immigration and smuggling more robustly' (Carrera and Guild, 2016:1). It also tripled the budget for Frontex and the border surveillance operations – Triton (Central Mediterranean) and Poseidon (Greece). In May 2015, the *EU Action Plan against Migrant Smuggling* was published in support of this agenda and EUNAVFOR, known as 'Operation Sophia', was established. Operation Sophia explicitly focused on the 'disruption of the business model of human smuggling and trafficking networks in the Southern Central Mediterranean' by 'efforts to identify, capture and dispose of vessels and enabling assets used or suspected of being used by migrant smugglers or traffickers' (EU, 2016). During 2015, attention shifted to the Eastern Mediterranean route as increasing numbers of people crossed from Turkey to Greece (Crawley et al, 2016).

Although the European Commission (EC, 2016) has cited 'saving lives at sea' as a driver of its border operations, these have primarily focused on stopping the smugglers rather than rescuing migrants and refugees (Achilli, 2015). In May 2016, a Europol-Interpol report found that more than 90% of migrants and refugees travelling to Europe used smugglers (Europol-INTERPOL, 2016). The report authors anticipated that as increased border controls were exerted, smugglers would diversify the routes they used. In February 2017, a UNHCR (2017) report confirmed that border operations had not stopped people from moving.

One of the primary characteristics of the contemporary 'undesired' migrant is their 'irregular' mode of entry. As will be discussed further in Chapter Six, migrants and refugees using these modes of entry have been discredited in public and political discourse. However, the explicit vilification and abandonment of certain categories of people, particularly children, has been difficult to reconcile with states' professed civility and humanitarian principles (see Chapter Four). European governments have been reluctant to ease restrictions, particularly considering strong anti-immigration sentiments among parts of their electorate. Yet, as the refugee crisis heightened, governments faced increasing critique from other parts of their electorates and from NGOs working in the field. In Australia there has been vocal public support for people who travelled irregularly by boat to Australia and were detained in mandatory offshore detention on Manus Island and Nauru.

In this context, facing a challenge to their proclaimed international moral status as civilised nation-states, the notion that deterrence efforts were aimed at 'breaking the smugglers' business model' became a central tenant of government border enforcement discourses in Australia and the UK, and on a more limited basis, and policy-specific context in the US. Through expressing outrage at the actions of the smugglers, governments engaged in 'interpretive denial' (Cohen, 2001) by shifting the blame on to these 'Other' evil doers and, in doing so, cleansing themselves of guilt. Not only did they absolve themselves of the responsibility for the suffering of migrants and refugees, through this face-saving manoeuvre governments positioned themselves in the role of moral rescuer saving brown victims from brown 'savages' (Spivak, 1988). The following section examines how emotions engaged with in this narrative produced the vilified character of the people smuggler and simultaneously the passive and dependent migrant or refugee in need of saving.

The people smuggler as 'evil-doer'

In Europe and Australia, government responses to people smuggling have been articulated through the metaphor of 'war', reinforced through the actual deployment of military forces on the ground in anti-smuggling operations. On 4 October 2013, in the first of regular press briefings on the progress of OSB, the then Australian Minister of Immigration and Border Protection, Scott Morrison (2013), stated, 'We're not running a taxi service here or a reception centre. We are running a *military-led* border security operation'. He went on to announce that '*the full arsenal* of measures represented in the Coalition's policies to stop the boats remain available to be deployed by the government' [italics added]. A year later, responding to critiques of the secrecy surrounding some border operations, including boat turnbacks, Prime Minister Abbott (2014) informed Channel 10 News that releasing information would help people smugglers, declaring that 'we are in a fierce contest with these people smugglers and if we were at *war*, we wouldn't be giving out information that is of use to the enemy' [italics added]. Meanwhile, a leaked EU strategy paper proposing an air and naval campaign to target people smugglers in Libyan territorial water stated this would lead to 'collateral damage' (Traynor, 2015b).

Massoumi (2015) has described the concept of the 'war story' as 'the official, state-sponsored story about why we go to war and how the war is won' (Massoumi, 2015:722). It 'gives coherence and order to wars that are often complex and confusing', making use of familiar dichotomies such as friend and enemy, aggression and defence, and war and peace (Massoumi, 2015:722). She observes that these stories often rely on gendered essentialist clichés; for example, Muslim women were oppressed victims who could be protected and saved through the 'war on terror'. In the war on people smugglers, migrants and refugees have been positioned as weak victims, often through an emphasis on the rescue of women and young children. For example, on 15 May 2015, the UK Border Force (Home Office, 2015) issued a press release with the headline 'Border Force cutter in Mediterranean migrant rescue mission'. It was stated that the British ship named 'HMC *Protector*' [italics added] 'was deployed by Operation Triton to save over 100 people ... including three small children and three heavily pregnant women'.

In the 'War Against Smugglers' story, emotions have played a central role in the character development of the figure of the evil smuggler who is portrayed as the arch foe. In a similar discursive mode to that used in constructing the figure of the threatening migrant, smugglers have been dehumanised and presented through a racialised and gendered lens as the dangerous and criminal Southern man. Not only have they have been dehumanised, but part of this characterisation has been developed through the assertion that *they* dehumanise the migrants and refugees they transport. They treat them as goods to be traded, rather than people, and exhibit a lack of care and appropriate sentiment, unlike humanitarian (Western) rescuers. Speaking in 2014, Scott Morrison (2014) said, 'I'm not going to second guess the mindset of criminal groups that put people at risk on the high seas. I'm not going to second guess what it will take for them to stop taking advantage of people. But be in no doubt they no longer have a product to sell'. He stated the Australian government were trying to get the message through to potential migrants, but 'if it takes for people to see the planes going across from Christmas to Manus, if it takes for people to see that we are true to our word, well, we are making sure of that'. To successfully prevent smuggling, this situation cannot be approached through our emotional reasoning and sensibilities, but instead, through the imagined reasoning of inhuman criminal smugglers, who are so different from us. The smugglers have forced the Australian government to take such extreme measures which they would rather not have to do. Through this compassionate violence, the government is being cruel to be kind and to save lives.

Overseas public information campaigns

This discursive characterisation of the people smuggler, in relation to other actors in the scene, is now explored through an analysis of Australian and US government OPICs launched as part of the war on people smuggling. OPICs have been a feature of state border control policies since the 1990s; they are 'marketing campaigns disseminating advertisements in migrant source and transit countries to pre-emptively deter irregular migrants' (Watkins, 2017:3). These have been described as one means of border externalisation processes whereby borders are stretched beyond the immediate sovereign territory (Mountz, 2010; Watkins, 2017).

The Danger Awareness Campaign (US)

In the spring and summer of 2014 there was a sharp increase in the number of unaccompanied children from El Salvador, Honduras and Guatemala crossing the Mexico – US border to escape gang violence and conflict (Krogstad, 2016). In the first six months of the fiscal year 2014, there were 28,579 apprehensions of unaccompanied children and 19,830 apprehensions of children and their families. These numbers decreased in the spring and summer of 2015, but rose again from August 2015. In the first six months of the fiscal year of 2016 there were 27,754 apprehensions of unaccompanied children and 32,117 apprehensions of children with families (Krogstad, 2016).

In late June 2014, President Obama wrote to Congress to update them on his administration's response to this migration (Obama, 2014a). He announced that he had directed the Department of Homeland Security and the Federal Emergency Management Agency to coordinate the government-wide response. He was now requesting the support of Congress in ensuring emergency legislation would be passed to enable aspects of this strategy to be enacted. Towards the end of the letter Obama referred to meetings his administration had held with Central American government leaders, and the proposed allocation of US resources to assist these governments in tackling root causes of migration and to support the re-integration of people deported from the US.

However, the letter began with, and was dominated by, a focus on the role of smugglers and the dangers they posed to migrants, especially children. In the first paragraph, Obama set the scene by stating, 'The individuals who embark upon this perilous journey are subject to violent crime, abuse, and extortion as they rely on dangerous human smuggling networks to transport them through Central American and Mexico'

(Obama, 2014a). His government's strategy included increased powers to remove and repatriate people (including children) who had recently crossed the border. Although he used the term 'unlawful migrants' once (halfway through the letter), the actions outlined in his strategy were framed throughout the letter by an expressed will to safeguard vulnerable migrants and to deal with the smugglers, who were identified as the people primarily responsible for the harm and suffering migrants experienced. This can be seen through the following statements made in the letter, in which Obama (2014a) announced that his administration was responding to the migration by:

> [1] fulfilling our legal and moral obligation to make sure we appropriately care for unaccompanied children who are [2] apprehended while taking aggressive steps to surge resources to our Southern border to [3] deter both adults and children from this dangerous journey, [4] increase capacity for enforcement and removal proceedings and quickly return unlawful migrants to their home countries ... [5] We are working with our Central American partners, nongovernmental organizations and other influential voices to [6] send a clear message to potential migrants so that they understand the significant dangers of this journey and what they will experience in the United States.

Care and aggression are explained as compatible responses (1, 2), linked together through the desire to eliminate danger and harm. Care is coupled with, and drives, an 'aggressive' 'surge' of resources to deter migrant travel. This is allegedly for their own good, to prevent people from embarking on dangerous journeys (3) and from facing the ominous threats of what might be done to them by the US government itself. Aggression and implied threats are used as a form of tough love or benevolent responsibilisation which persuades migrants to make the right choices (Harrison and Sanders, 2014). These interventions have an educational element as through enforcement accompanied by collaboration with 'influential voices' (6) they seek to make migrants 'understand' (6) that they should be afraid of the journey and let this emotional reasoning guide them to a rational judgement to stay put.

A key aspect of these responsibilisation efforts has been awareness raising among potential migrants to counter misinformation from dishonest smugglers. In July 2014, US Customs and Border Enforcement launched *The Danger Awareness Campaign*. This comprised of billboards, radio and television advertisements in Spanish in Central America, with multiple versions targeted specifically at Honduran, Salvadorian and Guatemalan migrants and their families (CBP, 2014a). The campaign was also used in US cities with large Central American immigrant populations to target families and friends who may fund migration journeys.

The US Customs and Border Patrol (CBP) (2014a) stated that the campaign had three central messages: 1) 'the journey is too dangerous', 2) 'children will not get legal papers if they make it', 3) 'they are the future – let's protect them'. As is often the case with public information campaigns (Jones et al, 2017), it aimed to stir up emotions of fear and anxiety in the audience to nudge them towards the desired actions. The smuggler was a central protagonist in the campaign stories. However, despite their central role, they were never visible in the images used. Instead, they were an ominous presence, felt and alluded to, but not seen and known in full human form. For example, in the TV public announcement called 'Sombras' (Shadows), the smuggler was depicted as a shadow figure projected against the wall of a building with his finger pointed aggressively at the shadow figure of a boy who leaned away as the smuggler loomed over him (CBP, 2014a). The smuggler told the boy he would soon have his documentation to travel to the US. The boy asked what to do if it went wrong. The smuggler told him not to worry, that his papers would arrive, and he should hand over his money. The woman voiceover then said that the smuggler was wrong, and that it was increasingly difficult for 'our' children to get papers in the US. They were falling victim to traffickers, thugs and rumours. They are our future and we must protect them. The shadow of the smuggler then transformed into the shadow of a coyote [a term by which smugglers are known] as he snatched the boy's money and ran away. Thus, his deceit was uncovered, and his true animal character and absence of human moral values revealed. In the billboard posters, the smugglers were not visible at all. The posters featured images of lone children in the desert with the same tag line – 'they are our future and we must protect them'. We are to deduce that these young boys were abandoned in the desert by callous and cruel smugglers who gave their families misinformation and false promises.

On the CBP website, these public announcement posters and videos appeared alongside contrasting imagery of CBP officers (CBP, 2014b). The images again depicted migrants in distressing situations, collapsed on the ground or struggling to cross the Rio Grande river. However, the other key figure in the image was now the CBP officer; they were visible and shown helping migrants in distress. One photograph showed a male officer pulling a woman out of the river. In another photograph, a male officer provided first aid to a woman who had collapsed after crossing into the US, while a child stood next to them. They were the heroes of

THE POLITICS OF COMPASSION

the moment, compassionate and morally righteous white American men saving brown women and children from the cruelties inflicted on them by savage and inhumane smugglers. In his statement on addressing the humanitarian challenge, CBP Commissioner Kerlikowske stated, 'I have seen CBP employees respond to these difficulties with professionalism and compassion. They've made heroic efforts with these children; rescuing them and caring for them in the most humane and compassionate way' (CBP, 2014b).

'No to people smuggling' (Australia)

This section explores how smugglers are portrayed in OPIC videos featured on the Australian Department of Immigration and Border Protection's YouTube channel (2014a), which is called 'No to people smuggling'. This is examined alongside an OPIC which ran in 2010 and targeted Afghan and Sri Lankan 'potential irregular immigrants' living in Malaysia (Porter Novelli, 2012; Watkins, 2017).

The Australian Department of Immigration and Border Protection has invested in OPICs to publicise its border enforcement measures. In his analysis of these campaigns, Watkins (2017:3) argues that the campaign narratives 'normalise a spatial imagery deterring irregular migrants through portraying 'home' as safe and financially stable while clandestine boat travel to Australia as dangerous and destined to fail'. There has been a focus on the dangers of the water, the conditions people will face in offshore detention, and at the hands of smugglers (Watkins, 2017). The ocean is depicted as dangerous and ominous to generate emotions of 'fear, sadness, hopelessness, panic and tragedy' (Watkins 2017: 12). This is de-contextualised as we do not see what people have left behind or hear about Australian policies that make these routes a necessity. In attempting to stoke fear about the prospective journey, the hopeful story of migration is rearticulated into one of certain despair; thus, redefining the 'truth' about irregular immigration and nudging prospective migrants into the desired course of action, that is staying put.

These OPICs have branded migrants who travel 'irregularly' as 'illegal' because they travel without legal authorisation. They are chastised for travelling 'the wrong way' and warned about the aggressive and punitive enforcement measures they will face (Department of Immigration and Border Protection, 2014a). However, another central message in the OPICs is that these measures combat the criminal networks of people smuggling by destroying their 'business model' (Barker, 2013). This can be deduced by the title of the 'No to people smuggling' YouTube channel on which the videos are hosted.

In 2010, the advertising agency, Porter Novelli (2010, 2012) was commissioned to research, design and deliver an advertising campaign targeted at Afghan and Sri Lankan refugees in Malaysia. This included a series of information posters and videos to be played to refugees in Malaysia. The videos showed Afghan and Sri Lankan people telling the story of their failed migration attempts. The videos were shot in close-up to 'enhance the impact of their stories by focusing on the person telling the story and the emotions they portrayed' (Porter Novelli, 2012). One poster series consisted of three posters (Porter Novelli, 2010). As with the videos, each poster had a close-up portrait of a person against a black background and, in combination with the text, appeared designed to elicit feelings of sadness and fear. The first poster depicted an old woman, her face in pain and on the verge of tears as she numbly gazed into the middle distant. The text read: 'I lost my son. The people smuggler's boat sank half way. The boat was overcrowded, nobody survived. People smugglers will lie to get your money. They don't care if you get to Australia or not. You are the same to them dead or alive. It's not worth the risk'. The second poster was of a middle-aged male smuggler. The text read: 'Will you trust him with your life savings? People who make money from smuggling or trafficking people are criminals. Why trust your life savings to criminals? Why trust your life to somebody who doesn't care if you survive the journey or not? Don't be fooled by the smugglers or your family could be left to pay for your mistake'. The third poster was a close-up of a young child staring into the camera over the shoulder of her mother who carried him and turned away from the camera. The text read: 'I dreamed of a good future in Australia. But now I may be sent back to Afghanistan. The people smugglers told me it was easy once I got to Australia. But they lied to me. The Australian government is getting tougher. My money is gone, my dreams are gone. My family will pay the price'. The tag line for all posters stated: 'The Malaysian and Australian Governments are working closely against people smuggling and human trafficking. The likelihood that you will be caught and imprisoned is now very high. Everyone loses'. The same composition was used in the posters directed at Sri Lankans and Afghans. However, in the Sri Lankan posters all the people featured, victims and perpetrators, were Sri Lankan and in the Afghan posters they were all Afghan.

As with the US Dangers Awareness Campaign, the adverts depicted a snapshot of the story, with no context of the situation they are escaping, or a deeper and fuller account of their life story. Although the 'tough' Australian policy was referenced, this was framed as a response to 'criminality'. The role of Australian border officers was to step in and resolve the chaos that had been created by these other actors. The smugglers were presented as criminals and, therefore, deceptive. They 'lie to get your money', 'lied' about the ease of the journey, and passengers were 'fooled by promises' from the smugglers. Their untrustworthiness and flawed characters were so inherent that these personality traits could be read through the bodies. Each poster series depicted the smuggler as a dark-skinned man of the same nationality as his passengers. Each man stared into the camera with what presumably was meant to be read as a menacing expression. The audience was asked 'Would you trust him with your life savings?'

This mirrors the common contemporary characterisation of people smugglers. As Sanchez (2017:9) writes, 'around the world, many of these tragedies are attributed to the actions of migrant smugglers, who are almost monolithically depicted as men from the Global South organised in webs of organised criminals whose transnational reach allows them to prey on migrants and asylum seekers'. They are the 'Other' evil wrong-doer on whom blame can be placed (Douzinas, 2007). Since, as criminals, making money is their primarily motivation, they are presented as lacking in humanity. The smuggler 'doesn't care if you survive the journey or not', so they overpack the boats and have no qualms about deceiving customers about the conditions of the journey and prospects on arrival. This narrative is reiterated in government statements in which detention and boat turnbacks are presented as necessary interventions to break the smugglers' 'business model' by denying them the product they wish to sell. One year after the Coalition government's victory in the 2013 elections and the introduction of OSB, the Immigration Minister, Scott Morrison (2014), stated that, 'turning back boats where it is safe to do so' and 'processing and resettling illegal maritime arrivals offshore is denying people smugglers the product they seek to sell, a permanent protection visa and citizenship in Australia'. This claim about the business model was also present in European government discourses on smuggling in the Mediterranean Sea during the refugee crisis.

In this justification, the smugglers' lack of care for others and their dehumanising practices are, in turn, mobilised in government discourses that dehumanise the smugglers. Smugglers are not truly human since they do not display compassion. Distaste is expressed at the way in which smugglers have broken the bounds of moral decency and transformed a humanitarian need into a business opportunity. This characterisation also appeared in videos on the 'No to people smuggling' YouTube channel. For example, in 2012, a video was produced called 'Safety Gear' (Department of Immigration and Border Protection, 2012). It featured two young male people smugglers on a beach, preparing a small boat to carry their passengers to Australia. Opening the scene, one man remarked that there was a storm coming, but 'it's not our problem'. They then proceeded to remove the boat's oars, fresh water, spare petrol, first aid kit and life jackets, being careful, of course, to 'save two for us'. In 2014, the infamous 'No Way' video was released (Department of Immigration and Border Protection, 2014b). The subheading was 'You will never make Australia home'. Set against the backdrop of a foreboding scene of a choppy ocean, the head of the Border Force warned prospective migrants 'Do not believe the people smugglers. These criminals will place your life and your family's life at risk. All for nothing'.

Yet, the critique of the smugglers' 'business model' is expressed by governments who have themselves transformed previously humanitarian, welfare and or public services, such as health services and education, into marketised industries under neoliberal governance (Harvey, 2007). Instead, similarly to the Dangers Awareness Campaign, the figure of the inhumane smuggler is juxtaposed with the Western border officials or civilians who, having been invisible so far, enter the scene at this point to rescue vulnerable people, and prevent further harm. In doing so they are celebrated for their compassion. For example, in December 2010, a boat carrying people seeking asylum sank off the coast of Christmas Island. Speaking at a press conference called in response to the event, the Labor Prime Minister Julia Gillard (2010) stated,

> [1] I know the nation is shocked by what we have seen. [2] We condemn the trade of people smuggling, it is an evil trade, [3] but I believe Australians are responding to these events as human beings. [4] We're seeing other human beings in distress and imagining to themselves – how would I feel if I was in those circumstances, how would I feel if I lost my wife, my husband or my child in such rough and dangerous seas. [5] I think we are seeing Australians respond with the kind of compassionate response that as Australians we are known for.

The smugglers were 'evil' because they risked lives and through this 'trade' turned human lives into business opportunities (2). In contrast, 'the nation' expressed the appropriate response which is 'shock' (1). Australians reacted to these events 'as human beings' (3). As in the responses to Alan Kurdi's death several years later, Gillard imagined how she would feel if she had a close family member on board that boat (4) and imagined that other Australians were thinking the same. Therefore, the appropriate human response is compassion and this emotion is claimed as an inherently Australian trait (5) and something to be proud of.

There is well-documented evidence about the horrific violence, abuse and exploitation many people face at the hands of people smugglers (Kingsley, 2016). However, the simplistic representation of smugglers as a homogenous group of people operating in well-organised networks has also been contested. Achilli (2015) argues that smuggling networks are characterised by heterogeneity and involve a highly differentiated, yet flexible structure. There are several roles in these structures, but these are not bound into set hierarchies and long-term networks. Meanwhile, Sanchez's (2017) research on the US–Mexico border has highlighted the involvement of women and the gendered roles in the smuggling procedure. She observes that smuggling does not simply generate large profits for organised criminal networks, but is also used as a supplementing income-generating strategy to cover basic needs in local economies. Meanwhile, she argues that although many people face violence from smugglers, we also need to understand how relationships between migrants and smugglers emerge and how migrants rely on their services in quite complex ways. In doing so she (2017:10) problematises the 'dichotomous script of smugglers as predators and migrants and asylum seekers as victims', observing that such a script 'silences migrants and asylum seekers' efforts to reach safety, but also the collective knowledge their communities use to secure their mobility amid increased border militarization and migration controls'.

The threat of the future smuggler

The war against people smugglers is now a long-standing feature of Australian border enforcement. Even as boat arrivals have dissipated, these enforcement measures remain and are justified through the need for permanent vigilance. Speaking about the deal announced in 2016, to resettle refugees from Nauru and Manus to the US, the Immigration Minister, Peter Dutton (2016b) spoke about the dangers of the Australian government being seen to soften their stance on detention. He stated that if he talked about children being released, smugglers as 'sophisticated, organised criminals' would begin messaging on social media to encourage people once more to get on their boats. It was not that the Australian government wanted to detain people, but that the actions of smugglers left them no choice; showing humanity and compassion to children could get them killed.

Just as governments issue updates about the number of attempted terrorist attacks which they have prevented (Mythen and Walklate, 2006), since the launch of OSB, the Minister of Immigration has delivered regular updates on the successes of OSB in thwarting people smuggling ventures. Dutton's January 2015 update (Dutton, 2015a) stated, 'Operation Sovereign Borders delivers six months without a successful people smuggling venture'. People smuggling has ceased *for now*, but a reminder was issued of what could happen were the operation to end; the press release warned that, 'when the Rudd and Gillard Governments abolished the Howard Government's proven border protection policies more than 50,000 people illegally entered Australia on more than 800 boats'. Therefore, 'we need to be *ever vigilant* because the smugglers and crime gangs that engage in people smuggling are looking constantly for opportunities to subvert our efforts' [italics added]; this a permanent emergency.

The idea of the smuggler lurking in the wings, ready to relaunch their death boats, echoes contemporary security discourses on terrorism. The never-ending war against the smuggler has parallels with the never-ending war against terrorism (Giroux 2002). Giroux (2002) argued that this has resulted in the state of emergency becoming business as usual. The terrible events of the past never end; instead, they endure into the present and continue forward into anticipatory projections of possible catastrophic futures. The focus on the smuggler is a symptom of what Amin (2013:6) has described as the 'catastrophist politics of societal management'. Through this approach, a 'just in case' structure of provisions is displaced by a 'just in time' structure of preparations. This relies on anticipatory intelligence that is used to develop a 'hyper-vigilant environment' in which dangerous enemies can be identified, tracked and stopped before they cause us harm (Amin, 2013:6).

The criminalisation of humanitarianism and solidarity

The war on people smugglers has been used to justify actions that are framed as forms of tough love; what appear as hard-hearted policies deter people from using people smugglers and save lives. Conversely, the actions of humanitarian organisations and individuals which provide support and care for people suffering on their migration journey have been criminalised. In 2010, the Australian government made it an offence to provide advice or material support to help someone seeking to travel to Australia through irregular routes; this also applied to support provided for humanitarian rather than commercial reasons and so was aimed at family members, refugee communities and supporters (Barker, 2013). There has also been a criminalisation of solidarity in the EU where criminal sanctions have been used against people who provide humanitarian assistance to people migrating through irregular routes to Europe (Carrera and Guild, 2016). This became increasingly prescient as the refugee crisis heightened in Europe in 2015 and more people became involved in offering humanitarian support to refugees and migrants. In the summer of 2015, refugees arriving in Denmark began walking to the Swedish border. Seeing exhausted people walking along the highways, often with children, Danish citizens assisted them by providing food, clothing, shelter and in some cases transport. Subsequently, 297 Danish citizens were charged with human trafficking (Nielsen, 2016). There have been similar cases of volunteers being charged in Greece after assisting refugee boats (Nielsen, 2016). Meanwhile, in the UK a British man was charged after transporting a child to her family in the UK after she had been stranded in Calais (Halliday, 2017). In February 2017, the Head of Frontex (the European Border Agency), Fabrice Leggeri, stated that charities rescuing refugees and migrants in waters close to Libya were encouraging smugglers to take more risks with people's lives because they could rely on them being rescued near the start of their sea journey, although research evidence refutes these claims (Heller and Pezanni, 2017). He suggested that these rescue missions should be re-evaluated as refugees and migrants were using charity boats like a 'taxi service' (Kingston, 2017).

In the permanent state of emergency in the war against smugglers, good citizens are expected to rally together behind the government and not to undermine its efforts. Writing about the war on terror, Giroux (2002:336) observes that under this rationale, instead of 'courage, dialogue and responsibility', it is 'silence and complicity' which is demanded. Commenting on his response to 9/11 and the war on terror, President George W Bush countered critics by declaring that his job was 'not to 'nuance'; nuance was seen as a form of anti-patriotism (Berlant, 2005:46). If you love the nation, there is no nuance. If you care about saving people's lives, there is no nuance. Attempting to add complexity to the smuggling war story, expressing dissent or questioning this response was presented as demonstrating a lack of care.

Conclusion

It is now well-established that emotions of fear and anxiety have been mobilised by governments to garner support for immigration border enforcement and securitisation. In this chapter, it has been shown how it is not only citizens' emotions that have been stirred and governed in this way, but that government OPICs have also been used to generate these emotions, including sadness, among prospective migrants and their families to nudge them into desired actions.

While compassion has been engaged with to mobilise resistance to immigration enforcement and exclusions, it has also been appropriated by governments and combined with the professed emotion of outrage, to justify further violence. In doing so governments have engaged in a form of interpretive denial (Cohen, 2001). They cannot deny that migrants and refugees are dying and suffering harm on their journeys. However, the lens has been refocused away from actions of minority world states on to the figure of the 'Southern' male people smuggler, and humanitarian actors, who have been framed as assisting criminality.

Note

[1] It later emerged that the Conservative government had already begun launching drone strikes in Syria against British IS recruits in August 2015, in the weeks before Alan's death.

6

Withholding Compassion

Introduction

Humanitarianism is understood as a form of 'soft power'; its perceived absence is a source of stigma that damages state reputations on the international scene. Governments proudly declare and celebrate the humanitarian qualities and actions of the nation-states they represent. In his speech to the 2016 UN Summit for Refugees and Migrants, the Australian Prime Minister Malcolm Turnbull declared that Australia has a 'generous' humanitarian programme and the best refugee policy in the world (The Australian, 2016a). Speaking in 2015 on the UK's response to the refugee crisis, the former British Prime Minister, David Cameron, stated that 'this is a country of extraordinary compassion always standing up for our values and helping those in need'.[1] Yet despite this boasting, the UK and Australia have faced sharp critiques over their refugee and asylum policies. Meanwhile, although at the UN Summit in September 2016, President Obama implored people to 'open up their hearts', his administration oversaw the largest number of immigration deportations in US history (Nicholls et al, 2016). This chapter explores how governments have legitimated the withholding of compassion from undesired migrants and refugees in the context of their public commitments to compassionate policies.

While a broad definition of compassion may be generally agreed on – it is a painful emotion directed towards alleviating another's suffering – there is significant ambiguity in this definition. This has led to a contestation of the emotional script of compassion and debate about: a) the criteria that need to be fulfilled to be seen as someone worthy of compassion; b) the terms of that relationship, including the power disparity; and c) the desired interventions and outcomes.

Continuing with the theme of compassionate refusal from Chapter Five, this chapter examines how a narrow and highly conditional definition of compassion has been used to justify the *expulsion* of people from the circle of concern. Drawing on Hochschild's theory of emotional regimes, this chapter explores the structure of compassion as an emotional regime in government discourse and its use in governance. It examines how 'feeling' and 'framing rules' (Hochschild, 1979) are used to establish who we are supposed to feel compassion for and under what circumstances. It is argued that models of compassion in government discourses enable the dual maintenance of both compassionate and hostile discourses and practices in ways that can be reconciled and legitimated.

Denying compassion

'When you know the events, you will open up your heart'. This slogan, recounted to me by an Australian refugee rights activist, had been used a few years before our interview to try to change public attitudes in the campaign against Australia's use of offshore immigration detention. Much of what occurs in the murky world of immigration enforcement is out of public view, if not beyond public knowledge. However, because of developments in media communication and consumption, and the activism of migrants and their allies we are also more aware than ever before about suffering and injustice (Boltanski;1999; Marciniak and Tyler, 2014). It is therefore increasingly difficult for governments to legitimately deny that suffering is happening.

Compassion has become a zeitgeist concept in public debates on asylum. However, despite this, immigration and asylum policies have become increasingly punitive and exclusionary. As Cohen (2001) has argued despite people's knowledge that suffering is taking place, suffering is often denied rather than *a*cknowledged; the experience of suffering, its causes, and/or implications are ignored, disavowed or reinterpreted, and compassion is withheld. In this chapter, it is argued that knowledge is different from *a*cknowledgement, which is a necessary component of a compassionate response. Compassion involves feeling and understanding someone else's experience as constituting suffering. This implies that there are criteria that must be met for an individual or social group to be accepted as legitimate subjects of compassion (Nussbaum, 1996, 2013). The feeling and framing rules of the emotional regime of compassion deployed by governments enforcing immigration restrictions are compatible with, and have enabled, a denial of some refugee and migrant suffering and, thus, a refusal of compassion. This chapter examines how the ideal subject of compassion has been constructed in government discourse and how this relates to Nussbaum's definition of compassion and critiques of this. It is argued that compassion is withheld from immigrants and refugees when their suffering is understood as not serious enough to merit compassion, when they are deemed to be at fault for bringing about their own suffering or in causing suffering to others; and when their story of suffering is, in a sense, one that is identified with too far and their pain is appropriated.

Despite the late 20th and early 21st century trajectory of shutting doors to migrants and refugees, there have been examples where the states have opened a window. This chapter explores two policy case studies that exemplify this; these are the Syrian Vulnerable Persons Resettlement Programme in the UK, and the Australian Syrian and Iraqi Humanitarian Programme. (The example of the Deferred Action for Childhood Arrivals administrative order in the US is discussed in Chapter Eight.) The second part of this chapter discusses the case of the election of Donald Trump to the US presidency to examine how 'suffering citizens' have become centred as *the* legitimate subjects of compassion, at the expense of migrants and refugees.

Government discourses of compassion draw heavily on the first two criteria of compassion outlined by Nussbaum – these are that the sufferer is experiencing *serious* suffering and that they are not at fault. The ideas of serious suffering and innocence have become conceptually linked so that if someone is perceived to have caused or intensified their suffering, it is concluded that their suffering could be alleviated by them taking remedial steps. Therefore, there is no need for compassion. In some cases, they are deemed to be guilty because they are judged to have caused someone else's suffering, and so are transformed into the perpetrator. In combining ideas of serious suffering and innocence in this way, the feeling rules in this model of compassion overlap with the concept of vulnerability. Indeed, both the UK and Australian humanitarian programmes for Syrian refugees use the terminology of 'vulnerability', which has been integral to the framing of these programmes.

Serious suffering – Syrian Vulnerable Persons Resettlement Programme

The vulnerable refugee

The UK declined to take part in the UN High Commissioner for Refugees (UNHCR) resettlement programme in response to the Syrian conflict and refugee crisis (Gower and Cromarty, 2016). However, the government faced cross-party pressure in parliament to engage in resettlement, while in an open letter to the Prime Minister on 17 January 2014, 25 charities called on the government to participate in the UNHCR programme (Merrill, 2014). The government had previously argued that such a scheme would encourage people to attempt dangerous journeys, risking their lives. The letter from the charities responded by asserting that refusing to assist in resettlement would increase the pressures in countries neighbouring Syria where large numbers of refugees were already being hosted, and that this would be a further push for refugees to move on towards Europe. On 29 January 2014, Theresa May (then Home Secretary), introduced the 'Syrian Vulnerable Person Resettlement Programme' (SVPRP)[2] which would provide a route for selected displaced Syrians who were deemed particularly 'vulnerable' to come to the UK.[3] In her oral statement to the House of Commons introducing the SVPRP, May began by reviewing the nature and scale of the problem.

> [1] I'm sure the whole House will join me in deploring the appalling scenes of violence and suffering which we have witnessed in Syria. [2] More than 100,000 people have been killed and the credible reports of systematic use of torture and starvation are simply sickening. [3] Millions of innocent people have fled their homes. [4] There are now more than 11 million Syrians in desperate need, including 6 and a half million people displaced inside Syria and more than 2.3 million refugees in neighbouring countries – at least half of them children. [5] The numbers are staggering and the scale of the crisis is immense.

May demonstrated that MPs were moved by the suffering and felt appropriate emotions (1); they were 'appalled' and 'deplore' the violence, mirroring the emotions of those who voiced concerns about the government's response. Next, in reviewing the scale of the problem, she established the boundaries of possible action, the scope for UK government action, and the remit within which they should be judged. Her analysis, based on the numbers (2–4), was that the scale was 'immense', 'staggering' (5); there was a sense of being overwhelmed and an implication that this was an extraordinary problem that could not easily be solved.

Having reviewed the scale of the problem and the context in which the government should be judged, May outlined the government's response to date.

[1] 'We are also leading the world in responding to the humanitarian disaster: [2] Britain is the second largest bilateral donor in the world after the United States. [3] We have provided £600 million for the Syrian relief effort so far, of which £500 million has already been allocated to support refugees and the internally displaced.'

There was a familiar celebration of the UK's humanitarian efforts; the UK was 'leading the world' (1) giving more financial aid to the region than other states (2, 3). This pride countered attempts to shame the government over lack of action. Later in the speech, May stated that, 'our country has a proud tradition of providing protection to those in need'. This defensive framing invited judgement on their recent actions to be based on knowledge and understanding of their longer historical record of action. As seen in Chapter Four, similar interpretations of the UK's history of hospitality have also been used by charities to *challenge* government policy by indicating how it diverges from the nation's true character.

These initial paragraphs set the scene for who was to be selected for the SVPRP. There were so many people suffering that the UK could not help them all. In this context where so many people fitted existing limited definitions of a 'genuine' refugee, further categorisation was needed to select those to be helped. May, thus, set out the criteria for the SVPRP.

'This programme – [1] the Vulnerable Person Relocation scheme – will be based on three principles. [2] First, we are determined to ensure that our assistance is targeted where it can have the most impact on the refugees at greatest risk. [3] The programme will focus on individual cases where evacuation from the region is the only option. [4] In particular, we will prioritise help for survivors of torture and violence, and women and children at risk or in need of medical care who are recommended to us for relocation by UNHCR. This is where we believe we can make a distinctive contribution as the United Kingdom. [5] For example, some of the worst abuses in the Syrian conflict involve the use of sexual violence.'

It is immediately noticeable that the term 'refugee' was absent from the title of the programme. Instead, the world 'vulnerable' was the dominant adjective or indeed noun (1). While government declarations about refugees have commonly identified people who are 'deserving' through the affix 'genuine' (Home Office, 2002), this was replaced here with the term 'vulnerable' and the associated term 'at risk' (2) and (4). Brown

(2014:10) has observed that 'vulnerability' has become a zeitgeist in British social policy, 'featured heavily in the language and practice of services interventions' and rooted in long-standing debates about 'deserving' and 'undeserving' people (see Anderson, 2013).

It could be assumed that simply being Syrian and a refugee would be enough to imply that a person was in a vulnerable circumstance. Yet, going beyond the well-established distinction between 'deserving' refugee and 'undeserving' asylum seeker (Sales, 2002), there was also a hierarchy of statuses within the category of refugee which was now split into 'refugee' and 'vulnerable refugee'. In the criteria for vulnerability set out in the announcement of the SVPRP, the focus on the suffering *body*, rather than the 'threatened body', was paramount (Fassin, 2012). The SVPRP was for people with medical needs, who had suffered torture or violence or sexual abuse (4) and (5). Even when other indicators of vulnerability were named, these appeared as essentialised identity markers attached to the body; the programme would help women and children who needed medical care or were at risk (4). Women were categorised with children. There was no mention of men or adults. Nothing was said about their biography or activities which would imply political engagement or agency. No fixed quota was established for the SVPRP and only 239 refugees were resettled under the scheme by September 2015 (Gower and Cromarty, 2016). However, following further political lobbying after the death of Alan Kurdi, the programme was expanded with a commitment to resettle 20,000 refugees during that parliament.[4]

The threatened asylum-seeking body has become increasingly discredited in political discourse, while the discourse of humanitarian care for the suffering body has assumed greater prominence (Fassin, 2005). Policies on asylum originated in a rights-based approach enshrined in the UN 1951 Refugee Convention. However, there has been a reassessment of the social worth of people seeking asylum. Fassin (2005) and Ticktin (2014) have reflected on the relationship between political and humanitarian modes of response to refugees and undocumented immigrants in France in the late 1990s and early 2000s. This period saw declining numbers of people granted asylum in France, but a rise in the numbers granted humanitarian leave to remain due to serious illness. This trend become embedded for a period through the introduction of the 'illness clause' in the 1998 Conditions of Entry and Residence of Foreigners legislation in France (Ticktin, 2014). This provision enabled those with a serious medical condition to attain legal status and rights of residency.

There is an extensive literature in refugee studies and humanitarianism on the politics of vulnerability and victimhood and how this framing can obscure and undermine the agency of refugees (Malkki, 1996; Fassin, 2005;

Chouliaraki, 2010; Ticktin, 2014; Kronick and Rousseau, 2015). Fassin (2005) asserts that from the late 1980s onwards in Europe, 'the threatened body' of asylum seekers was conflated with that of economic immigrants and suspicion was levelled against them. In this context, a refugee has often been presented as a figure of humanitarian rescue, qualifying for protection because of the *absence* of explicit economic aspirations (Long, 2013). Ticktin (2014:98) argues that, 'with humanitarianism as the driving logic, only the suffering or sick body is seen as a legitimate manifestation of a common humanity, worthy of recognition in the form of rights; this view is based on a belief in the legitimacy, fixity and universality of biology'. This is what Fassin (2005:372) terms 'biolegitimacy' which refers to 'the legitimization of rights in the name of the suffering body'. He argues that, 'the legitimacy of the suffering body has become greater than that of the threatened body, and the right to life is being displaced from the political sphere to that of compassion' (Fassin 2005:371). He asserts that while it used to be that the immigrant body was seen as legitimate if working, but disease was suspect, the reverse is now the case and disease is a social resource. Asylum seekers and undocumented immigrants become reduced to their physical life (or bare life) and are responded to through humanitarianism. However, Fassin (2005) argues that this is not simply a case of a separation of humanitarianism from the political; instead, increasingly the two have become conflated. There has been a '"humanitarianization" in the management of asylum seekers' (Fassin, 2005:372) as the category of asylum 'is increasingly subsumed under the category of humanitarianism'. The humanitarian integrates the political which in turn redefines it. Resettlement through humanitarian action becomes an act of generosity and compassion rather than a recognition of rights.

Policing the boundaries of vulnerability

Controlling interventions have been applied to 'vulnerable populations' under the auspices of care. Brown (2014:1) argues that, 'whilst it can be utilised in the pursuit of more "caring" interventions with those who are seen to be in need, vulnerability is also a concept relevant to debates concerning selective welfare systems and behavioural regulation'. However, control has also been exerted through the vigilant policing of the borders of vulnerability to eject those who are deemed not vulnerable and therefore unsuitable subjects of compassion. In social welfare 'the vulnerable' have often been constructed as those who are less accountable for their actions and who have less agency (Brown, 2015).

The SVPRP was expanded in direct response to the 'the heart-breaking images'[5] of the dead child and the resulting pressure on the government to do something to halt the mass drownings at sea. However, while hearts broke for those who died at sea, they hardened for those who survived and came ashore. At this point the weak transformed into the strong, and children became men. At the Conservative Party conference in October 2015, Theresa May (2015b) clarified who was not vulnerable and would not be considered for the programme. The programme excluded those who had made their own way to Europe. Speaking about people who had arrived in Europe, and specifically the UK, May said:

> 'The [current asylum] system is geared towards helping those most able to access it, and sometimes manipulate it, for their own ends – [2] those who are young enough, fit enough, and have the resources to get to Britain. [3] But that means support is too often denied to the most vulnerable, and those most in need of our help.'

It is implied that if people are genuinely in a serious state of suffering they lack agency (1). Suffering is primarily evidenced through the body; certain 'weaker' bodies are more likely to suffer (2). Later in the speech May (2015) stated that, 'three quarters of asylum seekers in Britain are men and the vast majority are in their twenties'; this intersection of age and masculinity disqualified them from the category of the vulnerable (Griffiths, 2015). Not only were they not legitimate sufferers, but in their 'manipulation' of the system (implying dishonestly) they undermined the government's ability to assist those 'most in need' (3); they were taking the places of more deserving people. This reflects the criminalisation of racialised and gendered bodies of male asylum seekers (Scheibelhofer, 2017).

Later in her speech, May (2015b) stated that people's 'desire for a better life is perfectly understandable, but their circumstances were not nearly the same as those of the people fleeing their homelands in fear of their lives'. Although describing these young men as manipulating the system, there was a note of empathy – she claimed to understand their situation – but not compassion. Their plight did not match her pragmatic framing rules (Hochschild, 1979) about who deserves compassion; there are hierarchies of vulnerability and it is a limited resource. Nor did it fit her moral framing rules (Hochschild, 1979) (compassion should be reserved for those *most* in need). Through completing their journeys to Calais, the 'fit' 'young' men not only evidenced that their suffering was not serious (they had been able to move and had not died), but that they were also at fault. Instead of being passive and therefore innocent, they exerted their agency and took control.

Australia also established a humanitarian programme in response to displacement in the Middle East (as part of the UNHCR resettlement programme). Although not explicitly mentioned in its title, the Australian Humanitarian Programme for Syrians and Iraqis also emphasised the vulnerability of people who would be resettled through this scheme. Concern for the welfare of people who are to be resettled through organised humanitarian programmes has been used by the Australian government to vilify and exclude people who attempt to reach Australia through irregular maritime routes.

Innocence and fault

Queue jumping

On 9 September 2015, the Australian government announced that in response to the conflicts in Syria and Iraq it would make an additional 12,000 humanitarian places available (Bishop, 2015). Priority would be given to people who were: a) 'assessed as being most vulnerable – persecuted minorities, women, children and families with the least prospect of ever returning safely to their homes'; and b) based in Lebanon, Jordan and Turkey; humanitarian places would 'not be offered to people in Australia or regional processing countries who travelled to Australia illegally by boat' (Department of Immigration and Border Protection, 2016).

As with the SVPRP, 'vulnerability' was a key criterion, and the term 'refugee' was not mentioned in the statement on priorities. As in the UK, there was a focus on women, children and families. Crucially, potential beneficiaries had to have remained in states neighbouring Syria and Iraq, and not have travelled to Australia 'illegally' by boat. Even though they were refugees, this means of travel made their testimony irrelevant and they were expelled from a relationship of compassion. As seen in the case of the Calais boys and young men, two criteria for compassion – serious suffering and no fault – are interlinked. The Pacific Solution was justified through claims that it 'saves lives at sea'. Yet, those same people, having survived, were transformed into 'illegal' immigrants who were reprimanded for putting themselves and their families in danger. They were also deemed to be at fault because of how their behaviour impacted on refugees waiting in transit locations for resettlement opportunities (the valid subjects of compassion).

In 1990 the Joint Standing Committee on Migration published a report titled *Illegal entrants in Australia: balancing control and compassion,* which advocated a tough stance on future 'illegal' arrivals, but a compassionate one towards those present at that time in Australia (McGarth, 2005), setting apart the welfare of these two populations. Article 31of the UN 1951 Refugee Convention states that people seeking asylum should not be penalised for travelling without valid travel documents (Wazana, 2004). Yet, people who travel to Australia through irregular routes to seek asylum are labelled 'queue jumpers' (Gelber, 2003). As refugee rights campaigner, Owen, said, 'They are seen as cheating in some way. This is against the Australian notion of the 'fair go' which is wheeled out a lot. Its un-Australian to jump a queue'. There is a false perception that there is a queue in which people can wait their turn to apply for asylum in Australia. Instead, Australia operates a quota system, with a limited number of places available. The notion of a queue emerged out of the merging of the onshore and offshore elements of Australia's Refugee and Humanitarian Programme under the Howard administration (Suhnan et al, 2012). The government argued that more 'irregular maritime arrivals' (IMAs) meant fewer refugees could be accepted. A 'pushing in' analogy appeared repeatedly in celebratory announcements about the success of Operation Sovereign Borders in 'restoring integrity' (McKay et al, 2011). In a 2015 press release titled, 'Restoring integrity to refugee intake', Peter Dutton (2015b) declared that:

> '[1] After stopping the flood of illegal [elsewhere 'irregular'] maritime arrivals (IMAs) into Australia under Labor, the vast majority of refugees taken in by Australia will once again be from the world's refugee camps and other locations offshore. [2] The intake in the Special Humanitarian Programme (SHP) fell from almost 4,700 people in the last year of the Howard government to just 500 in 2012–13 while the number of IMAs taking their places rose from 200 to almost 5,000. [3] The thousands of IMAs in Australia who are still to be processed will not take the places of those offshore as they did under Labor.'

The language of 'restoration' implies a damaged system. Although most people arriving by boat were refugees, through their categorisation as 'illegal' and 'IMAs', they were contrasted to, and pitted against, a separate population of deserving 'refugees' (1). They had pushed in and 'taken the place' of genuine refugees who were first in line, and who were less mobile and thus in greater need (2, 3). There was a direct correlation between the numbers of IMAs and offshore refugees. As numbers of IMAs went up, numbers of offshore refugees would go down (2). There were a finite number of places which must be distributed fairly, in accordance with Australia's culture of 'fair play'. Like refugees and migrants in Calais, having exerted their agency and become mobile, IMAs were categorised as 'economic migrants'; 'genuine' refugees wait to be rescued and follow 'correct' procedure (McCay et al, 2011). Former Minister of Immigration, Scott Morrison (2014) summed this up by stating that, 'refugee resettlement is not an economic upgrade programme ... The refugee convention and refugee resettlement is supposed to be for asylum seekers not Centrelink [social security] seekers'. In targeting IMAs, the Australian government was celebrated as the fair and compassionate arbitrator who restored order so those most in need could be assisted. In the UK, similar claims were made by Theresa May (2015b) who advocated, 'an approach that combines hard-headed common sense with warm-hearted compassion. An approach with strict new rules for people who abuse the system in Britain, and greater generosity for people in parts of the world where we know they need our help'.

People who arrive of their own volition are constituted as a threat because they are perceived to have done something illegal (see also Chapter Eight on undocumented immigrants in the US). Ironically, although efforts to combat smuggling are done in the name of helping vulnerable migrants and refugees, Suhnan et al (2012) found that Australian public antipathy to people smugglers, engendered through the vilification of people smuggling in the government discourses, has led to prejudice against asylum seekers who became associated with the criminalised actions and characteristics of smugglers. This perception of their criminality is heightened through their mandatory internment in detention centres, signifying punishment (McKay et al, 2017).

Ingratitude

The inability to make the 'right' decision is deemed to be a moral flaw that needs correction, and has been managed through 'responsibilisation' (Harrison and Sanders, 2014). In the case of IMAs, their flawed decisions to travel through irregular routes has been punished through detention to deter others from taking this route. Yet being detained is also supposed to persuade people to make the 'responsible' decision to return to their countries of origin. If people resist attempts at responsibilisation, their categorisation as being morally flawed is reinforced. In the case of detainees, part of this moral failure has been their perceived ingratitude for the 'compassion' and 'care' shown to them.

Despite testimonies that detention causes serious suffering, the Australian government has engaged in literal denial that the conditions in detention centres are inhumane (Cohen, 2001). Interpretive denial has also been used to explain suffering as being caused by the actions of detainees themselves, and implicatory denial is evident in the denial of the government's responsibility for this suffering (Cohen, 2001). This can be seen in the responses to self-harm and incidents of protests in the detention centres.

On 2 May 2016, Hodan Yasin, a 21-year-old refugee woman held in detention on Nauru, doused herself in petrol and set herself alight; she suffered 70% burns (Doherty and Davidson, 2016). This occurred days after the suicide of a 23-year-old Iranian man, Omid Masoumali, again through self-immolation after he was driven to despair by his prolonged and indefinite detention on Nauru.

Yasin had fled Somalia with her family to seek asylum in Australia. Classified by the Australian government as IMAs, they were sent to Nauru. In November 2015, Yasin was injured in an accident on the island and transferred to a hospital in Brisbane for treatment. On 27 April 2016, she was forcibly returned to Nauru. Witnesses saw Australian Border Force guards carry Yasin out of the Brisbane immigration transit accommodation; they heard her screams as she pleaded to stay (Doherty and Davidson, 2016). Her self-immolation took place less than a week after her return to Nauru; it was reportedly her second suicide attempt. Witnesses, including the medical staff who treated her in Nauru and Brisbane, saw the horrific injuries inflicted on her body. The incident and injuries were widely reported on in both domestic and international news media; this suffering was known.

Yet knowledge of Yasin's suffering did not induce a compassionate response towards her from the government. Two days after her self-immolation, Peter Dutton (2016c) delivered a speech at a press conference in Canberra. After praising the care of the medical staff, he expressed 'grave concern that this person would resort to such an extreme act of self-harm'. In a denial of her humanity he did not say her name; instead referring to her as 'this person' or the 'patient'. Interpreted through an understanding of bodily self-harm as political protest (see Chapter Seven), her suffering was explained as a manipulative act. He went on to discuss recent protests by detainees in Nauru, implying that her self-harm was part of this wider context of protest.

In a well-established narrative used in response to previous protests on Nauru and Manus (Gleeson, 2016), Dutton dismissed the legitimacy of their protests through a literal denial that conditions on Nauru are inhumane: 'the recent protests in Nauru are not protests against living conditions, they are not protests against healthcare and are not protests at the lack of financial support' (Dutton, 2016c). As proof of this, he listed the increased number of health professionals who had been employed and the investment in the medical clinic. He reinterpreted protests and self-harm as attempts to blackmail the Australian government into resettling detainees in Australia. In doing so he blamed detainees, but also the 'advocates' who support them and were 'causing serious harm', much as NGOs operating in the Mediterranean have been blamed for enabling the smuggling business (see Chapter Five).

Once again, the suffering of 'IMAs' was not just refuted, but also identified as harming more deserving subjects of compassion; in this case those future lives which could be lost at sea:

> No actions they take will lead the government to deviate from its course. We are not going to allow people to drown at sea again. People have paid thousands of dollars to come to Australia and they haven't arrived in Australia and they are frustrated by that and I can understand that. ... I'm not going to allow women and children at the hands of evil people smugglers to go to the bottom of the ocean. (Dutton, 2016c)

Dutton declared that he was not going to allow women and children to die. The very same women and children, having survived, were now detained on Nauru. This apparent category overlap was resolved; in the process of surviving they became agentic people resisting and responding to their suffering, and were transformed into cynical 'undeserving' fraudsters to be expelled from the relationship of compassion.

Peterie (2017:1) asserts that in contrast to the weak and passive ideal subject of compassion (the suffering victim face of the Other [Douzinas, 2007]), strong and agentic IMAs may be understood as having similar possibilities to the Australian people; thus, they pose a threat which speaks to the 'fears and insecurities of the Australian people'. The final section of this chapter examines the appropriation of suffering and how increasingly in debates on migration and asylum, populations in the minority world have not only been positioned as 'saviours' (Douzinas, 2007), but have also been portrayed as people who are themselves suffering and in need.

Feeling their pain

Nussbaum (2013) identifies the third criteria for compassion as the eudaimonistic judgement that the other person's well-being matters in our schemes and goals. This can happen through identifying similar possibilities between the other and us, while the absence of this affinity can drive fear and hostility. However, paradoxically, its presence – seeing another's suffering as our possibility – can also be a catalyst that drives hostile feelings and leads to a withholding of compassion. Reflecting on the refugee crisis, the late Zygmunt Bauman (Evans and Bauman, 2016) suggested that the sight of large numbers of people fleeing to Europe reminded many in Europe of their own insecurities and vulnerabilities, fuelling anxiety and fear.

Writing in the aftermath of 9/11, Hochschild (2002) observed that the attacks had a disorientating effect on established emotional regimes, which then required readjustment. Through the terrorist attacks, the 'the iconic targets – the World Trade Centre and the Pentagon – the nerve centres of global capitalism – were revealed as shockingly vulnerable' (Hochschild, 2002:117). If people in these centres of power could be wiped out in an instant, this could happen to anyone. While we might identify shock events such as terrorist attacks and financial crises as catalysts for such feelings, social theorists have also argued that we live in a broader and more ambiguous state of ontological insecurity (Bauman, 2004). Hochschild (2002:119) asserts that in such disorientating times people go into emergency mode and 'turn to national authority figures for guidance about what we ought to feel'. These 'feeling legislators' (Hochschild, 2002:121) help to institute a new emotional regime which 'reorders suspicion' and returns us to a 'nervous normal'. In this new emotional regime, there is a new stratification system, 'the haves are those above suspicion, the have-nots are those who are obvious objects of it' who may cause us harm (Hochschild, 2002:125),.

On 9 November 2016, the Republican President-elect, Donald Trump, gave his victory speech (CNN, 2016). He congratulated the Democrat candidate, Hilary Clinton, on her hard-fought campaign. He said he would bring the country together and govern for all Americans. There was no mention of immigration in his speech and the tone was a sharp departure from his campaign speeches. Immigration had been a central campaign issue; exit polls indicated that for the majority (64%) of those who voted for him immigration was the most important issue (Huang et al, 2016). His campaign promises had included plans to deport the approximately 11 million undocumented immigrants in the US; to build a border wall between the US and Mexico; to end the executive orders introduced by President Obama that gave some undocumented immigrants deferrals on deportation; and to ban Muslim immigration (Trump, 2016a).

As with the vote for Brexit in the UK, an explanatory narrative has been built in public commentary around the plight of the 'left behind' Trump voter; older, white, less educated, working class and often male, voters on low incomes (Barr, 2016; Swaine, 2016). Yet 49% of university-educated people also voted for Trump.[6] Meanwhile, the people who have suffered the most from the 2008 financial crisis and subsequent austerity measures in the US and Europe are in fact women of colour (Emejulu, 2016). Much election analysis centred on class; the persistent reference to the 'white working class' in effect dismissed the classed experiences of people of colour who form a significant proportion of working class populations (Emejulu, 2016). It is beyond the scope of this book to provide a full analysis of the factors explaining voting behaviour in the election. However, the polling of voters revealed that there was evidently a disjuncture between how supporters of Trump and populist rhetoric elsewhere felt about their economic and social status, and their actual material conditions in practice. As Ioanide (2015) has argued, when it comes to racism, emotion is key since 'feelings trump facts'. Evidence indicates the relative prosperity and well-being of white populations compared with many migrants and other racialised minorities. However, these facts appear to have been overridden by the *'feels-as-if'* story (Hochschild, 2016:135) that feelings tell. Voters were persuaded by this 'feels-as-if story' which resonated with their 'deep story'. In post-truth politics (Davis, 2016) people may be sceptical of 'factual' evidence, but are more convinced by stories of feeling through which they understand their world. In the remainder of this chapter it is argued that through the feeling rules engaged with in Donald Trump's narratives, white citizens were imagined as the true victims and righteous subjects of compassion. This built on a political narrative trend in which, as Fasenfest (2016:3) writes, 'the patina of victimization is applied in a sort of perverse reversal. Victims of discrimination and exclusion are suddenly cast as the perpetrators of these same actions, with cries of "reverse discrimination" and a general assault on efforts at multi-cultural and racial diversity in societies'. There is a rejection of the feeling rules that are seen as being imposed by a 'liberal elite' (Hochschild, 2016). However, in this rejection those feeling rules are not so much dismantled, but rather appropriated and reworked so that 'their' pain becomes displaced by 'our' pain.

Trump succeeded in tapping into this 'deep story' of the white citizen 'victim'. This was apparent from the moment he announced his candidature, and declared that 'the US has become a dumping ground for everybody else's problems'. He infamously stated, 'When Mexico sends its people, they're not sending their best ... They're sending people that have lots of problems, and they're bringing those problems with us. They're bringing drugs. They're bringing crime. They're rapists. And some, I assume, are good people' (Trump, 2015). His engagement with the rhetoric of white suffering is now explored through an analysis of his 31 August 2016 campaign speech about immigration to an audience in Arizona during which this narrative was most clearly set out (Trump, 2016b):

> [1] 'Today, on a very complicated and very difficult subject, you will get the truth. [2] The fundamental problem with the immigration system in our country is that it serves the needs of wealthy donors, political activists and powerful, powerful politicians. It's all you can do. Thank you. Thank you.'

> [3] Let me tell you who it does not serve. It does not serve you the American people. Doesn't serve you. [4] When politicians talk about immigration reform, they usually mean the following, amnesty, open borders, lower wages. [5] Immigration reform should mean something else entirely. It should mean improvements to our laws and policies to make life better for American citizens.

> Thank you. [6] But if we're going to make our immigration system work, then we have to be prepared to talk honestly and without fear about these important and very sensitive issues. [7] For instance, we have to listen to the concerns that working people, our forgotten working people, have over the record pace of immigration and its impact on their jobs, wages, housing, schools, tax bills and general living conditions.

> [8] These are valid concerns expressed by decent and patriotic citizens from all backgrounds, all over. [9] We also have to be honest about the fact that not everyone who seeks to join our country will be able to successfully assimilate. Sometimes it's just not going to work out. [10] It's our right, as a sovereign nation to choose immigrants that we think are the likeliest to thrive and flourish and love us.

In these first three paragraphs, immigrants were not mentioned once directly. Instead the 'American people' were the central protagonists in the story. Trump began by saying the audience will get the truth (1). Throughout the speech he frequently proclaimed that he would give them 'truth' and 'honesty' and would do so 'without fear' (6), rhetorical devices that are often used when the speaker is aware that the issue they are talking about may be regarded as controversial (Edwards and Fasulu, 2006). The first actors he then referred to are 'wealthy donors, political activists and powerful, powerful politicians' who he stated are the chief beneficiaries of the immigration system. They prioritised the needs of immigrants. Trump rejected these feeling rules and the 'American people' are presented as those most in need of care because their needs have not been served.

In the third and fourth paragraphs, he identified these 'American' people more precisely. These people regained their social status as the central protagonists in the American story. Their needs and feelings mattered; they were the real victims because they had been forgotten (he often used the term 'forgotten' in his campaign speeches). Other people only entered the story in terms of how they were encountered by and affected the feelings and lives of the 'American people'. Although in other speeches Trump used the term 'working class', in this speech he dropped 'class' to refer to 'working people' (7). This defined the boundary of the defended group, but was sufficiently loose and abstract enough to avoid some of the ideological and policy obligations and socialist politics that might be expected on hearing these terms. It was broad enough to include those who may *feel* a loss of economic and social status, but may not identify or be identified as 'working class'.

It was only at the end of the fourth paragraph that Trump first mentioned immigrants, although he referred to them as 'people who seek to join *our* country' [italics added]; it was a reminder to the audience of who should have a say in and control in this encounter. Before he began to discuss specific concerns about immigrants, he prefaced his critique with a defensive statement about the 'valid' concerns of 'decent' and 'patriotic' people. Speaking defensively, he presented those who might express these feelings as marginalised potential victims. They felt 'fear' to speak 'honestly' (6), with the implication that they would be attacked for doing so. At this point Trump's reservations about immigrants were expressed as emanating from his love and care for the American people, rather than hostility to immigrants; it was not anything personal, 'it just doesn't work out' (9), because they did not have the requisite economic and social skills, but also because they did not feel for the nation in the way they should, they did not 'love us' (10).

His tone then changed as he began to portray immigrants as the perpetrators of harm, who not only did not love US citizens, but actively hurt them. He began with the issue of criminality:

> Countless innocent American lives have been stolen [2] because our politicians have failed in their duty to secure our borders and enforce our laws like they have to be enforced. [3] I have met with many of the great parents who lost their children to sanctuary cities and open borders.

His narrative of the suffering of US citizens drew on key aspects of the criteria for compassion identified by Nussbaum (2013). Serious suffering had occurred; 'countless' lives had been lost. These were 'innocent' people, but also, importantly, 'American lives' (1). They were 'our' people. He established that it was Hilary Clinton and the Obama administration who were responsible and to whom outrage should be directed (2). While pro-migrant and refugee activists held state border security policies as responsible for mass death at sea in the Mediterranean, according to Trump border security was at fault, but because it was too *lax*. He then proceeded to name some of the victims of weak border controls and to tell their individual stories.

> [1] This includes incredible Americans like 21-year-old Sarah Root. [2] The man who killed her arrived at the border, entered Federal custody and then was released into the U.S ... He was released again after the crime, and now he's out there at large. [3] Sarah had graduated from college with a 4.0, top student in her class one day before her death.

In naming them and telling their stories (and introducing their families on stage) they are humanised rather than simply part of the 'many' who have died[7] (1). Their innocence and deservingness was also highlighted, as often happens in migrant and refugee anti-deportation campaigns; they were young and academically able with promising futures ahead (3), or old and vulnerable, and good, kind people. While we have become used to hearing about the deaths of immigrants attempting to cross borders, Trump spent much of the speech turning this narrative around to suggest that it was *US citizens* who were dying because of immigration policy and who were the real victims. In fact, migrant deaths and suffering were not mentioned at all.

He then claimed that immigrants were also causing economic harm:

[1] Most illegal immigrants are lower skilled workers with less education, [2] who compete directly against vulnerable American workers, and that these illegal workers draw much more out from the system than they can ever possibly pay back. [3] And they're hurting a lot of our people that cannot get jobs under any circumstances.

He used the term 'illegal' throughout his speech (1). Even when stating that many 'illegal immigrants are good people', the prefix 'illegal' positioned these people as at fault. They were the powerful aggressors who competed against the 'vulnerable' American worker who deserved our compassion (2). The 'illegal' workers drained the system and did not pay back; they were not playing by the rules (2) and therefore had an unfair advantage over 'our people' in the job market (3). Like 'working people', 'our people' was broad and ambiguous enough to allow a range of citizens to imagine that they were 'our people', but given his derogatory comments elsewhere about Mexicans, African Americans and Muslims, it could also be implied that 'our people' were white.

In her description of the deep story of right wing Tea Party supporters, Hochschild (2010:136) uses the analogy of waiting in line. In their 'deep story' the protagonist is standing in a long line leading up to a hill. They have done everything right but, 'the line is barely moving and you can't see how close the American Dream is. The American Dream is a story of progress but you are not sure you are progressing and there is insecurity' (Hochschild, 2016:136). Then they see people cutting in to the line ahead, pushing them further back. They are compassionate people, but cannot sympathise with and help people who are not playing by the rules and who may even be harming them. It is US citizens who are now 'vulnerable' and in need of compassion. As mentioned earlier, Waite et al. (2014) observe that the 'capacity to hurt' can be understood as both *being* hurt and *doing* hurt. While it has been evidenced that immigrants are harmed by unjust immigration policies, Waite et al. (2014) found that some established citizen populations saw immigrants as *perpetrators* of hurt. This discourse was drawn on in Trump's speech. The migrant's capacity to inflict hurt on abandoned citizens has also been a key theme in populist politics in Europe and therefore hate or fear expressed towards migrants has had a defensive emotional response (Amin, 2013).

In concluding his speech, Trump issued a reminder of what the primary motivations for his policies and feelings were. He stated:

There is only one core issue in the immigration debate, and that issue is the well-being of the American people. ... We will be fair, just, and compassionate to all, but our greatest compassion must be for our American citizens.

In framing this scenario as a need to prioritise among competing claims for compassion, it was presented as an obvious choice to prioritise those who are closest to 'Us' and whose welfare is therefore paramount in our life goals (Nussbaum, 2013). In setting out the plight of US citizens through a similar logic to that used to make the case for immigrants, there is a flattening out of experience; we all suffer. The only measure that counts is the strength of feelings of hurt, which is divorced from wider material contexts and evidence of structures and histories of oppression.

Conclusion

Governments proudly declare and celebrate their nation-states' humanitarian qualities as a reflection of their civility and good moral standing. Compassion has frequently been claimed as a driving force motivating responses to migrants and refugees. Yet this is in a context of enduring restrictionism and exclusion. Chapter Five examined how compassion has been appropriated to justify these violent actions, while the current chapter has explored how, having proclaimed to be compassionate, governments have sought to legitimise the expulsion of some people from a relationship of compassion by demonstrating how they fall short of the necessary criteria for compassion. Chapters Seven and Eight now examine how migrant and refugee rights campaigns have sought to respond to this.

Notes

[1] Hansard HC Deb. cols. 23-24 7 September 2015.
[2] This was initially referred to as the 'Vulnerable Persons Relocation scheme'.
[3] Hansard HC Deb. Cols 863-864 29 January 2014.
[4] By the end of March 2017, 7,307 Syrian nationals had been resettled in the UK through the SVPRP (Rudd, 2017).
[5] Hansard HC Deb. cols. 23-24 7 September 2015.
[6] Of those in the UK who voted for Brexit, 59% were middle class (Dorling, 2017)
[7] A similar shift from a focus on the 'mass' to the individual story can be seen in refugee and migrant activism.

7

Outrage, Responsibility and Accountability

Introduction

The death of Alan Kurdi illustrated the power of compassion as a force for mobilisation and as a channel for interrupting hostile immigration and refugee discourses. However, as discussed in previous chapters, the discourse of compassion has also been appropriated by governments in ways that have led to the accommodation and reinforcement of oppressive immigration regimes.

Through returning to the use of testimony in resistance (introduced in Chapter Four) Chapters Seven and Eight examine how migrant and refugee rights activists have reimagined and recovered 'compassion' to challenge violent and repressive immigration regimes and hold those responsible to account. This is considered, in this chapter, through a discussion of the campaign to end Australia's use of offshore immigration detention on Manus Island and Nauru. The focus in this discussion is on the #LetThemStay protests which took place in early 2016 against the deportation of refugees from Australia to the offshore detention centres, the protests by people detained in these centres, and the #BringThemHere campaign being waged by supporters in Australia (ongoing at the time of writing). This case study explores the power and limitations of the physical body as a mode of testimony. This addresses the context of the longstanding denial and discrediting of other forms of testimony by the Australian government, and the obscuring from public view, and physical proximity, of the violence of Australia's immigration and asylum enforcement. The case study outlines how protestors used the physical sites of their bodies and public spaces to protest the use of offshore detention. The discussion reflects on the challenge of enabling the face-to-face encounter that

Levinas (1979) argued produces ethical responsibility, when so much of the violence of immigration and asylum enforcement is obscured from public view. It is posited that physical protests and bodily testimony have been mobilised to produce pathways to such an encounter. Meanwhile, in the context of the denial and discrediting of other forms of testimony and the appropriation of a discourse of compassion by the government, these protests have been used to rearticulate relationships of care and compassion, and to direct outrage towards the causes of suffering.

Attempts to alleviate suffering are crucial in the action-orientated emotion of compassion. Compassion should generate outrage (that other key moral sentiment in addition to compassion) and potentially shame (when reflecting on one's own culpability). While compassionate action can be directed into care, solidarity and support towards those who are suffering, the lens must also be turned to put a spotlight on, make visible and hold to account the causes of suffering and the perpetrators.

Blood on their hands – absent bodies and accountability

Trafficked to Nauru and Manus

> We were four-hundred people.
> Four-hundred lost souls in a tightly confined space.
> Four-hundred prisoners
> All anticipating the nights
> So we could leave
> and enter our nightmares
> (Behrouz Boochani, 2017:22)

Behrouz Boochani is a Kurdish-Iranian refugee journalist who, at the time of writing, has been incarcerated in Manus detention centre for four years. During this period, he has documented his and other detainees' lives, highlighting the systemic violence, abuse and neglect they face (Boochani, 2018). His work has been published in *The Guardian* and other media outlets. Ali, known by the pen name Eaten Fish, is an Iranian asylum seeker and cartoonist. He was also detained on Manus Island for four years, but, at the time of writing, has just been resettled in Norway. Eaten Fish is suffering serious mental illness which was exacerbated by his time on Manus where he suffered violence, including sexual assault. His graphic cartoons chronicled his experiences in detention – the capture of 'boat people' by Australian border force, sexual abuse in Manus, the deaths of fellow detainees, and his declining mental health, all taking place under the watchful eye of the camp's CCTV (Perera and Pugliese, 2016).

Yet despite the existence and circulation of these first-hand testimonies of systematic human rights abuses in detention, the centres continued to operate. Boochani (2017:20) reflected on this and some of his frustration in using journalism as resistance stating that, 'the government propaganda was too strong and my voice was lost. Now after three years I realise that the Australian people still do not know exactly what is going on here. It seems that no one recognises the situation is a form of systematic torture; they do not see the reality'.

Implicatory denial

In 2014, an Iranian asylum seeker, Reza Berati, was murdered during a violent attack on the Manus detention centre by local men. In that same year, Hamid Kahazai died there from septicaemia. In a press conference, the then Minister of Immigration, Scott Morrison (2014), declared that Reza's death was a 'terrible tragedy', while he was also 'saddened' by the death of Hamid. He observed that 'where there are issues that need to be addressed at the processing centres, the government has taken action to support the Papua New Guinea (PNG) and Nauruan governments who run these centres'. Two years later, *The Guardian* leaked the Nauru files which detailed 2,116 cases of abuse against detainees that had been reported and recorded by detention centre staff between 2013 and 2015; more than half of these cases related to children (Farrell et al, 2016). The leak of these files followed two suicide attempts in the detention centre in April 2016. A week after the leak of the files, the Minister of Immigration, Peter Dutton, expressed his frustrations at the media who reported the abuse and at third sector organisations, namely Save the Children, who he accused of leaking the files. He stated that, 'The trouble, frankly, with the approach of *The Guardian* and the ABC has been to trivialise the very serious issues by trying to promote the 2,100 reports as somehow all of those being serious when they're not' (Peter Dutton quoted in Farrell and Karp, 2016).

In each of these instances, there was a denial of culpability on the part of the Australian government. Firstly, described as 'tragic' and 'sad' events, the deaths of asylum seekers on Manus were presented as an accident rather than resulting from systematic neglect and abuse. Even where it was acknowledged that there may be issues to be tackled within detention facilities, this was not in relation to the violence of their very existence, created and funded by the Australian government, but rather due to their mismanagement by the impoverished former colonies who have been outsourced by Australia to operate these centres. The remainder of this chapter examines how campaigns in the offshore detention centres and in Australia have sought to respond to this denial of responsibility, and protest the use of offshore detention.

Physical testimony

Developments in global communications mean that we are regularly brought face to face with geographically distant suffering through our television screens and through social media, in the latter case often through direct communication from those who are suffering, as well as through third parties such as NGO staff and journalists. Despite challenges in accessing platforms, migrants and refugees in the societies that receive them have provided accounts of their circumstances and have advocated for their own rights and needs (McNevin, 2011; Marciniak and Tyler, 2014). However, immigration bureaucracies have also attempted to create and preserve social distance between migrants, refugees and audiences who may respond to their testimony, to undermine efforts at community building, solidarity and resistance (Schuster, 2005). Although border enforcement has become increasingly visible and embedded in everyday life in our communities (CRMRB, 2015), simultaneously much of the work of border enforcement also operates out of view. Immigration detention estates have expanded, and borders have been exported beyond the physical boundaries of nation-states (Mountz, 2010). This obscures the violence of border control and limits the ability of those who are affected to get their testimonies heard.

One example of these practices has been Australia's use of offshore immigration detention centres in the Pacific islands of Nauru and Manus Island. This section explores how efforts to resist and end offshore detention have engaged with the fundamental tasks and perils of bearing witness, discussed in Chapter Four (Kurasawa, 2009). For witness bearing to take place, testimony must reach its audience in a form that is comprehensible and that induces empathy. The inaccessibility of Australia's offshore detention facilities, restrictions on media access (Gleeson, 2016), and Australian government denials have limited opportunities for visual and verbal testimonies to be heard directly and for direct engagement to take place. In this context the bodily testimonies of refugees and their Australian supporters – that is testimony inscribed on the body or performed through the body – has taken on an important role and been used to enable the process of witness bearing.

First, as the political identities and verbal testimony of people seeking asylum as rights holders is increasingly disbelieved, or overridden by the reinterpretation of their threatened body into the threatening body, bodily testimony of vulnerability and suffering has become a last resort of access to recognition (Fassin, 2012). Yet even this, as it has been reclaimed, made active and understood as a political voice (Tyler, 2013), has been discredited by the Australian government.

Second, immigration bureaucracies construct and preserve social distance between migrants and refugees and the political administrations and public in receiving societies, including by physically expelling people to the margins, as in the case of offshore detention (Gill, 2016). In this context, both refugee and Australian protesters have held physical space, and have used their bodies to bring the bodies of refugees ashore. It is argued that in the Australian context where the government has appropriated the discourse of compassion to justify its actions, this has become a powerful means through which protesters have reclaimed the discourse of compassion and redirected attention and outrage to the actions of the government.

Protesting Australia's offshore detention estate

Refugees who have survived the journey to Europe have been allowed to land, have been interviewed by journalists, and have interacted with people in the states where they arrived. Yet on the other side of the world, since 19 July 2013, 'irregular maritime arrivals' trying to reach Australia by boat have been intercepted by the Australian military in the water operations which, supposedly for national security reasons, are surrounded in secrecy. They have then been transferred to offshore detention facilities and detained indefinitely. They have not been allowed to claim asylum in Australia, although Australia is a signatory to the UN 1951 Refugee Convention. The convention recognises that people seeking asylum may not be able to travel through regular legal channels and should not be sanctioned for using irregular routes (Wazana, 2004). As of 31 May 2016, of the 1,194 people transferred to offshore detention in Nauru and who have had their claims for asylum assessed by the Nauruan government, 915 (77%) have been found to be refugees. Meanwhile, 541 of the 551 people transferred to Manus Island detention centre whose asylum claims have been assessed by the PNG government have been found to be refugees (98%) (Karlsen, 2016). In the UK and elsewhere, there has been a reported culture of disbelief around the testimonies presented by people seeking asylum (Griffiths, 2012). However, through the Pacific Solution, the Australian state has discredited asylum testimonies at a whole other level. Even if it is acknowledged that people arriving by boat are trying to claim asylum, the fact that their bodies arrive through this irregular route means that their verbal testimonies account for little. Australia refuses to let them seek asylum in Australia. In this scenario, their ability to verbally attest to their suffering is curtailed through the denial of their arrival.

Captured in offshore detention, people do not have opportunities to interact with Australian citizens and residents, unlike refugees and migrants living in communities in the societies that receive them. They do, however, encounter Australian citizens working in the detention centres. As evidenced in the Nauru files, detainees have reported abuse and harm to staff, while staff whistle-blowers have reported abuse to the Australian media and public (Farrell et al, 2016; Gleeson, 2016). Since the passage of the Border Force Act 2015 it has become illegal to do so, although many former staff continue to speak out and no one has been prosecuted yet[1] (Gleeson, 2016). Detainees have also been in contact with advocates in Australia to whom they have provided first-hand accounts of their cases, abuse in detention and day-to-day life there through oral and written testimonies, cartoons, undercover video footage and photographs, which have also been released to the media (Boochani, 2016; interviews with Australian campaigners). However, this abuse is not happening in Australia. Most Australians never encounter the camps in their day-to-day lives; they will not meet the detainees, and will not even see them on television or social media unless they actively try to do so. The detainees' bodies, and so in effect *they*, are absent from daily life in Australia. Meanwhile, the government has consistently denied and discredited accusations of abuse in detention, while making the 'compassionate' case that this is the most humane option because it 'saves lives at sea'.

Asylum and 'irregular maritime arrivals' have been at the centre of political debate since the late 1990s, and particularly since the first introduction of the 'Pacific Solution' in 2001. However, after years in which there was little shift in political discourse and government policy, over the course of 2016 a series of events indicated that some change was taking place, although the government remains adamantly opposed to bringing offshore detainees to Australia. A key turning point in the debate was the success of the #LetThemStay campaign in 2015-16, followed by the Nauru and #BringThemHere protests which gained momentum following a series of events in early and mid-2016.

#LetThemStay

Since 2013, detainees held in offshore detention have not been allowed to claim asylum in Australia. However, some people with serious medical conditions have been transferred from offshore detention to Australia for treatment.

In 2015, the Human Rights Law Centre (HRLC) brought the case of plaintiff M69 to the High Court to challenge the government's use of offshore detention (Webb, 2016). The M69 case was that of a Bangladeshi woman who was receiving medical treatment in Australia, had a child born in Australia, and was facing deportation back to Nauru. The centre argued it was unconstitutional for Australia to use offshore detention because it was not authorised by a valid Australian law and infringed constitutional limits on the government's power. An internal Department of Immigration document stated that this litigation was, 'likely to cause problems with being able to remove transitory persons' and that it was 'therefore important to return as many transitory persons as we can, as soon as possible' (Webb, 2016). Over the next three months the Human Rights Law Centre and refugee organisations identified 267 people at risk of being returned to Nauru. The centre filed proceedings to seek to prevent these deportations. In June 2015, the government amended the Migration Act retroactively (after the case began) with Section 198 AHA. This allowed for Australia's participation in the plaintiff's detention in a foreign country. The High Court ruled in favour of the government, finding they could lawfully return refugees to offshore detention, although they were not obliged to do so (Webb, 2016). In early 2016, the #LetThemStay campaign was launched in Australia to protest and prevent the removal of the 267 people to Nauru, including 72 children of which 37 were babies who had been born in Australia.

The babies became the face of the campaign, following a pattern seen in other anti-detention campaigns around the world, and also in Australia where in recent years organisations, such as ChilOut and Grandmothers Against Detention of Refugee Children, have focused on child detention. The national campaign organisation GetUp! (2016) featured some of the babies on its web page for the #LetThemStay campaign. Each baby was pictured in a close-up photograph on their own, often smiling at the camera. The photographs looked like they were from family photograph albums. Underneath each photograph was a short story about the baby in which the parents expressed their love and pride in their children, and their hopes and dreams for them; these were ordinary everyday stories about family and love which other parents might identify with and which individualised and humanised the people at risk.

Thousands of people took to the streets in the #LetThemStay rallies across Australia calling for the 267 people to be allowed to stay and for an end to offshore detention. Although the government won the High Court challenge, these protests succeeded in (at least temporarily) preventing the return of 150 people, including the 37 babies. Families were released into community detention and single men were detained in centres in Australia. It was not an end to offshore detention, but the outcome did nevertheless buoy refugee advocates and activists. As Owen, a refugee rights campaigner, observed, this was 'the first successful pushback' against the government on refugee policy for several years.

Although not part of the M69 case, a one-year-old child referred to as 'Baby Asha' also become a face of the campaign. Baby Asha was born to parents seeking asylum in Australia. They had been removed to Nauru in June 2015 when Asha was five months old, despite advice from the charity Save the Children that this would be 'potentially catastrophic'. Asha developed gastroenteritis within a week of her arrival on Nauru. The family were returned to the Lady Cilento hospital in Brisbane at the end of 2015 after Asha was severely burned in an accident on Nauru. In early February 2016, Asha's family were told that they faced imminent removal to Nauru once her treatment was complete. However, hospital doctors refused to discharge her because she did not have a safe home to go to (Doherty, 2016a). Several hundred protestors gathered outside the hospital in support of Asha's family and the doctors; they maintained a vigil at all the hospital exits to prevent her removal (Doherty, 2016b). After a one-week stand-off, the baby was discharged with her mother into community detention in Australia (Doherty, 2016c).

#CloseTheCamps and #BringThemHere protests

On 20 March 2016, men, women and children being detained on Nauru began a peaceful daily protest against their detention and the delay in the processing of their asylum claims (Butler, 2016). Many had been detained since the offshore detention policy was reintroduced in 2013. They had been promised that the Nauru government would complete the processing of their asylum claims by October 2015. Two and a half years later they were still waiting. Their 1,000th day in detention was 20 March 2016. Each day at 4 pm they walked to the gates of the compound where they displayed protest banners and chanted their appeals to the Australian government and people, and the international community. Some of the banners they held were direct appeals for care and compassion – 'Australian people open your hearts and close camp' (CNN International, 2016).

These were alongside statements of outrage which identified and held to account those instituting policies that directly caused their suffering. For example, one banner read, 'you are accused, kids abused'. Although the island is inaccessible to journalists, detainees shared photographs of their protests with advocates in Australia who in turn shared these through social media and to media outlets.

The #LetThemStay rallies and the protest outside the Lady Cliento Children's Hospital received significant attention in national and some international media (Webb, 2016). The renewed media and public focus on offshore detention remained. In April 2016 the PNG Supreme Court found that the Manus Island detention centre was illegal and ordered it to be shut down. That month there were also reports of serious incidents of self-harm in the Nauru detention centre. In April, Omid Masoumali committed suicide on Nauru after self-immolating while UN High Commissioner for Refugees (UNHCR) representatives were visiting the detention centre, calling out, 'this is how tired we are; this action will prove how exhausted we are. I cannot take it any more' (Doherty and Davidson, 2016). Then, on 10 August, the Nauru files were leaked by *The Guardian* in a story covered extensively around the world and leading to widespread condemnation of Australia's offshore detention centres by the UNHCR and other national and international human rights organisations (Davidson and Doherty, 2016; UNHCR, 2016). People detained on Nauru continued their daily protests in the aftermath of the Nauru files. Meanwhile, across Australia, thousands of people took part in rallies and vigils outside legislative and government administration buildings, calling for an end to offshore detention. Vigils also took place outside the Australian embassies in the UK and Japan; at the London vigil protestors spent 10 hours reading aloud testimony from the reports (El-Enany and Keenan, 2016). As George, a refugee rights campaigner, said, the government was holding firm but 'the backlash is growing. That's pretty profound because that was not the case before'.

The suffering body as testimony

As this book was being completed, the Manus Island detention centre was facing imminent closure following the legal ruling in PNG. However, the Australian government stated that those who were refused asylum would be returned to their countries of origin, while those granted refugee status would never be allowed to settle in Australia (Doherty, 2017). Since the launch of Operation Sovereign Borders, offshore detainees have only been allowed to enter Australia when they have suffered serious ill health or physical harm to their bodies in detention; this reluctant invitation has then been rescinded once the physical body is healed. This reflects the pre-eminence of the suffering body as a route to recognition following the delegitimising of the threatened body (Fassin, 2012).

The response to the Nauru files also exemplified this phenomena. People seeking asylum have been detained indefinitely since 2013 and denied the right to apply for asylum in Australia. However, although there has been international media coverage of Australia's disregard of people's legal right to claim asylum, it was the testimony of the physical abuse of children's bodies which generated the unprecedented scale of outrage and condemnation from across the world. It was the captured, harmed, passive and unnamed bodies, witnessed through third-party testimonies who were recognised, rather than the resisting, mobile bodies asserting their right to apply for asylum.

In many cases of resistance to human rights violations around the world, people seeking asylum have transformed the suffering body itself into a testimony of strength and agency. As Nair (2012:784) has observed, 'the lived experience of displacement is corporeal, and so too the translation of this experience into politicised dissent. In response to an absence of adequate economic and political platforms, the body of the displaced becomes a prime site of a simultaneous experience of dispossession and protest'.

In February 2017, Eaten Fish (the Iranian asylum seeker cartoonist) went on a 19-day hunger strike, after his reports of being sexually assaulted were dismissed by immigration authorities who returned him to the main compound in Manus to live among the perpetrators of the abuse (Robertson, 2017). After the denial of his verbal testimony, his emaciated body functioned as tangible physical testimony of his suffering and needs. Speaking on Facebook about his actions, Eaten Fish said, 'I did protest because I need safety ... Protection ... I don't want to die. I do not want to be made to suffer anymore. I need proper treatment. I need safety and peace more than food' (Robertson, 2017). There have been hunger strikes before on Manus; in 2015, up to 700 men detained on the island went on hunger strike, with some men also sewing their lips together to protest the conditions in the centre, the delays in processing their asylum claims, and plans to forcibly resettle them in PNG (Doherty, 2015).

There are parallels here with the case of Abas Amini, a Kurdish-Iranian man seeking asylum in the UK who sewed his lips, ears and eyes in protest at the British government's decision to deport him (Tyler, 2013). Tyler (2013:101) has described this as a practice of 'grotesque mimicry' through which Amini 'wanted to make the everyday violence of xenophobic discourses and practices visible in another register'. She argues that such 'political instrumentalisation of abjection' can 'move us beyond the deadlock of normativity and abjection'; Amini 'refused to be the abject other of the British state or a (passive) object of humanitarian protection' (Tyler, 2013:101). By acting out his abjection, he transformed his abjection into political speech which 'challenges us to confront him as a political activist' (Tyler, 2013:101). Although this was an expression of being made abject, through these performative acts of resistance this violence was made visible while the exertion of agency and control resisted the abjection.

Bringing bodies ashore

Proxy bodies

Undocumented people in the US and other migrants living in societies that receive them have also used bodily occupations of public spaces to resist their invisibility and enact themselves as political subjects (Isin, 2009; Schwiertz, 2016). In doing so, they have resisted oppression by occupying and passing through public spaces and defying the political invisibility that has been imposed on them by the state. In the US, this has also included protests outside federal buildings, immigration detention centres, state and federal legislatures, and occupation of Senators' offices (including then President Obama's 2012 presidential campaign offices) (Nicholls, 2013; interviews with US activists). It has been clear who is to be held accountable for the suffering and violence they have experienced. Meanwhile, due to extensive media reporting and NGO documentation, the suffering of refugees journeying to Europe during the refugee crisis has also been visible, even if they have limited power to control the narrative. Their faces are seen, some of their names are known, and those who have arrived have entered a shared physical space – Europe. There is some proximity to their audiences as they have arrived, even if they are in a liminal position. However, it has been more challenging for people who are in immigration detention, and particularly in offshore detention, to achieve a comparable encounter with those who might witness their suffering and to whom they can address the demands.

Empathy does not necessarily lead to action, while there have been concerns that compassion was depoliticised during the refugee crisis when some NGOs emphasised their political neutrality and framed the emergency as a humanitarian crisis (Stierl, 2016). In the daily #CloseTheCamps protests at the gates of the camp on Nauru, people did not simply ask for compassion, but held Australians to account; a banner they displayed stated, 'don't stop the boats by killing us in offshore' ('Such a Human', 2016). Images of these banners were shared by advocates and activists in Australia on social media. However, while people on Nauru held physical space and voiced their demands and accusations, they could not physically access public civic space in Australia and address the public or government there directly.

Bridging this barrier, some Australian citizens and residents placed their bodies on the street and in civic spaces to engage in direct encounters with public and government audiences. The protestors outside the Lady Cliento Children's Hospital used their own bodies to physically block the exits and prevent the removal of Baby Asha and her mother. Meanwhile, both there and in the #LetThemStay and #BringThemHere rallies, physical space was occupied to make visible to the public the abuses taking place in detention and to address accusations to the government who fund and operate these facilities. There were also more direct confrontations in parliaments and other government buildings across Australia. On 30 November 2016, protestors from the grassroots activist group Whistleblowers, Activists and Citizens Alliance (WACA) Alliance disrupted Prime Minister's question time in the Australian parliament by chanting from the public gallery: 'murder, rape, torture and child abuse' (Belot, 2016). They went on to shout; 'we are here today because your policies are breaking our hearts because every day on Manus and Christmas Island is another day in hell'; and 'You are complicit in the murder, rape, torture and child abuse of refugees' (The Australian, 2016b). The following day, two members of the same organisation abseiled down the edifice of Parliament House after unfurling a banner which read 'Close the bloody camps now #justiceforrefugees'. Meanwhile, other members of the group stood in the waters of the fountain outside (which had been dyed blood red) with signs that read, for example, 'turnbacks are murder'.

Their chants and banners carried the same sentiments as the banners held by people protesting in Nauru. In this sense, in a domino effect, the bodily actions and chants of WACA protestors conveyed the pleas and accusations made by Nauru protestors, bridging the physical distance between victims and perpetrators. However, WACA protestors also conveyed the pain this policy was causing *them*; it was 'breaking *their* hearts' and 'shaming' *them* on the international scene. The plea was therefore also about the suffering caused to citizens who politicians, as elected representatives, claim a direct relationship and duty to; if the suffering of distant others does not move the politicians to act then what if pain is carried through and made visible through the bodies of citizens? This could be understood as an appropriation of pain since the Australian protestors become centred as the visible suffering subjects; indeed, news outlets covering these scenes in parliament focused on the protestors there, not in Nauru. However, the scenes in parliament could also be interpreted as an example of connected bodies and interdependent relationships of care. This is explored further later in the chapter.

However, before doing so, the following examples illustrate how some activist campaigns have also responded to the invisibility of migrants and refugees by metaphorically bringing their bodies ashore. Several campaign organisations and networks have engaged with arts practices to bring bodies ashore through material representation to stage face-to-face encounters. For example, in a recent art action, an Australian activist organisation, Mums4Refugees, planted 177 black cardboard silhouette figures of children in the sand at Bondi Beach in Sydney to represent the 177 children in detention on Nauru (to coincide with Sculptures by the Sea – an annual public sculpture exhibition).[2] The figures of the children stood in small groups and pairs, some holding hands as if they were playing on the beach, much as Australian children might do in their ordinary day-to-day life in Australia. This scene was reminiscent of the childhood holiday memories which were recalled by people who commented publicly on Alan Kurdi's death and counter-posed ordinary scenes of idyllic childhood with the tragic imagery of Alan's lifeless body in the sand (see Chapter Four). Yet while powerfully engineering a symbolic physical encounter, these shadow two-dimensional figures were silent and nameless, their stories told and interpreted by others.

The proxy presence of the Nauru detainees through material objects sits within a wider practice of art and performance activism. Thousands of people who set off on sea crossings to Europe never arrived, perishing instead in the mass watery cemetery of the Mediterranean. Performance activism has been engaged in the context of this refugee crisis on Europe's borders to mourn those who did not survive, while also taking grief beyond the private realm into the public as a means of building a political community and holding those responsible to account. Examples of this practice can be seen in the work of the Centre for Political Beauty discussed in Chapter One. Meanwhile, as Stierl (2016) documents, campaign groups have held public commemorations and vigils to grieve for people who died at sea. Such vigils have taken place on border sites such as Lampedusa (Italy) and Tunisia, but also in Berlin 'to connect the supposedly distant suffering of many with the role of geographically non-peripheral EU countries in the making of external border obstacles' (Stierl, 2016:177). To coincide with the UN Summit for Refugees and Migrants in September 2016, in the UK campaigners from the International Rescue Committee placed 2,500 used life jackets in a 'graveyard of life jackets' outside Westminster to represent some of those people who had died at sea during the crisis

(Pasha-Robinson, 2016). The purpose of the act was to urge politicians to do more to save lives, including expanding resettlement opportunities in the UK. Stierl (2016:175) has termed such actions 'grief-activism' through which there is 'a creation of a political community in scenes of collective grief', and which highlights how 'death is so intimately woven into practices of border governance' (Stierl, 2016:184). These practices make visible, reaffirm and mourn the lives that have been violently lost and they protest modes of governance which have made these lives disposable. Such public grieving is also bound up with, and voices, outrage. In new humanist approaches, recognising and mourning those who have died is a way of humanising those lives (Danewid, 2017). Butler (2009) has asserted that approaches that centre loss, grief and vulnerability can enable the building of political communities across cultural difference through recognising the precariousness of human life as a shared condition (Butler, 2009). This approach has, however, been critiqued for its ahistorical perspective, as discussed later in the chapter.

Connecting bodies and feminist ethics of care

In observing the bodily testimony of some Australian activists and discussing this with them, it became apparent that there were also both intentional and less intentional ways in which their actions demonstrated the *connectedness* of human bodies in interdependent relationships of care and the importance of a politics of care (Tronto, 1995). As well as amplifying and increasing the visibility of people detained offshore, the campaign strategies of some Australian activists invited critical reflections on their own identities and roles, and how their bodies might connect to those in detention, and other people living in Australia or around the world.

Several campaign and advocacy groups, established to protest against offshore detention, have been organised around the shared, often professional, identity of their members; for example, Doctors for Refugees and Teachers for Refugees. Groups have also been established that highlight the values that drive them, grounded in the 'positive' emotions of care, love and compassion, such as We Care Nauru and Love Makes a Way. Mums4Refugees and Grandmothers Against Detention of Refugee Children (henceforth referred to as the Grandmothers), two women's activist groups established in 2014, draw on both of these approaches through their use of kinship identity markers, which feature centrally in how they have used their own bodies in public space to bridge moral distances. In doing so they have identified and held to account those responsible for the suffering of people in detention and those who have a duty to respond. However, their actions can also be interpreted within a global context and history of maternal political mobilisation, as they have demonstrated an alternative mode of engagement rooted in care and solidarity.

Activists interviewed from each organisation explained how their kinship roles led them into establishing these groups. Angela explained how she began organising with the Grandmothers soon after she retired:

> I had started visiting [local] detention centre and I had also had my first grandchild. I think the whole thing for me, the passion is that looking after my grandchildren and nursing them and thinking that there is kids in detention at that time in Australia, and I visited them on a regular basis, but also on Nauru. I just cannot reconcile what my grandkids have, their lifestyle. There is no comparison to those kids that were in detention in Australia but also on Nauru as well. It's just a real connection ... I'll have them on a Wednesday then on a Thursday I might be visiting [local] detention centre.

Her experiences of her everyday grandparenting practices with her own grandchildren and visits to other children held in detention brought into sharp relief the disparities in these children's lives; as in the case of Alan Kurdi, it produced an intolerable clash between the ordinary and extraordinary. As seen in her to-and-fro thought process, this created a 'real connection' between these lives of these two sets of children and her care for them.

Like the Grandmothers group, Mums4Refugees is a network of members across several Australian cities. It has over 2,000 members who include mothers of all ages. As one of the founders, Elise explained, their impetus to establish their network also arose through the care role they performed in their daily lives: 'We have the odd auntie or foster carer so we are carers. We are women. We are carers. We met firstly on an online parents group'. Connecting initially through their own parenting identities and experiences, the founding members 'began discussing conditions in Nauru in late 2014, and we were strangers and we decided to get together'. She explained that they named themselves Mums4Refugees because 'we were mums and we made it a mothers' group and there was already a Doctors4Refugees and Lawyers4Refugees so we thought, go on, let's do Mums4Refugees'. In addition to advocacy work and online campaigns, both groups also regularly engage in protest and awareness raising activities offline. Drawing on observations at a direct action and a rally, and interviews with three activists from these groups (two Grandmothers and a member of Mums4Refugees), their campaign actions are now discussed to explore the power and tensions that emerge in the narrative of kinship care as a catalyst for mobilising an alternative politics of compassion in relation to immigration.

One of the key aspects of the Grandmothers' mission statement is to educate the public about asylum and one way they do this is through holding weekly vigils in central locations in their cities. The Grandmothers explained that they started with marches, but decided that a stationary vigil would give them more opportunities to talk with members of the public and share their message. Wearing their Grandmothers Against Detention of Refugee Children t-shirts, each week they stood in a central public location, distributed information, and sought to engage members of the public in discussions about detention. Meanwhile, both the Grandmothers and Mums4Refugees have also staged protests and direct actions at Department of Immigration offices, offices of government ministers, and at parliament.

While interviewing campaigners in Australia, I attended and observed a protest organised by Mums4Refugees and the Grandmothers outside a city's Department of Immigration offices. The women arrived at the protest with their babies and small children; one of the women was heavily pregnant. As the women set up their placards outside the offices, the babies slept or toddled around on the grass and around the placards and signs, occasionally being fed, comforted or entertained by their mothers and other women. Some babies wore bibs with protest slogans written on them. As the women lined themselves up for a photograph, carrying signs the spelled out 'Bring them here', the fire alarm went off and staff began filing out of the building. They walked past the women; some indifferent, others looking on smiling and stopping to sit on a wall and watch. Two police officers walked by and stopped to speak with two of the Grandmothers; no police presence was maintained, and no efforts were made to intervene. Approximately half an hour later two of the mothers slipped into the building and attached paper signs on the 'Australian Department of Immigration' metal plaque in reception. These signs were headed with the Australian government crest and read 'sponsoring rape since 2012' and 'sponsoring child abuse since 2012', referring to the date that offshore detention was reintroduced. No one intervened. The women came out and one shouted 'close the bloody camps', before everyone packed up and went on their way.

Maternal activism has an established history with some of the most famous examples coming from South and Central America in the 1970s and 1980s when groups such as the Madres de Plaza de Mayo in Argentina protested and demanded information from the government about disappeared loved ones (Taylor, 2001; Kumar Das, 2008). The 'maternal frame' 'centres women's activism on the metaphor of motherhood' (Kumar Das, 2008:59). Using the motherhood metaphor can continue and reproduce traditional motherhood roles and representations, but it has also (sometimes invoking these representations) been used as a political strategy. Nationalist movements often draw on nationalist discourses of mothers as the symbol of the nation who protect and reproduce national culture. Exploring this through the case of the US anti-immigrant group, Border Grannies, Johnson (2015:40) writes that, 'this has 'manifested as an emphasis on wives and mothers who accomplish the work of the nation as biological reproducers who uphold ethnic and racial homogeneity as well as transmit cultural markers that define the dominant in-group'. However, their symbolic status as guardians of the nation has also been deployed to question the nation's moral compass and direction, and to resist oppressive practices. Grandmothers are normally portrayed as kind and gentle domestic figures and not anticipated to be out on the street protesting. As the now iconic protest slogan attests to, 'you know your government has failed when your grandmother starts to riot!' (Klein, 2014). During a rally in response to the leak of the Nauru files, I spotted Josie, one of the Grandmothers, carrying a sign with this slogan. When interviewed for this research a few days earlier she had observed that the media and public often commented on the apparent incongruity of the political activist granny. She mentioned that in describing the scene at a vigil, one journalist had written '"there they were in the heat in their gardening hats and their comfort shoes", which is probably true actually!' Meanwhile, another (male) campaigner had suggested to the Grandmothers that they should knit a scarf while protesting. She pulled a face in frustrated amusement at these portrayals of them, and reminded me that many of the Grandmothers are feminists who had been involved in politics and activism since their youth in the 1960s and 1970s.

The campaign messaging from the Grandmothers and Mums4Refugees is framed in the language of human rights, social justice and care, rather than the maternal explicitly. However, during their actions these messages were inevitably also read through their gendered maternal bodies. The interruptions that their maternal bodies, 'out of place' in political action, elicited drew attention to their campaign. The Grandmothers said they were often photographed by passers-by, while media interest in both the Grandmothers and the Mums4Refugees campaign has focused on how their maternal identities shape their campaigns. Writing about Mexican activist mothers, Wright (2009: 219) found that the women connected to audiences who were not otherwise necessarily engaged with their campaign issue (femicide). She writes, 'by presenting their justice demands in terms of a mother's experience, the mother-activists seek to connect to their audiences by appealing to their fundamental humanity, a humanity in which a mother's bond with the child is regarded as central and morally sound'.

Tronto (1995) argues that care provides a useful lens for looking at moral and political life. She (1995:142) describes care as, 'a species activity that includes everything that we do to maintain, continue and repair our 'world' so that we can live in it as well as possible'. Human beings are interdependent, engaged in acts of care both as receivers of care and usually as care-givers also; they are bound together. Rather than rational beings pursing self-interest, people are enmeshed in relationships of care. They act politically not only on the basis of self-interest, but also on constellations of caring relationships and institutions that they find themselves in. According to Tronto (1995:142), care has four phases: 'caring about, attentiveness; taking care of, responsibility; care giving, competence; care receiving, responsiveness'.

The Grandmothers and Mums4Refugees engaged with a discourse of compassion through their performance of care in which their physical presence and protests highlighted how people exist in interdependent relations of care. Their gendered bodies and practices brought attention to the care needs of physically absent others (attentiveness), while putting a spotlight on duties people have towards each other, as well as the failures of some to perform their necessary roles in this web of care (responsibility and competence).

As Elise explained, the ethos of care is at the heart of their messaging:

> In a lot of our other actions we are asking for 'care and not cruelty'. I think this rationalising cruelty is something that we try to address in a really accessible way and we all need care to try to survive. Not just refugees, but we all receive care. We have all been cared for. We have had parents, or friends, or the state help us up and it's not a quality that just these people arriving by boat or by plane fleeing persecution need. It's what everybody needs just to sustain a healthy life.

In contrast to the limiting criteria for compassion engaged with in state practices that have been outlined in earlier chapters, Mums4Refugees rearticulate care as something that everyone deserves and needs – 'we all receive care'. In their daily practices and organising ethos, as well as their campaign messaging, Mums4Refugees perform care, while also highlighting and calling out its absence. Members bring their babies and children to the group's actions (whether due to the practicalities of care arrangements or in more intentional ways) where they interact with and care for these children who they in turn are raising to be caring human beings, as a placard at a protest attested to (New Matilda, 2016). This placard was displayed at a protest that was billed as a 'playgroup protest', mimicking that everyday social practice more commonly associated with parents and babies. The women had turned up with their toddlers and babies at the Prime Minister, Malcolm Turnbull's, constituency office which they then occupied as their children played with banners that read 'close the camps' (New Matilda, 2016). Another campaign organisation called Friends, Families and Feminists Against Detention held a 'pram jam', in which they brought their young children to protest at a regional parliament building. The women performed these everyday practices of care while protesting the lack of care that people (children, but also adult men and women) receive on Nauru and Manus. These actions shamed and chastised the government for its lack of care and its hypocrisy in treating asylum seekers as they do while professing to care about families. In the 'pram jam' action, one of the protestors was removed from the parliament building by police during the protest while her child continued to breastfeed. The ordinary practices of caring performed or imagined. even when less intentional, jarred against the horrors of detention and abuse that the women call out, reinforcing that this suffering is intolerable. These performances of everyday care alongside these stories of horror, were a reminder to audiences of their own care needs, practices and relationships of interdependence, but also the failure of society to care for others.

The idea of family and familial loss can be understood as fundamental human experiences through which empathy might be built between testifiers and witnesses who have this shared understanding. Drawing on Sara Ahmed's work, Wright (2009:220) suggests that in these scenarios empathy 'expands the sense of the audiences' own identity to include that of the testifier such that, as Ahmed explains, the testifier's experience of injustice becomes the audience's experience, and the testifier's quest for justice becomes the audience's'.

Although values of care have featured centrally in their messaging, kinship relationships of care were also read through their physical practices and bodily identities. The revered cultural status of mothers and grandmothers is often attached to conservative notions of family and nation, but the politics the Grandmothers and mums espoused was feminist and anti-xenophobic. The Grandmothers' campaign sat more comfortably within expectations of maternal politics given their focus specifically on ending the detention of *children*. However, as Elise explained, Mums4Refugees tried to re-centre the story of the universal need for care as the primary narrative in their actions, rather than the more limited and conservative notion of care for the vulnerable child or woman:

> We are a women's group and we focus on gendered stuff but once again there has been this particular problem that it's been get the *children* out, get the *mums* out, get the *women* out, and so we always try to strike that gendered balance with "no, single men are people too you know".

Postcolonial asylum and the limits of new humanism

Danewid (2017) has recently observed that often ethical theorising, whether liberal or poststructuralist, 'substitutes abstract humanity for historical humanity'. As argued in this book, this has meant that the refugee crisis has become articulated as an exceptional and contemporary crisis in European values and identity, and a redemption of the 'innocent', ethical and compassionate European. While this can be a powerful mobilising campaign message, it obscures the historical routes and colonial continuities in the causes and management and responses to the contemporary refugee and migrant crisis, and indeed asylum and immigration policy more broadly. As postcolonial asylum theorists have shown, contemporary asylum regimes in Europe are constituted through histories and ideologies of empire and colonialism (Farrier 2011; Mayblin, 2017). Meanwhile, attending more specifically to the contemporary migrant and refugee crisis, the recent concept of the 'Black Mediterranean' has placed the mass drownings of African migrants and refugees in the Mediterranean and the racial violence wrought in the context of empire, colonialism, transatlantic slavery and the birth of modern Europe (Saucier and Woods, 2014; Danewid, 2017).

The system of offshore detention used by Australia is also 'rooted in colonial ideology' as impoverished former colonies have been funded by Australia to host the violent detention centres (Boochani, 2017). Boochani (2017:20) argues that the Australian government has used Manusian locals against asylum seekers, stating that 'they are being sacrificed here too'. Writing about his 2017 film, *Chauka please tell us the time*, he observes that 'the Chauka is a beloved and symbolic local bird for the Manusians, yet the Australian government has put that name on the solitary prison and tortures under that name' (Boochani, 2017:20). John, an Australian activist, also cautioned that sometimes campaigns against offshore detention drew on colonial ideology:

So, there is this very strange amalgam of nationalism that says well we have abandoned people to perhaps an inferior culture. So, nationalism and hints of colonialism. The islanders of PNG are not fit. Therefore, Australia should provide protection. It has more to do with decency and we do this better than anybody else so let's bring them to Australia.

Recognition of the historical roots of contemporary asylum policy in Australia has perhaps been best captured and explored in alliances of solidarity that have been formed between some Aboriginal communities and refugees (including ex-detainees) in Australia. This was symbolised in a ceremony in Melbourne in 2016, in which Aboriginal elders issued Aboriginal passports to refugees symbolically granting them citizenship in their lands (RISE, 2016).

Conclusion

During fieldwork for this book, it was noticeable that, in comparison with the UK and especially undocumented rights campaigns in the US, refugee campaigners were significantly less visible in the Australian refugee rights campaign sector. This has been highlighted and critiqued by one of the few refugee-led campaign groups, RISE, which has called on Australian activists to step back and enable refugees to have greater visibility and voice. Chapter Eight moves to the US to explore how such debates have been engaged with in the undocumented youth movement there. It is argued that developments in the movement's organising and messaging strategies and content provide a useful example of how a shift from the notion of compassion that is felt at a distance to a practice of compassion as solidarity can be achieved, and the impact of this on approaches to responding to social injustice.

Notes

[1] Doctors have recently been exempted from this act (Hall, 2016).

[2] Love Makes a Way (2016), which also campaigns against the use of offshore detentions, has also made use of cut out paper dolls and cut out baby figures and baby grows in its actions

8

Self-Care and Solidarity: The Undocumented Immigrant Youth Movement

Introduction

> There was really no hope for me to go to college, so I was planning my life like, okay, I guess I'm not going to go to college. I'm going to start working or figure out how to work. Maybe. I had all these alternatives. Join American Idol! [laughs] But I realised you have to have a social security number even to join American Idol! [laughs] Because everything really depends on having a social security number. So, I guess my life is really going to stop now. (Set, undocumented young activist, Los Angeles)

In the early 2000s the undocumented youth movement emerged on to the scene in the US to campaign for the rights of undocumented young people, like Set, who had migrated there as children. The movement initially began as a campaign for a pathway to citizenship for a subset of academically successful undocumented young people. However, since 2010, and particularly after 2012, there was a shift in the messaging and priorities as the movement became more autonomous and more inclusive of the wider undocumented community. This chapter draws on qualitative interviews and participant observation conducted during two studies, in 2015 and 2017, with members of the undocumented youth movement in Southern California (see Chapter One). This is discussed alongside an analysis of speeches by the then-President Obama about the administrative relief known as Deferred Action for Childhood Arrivals (DACA).

Continuing with the theme of compassion in resistance, this chapter traces how the movement's use of storytelling as testimony evolved over time.

In the earlier years of the movement, young people's testimonies were constructed to be understood and empathised with by US citizens and the political establishment. As discussed in Chapter Four, testifiers are sometimes unable to present their experiences in the terms they would prefer because these would not appeal to those being addressed (Wright, 2009). This was problematic for undocumented young people who had to repress or alter aspects of their identities and experiences. These testimonies also reinforced the exclusion of others who could not enact the conditionalities needed to be recognised as 'deserving'. However, as the movement became increasingly youth-led, this began to change as dissenting and previously excluded narratives from within and beyond the movement were listened to and engaged with.

Social movements use narratives in outward-facing ways to build support for the movement's aims, and within movements to develop group consciousness. This chapter examines how these processes became intertwined as the undocumented youth movement developed. It is argued that as the movement built, storytelling was used to testify and witness each other's more authentic testimonies in a process of address and response in which there was an affirmation of the subjective agency of those suffering and their ability to respond. As Bassel (2017:11) has argued, political practices of listening can play a central role in challenging 'inaudibility and political inequality'. She states that effective political listening requires 'taking on roles of speaking and listening equally as interdependent peers' in seeking a path to the experience of others. This is not done by trying to inhabit the lives of others, or in speaking for someone else, but rather in seeking to experience the world 'as they construct it for us' (Bassel, 2017: 11). These horizontal patterns of exchange can also lead to making 'vertical claims on powerful actors' (Bassel, 2017: 11). It is argued that this shift from seeking to appeal to the compassion of a distant other, to a notion of compassion as suffering with one another in solidarity, has enabled a more inclusive, empowering and, therefore, more promising mode of responding to, and resisting, suffering and social injustice.

Undocumented young people

There are approximately 11.7 million undocumented immigrants living in the US; 2.2 million are children and young people who arrived as minors (Terriquez, 2015). These are people who migrated to the US, but lack documentation authorising their presence there. In 2012, President Obama introduced DACA. This gave eligible undocumented young applicants a two-year renewable deferral of deportation and provided them with a social security number, although no pathway to citizenship. DACA was in response to the plight of young people, like Set, who were living in limbo. Undocumented children are eligible to attend elementary and high school in the US (Zatz and Rodriguez, 2015). However, on graduating high school their pathways diverge from their peers. They are ineligible for many university financial loans, and in some same states have been treated as out-of-state or even international students for fees purposes. Before 2012, they did not have a social security number and so could not work legally. As undocumented immigrants, they and their families also faced the prospect of deportation in a context where it had become increasingly difficult to legalise their status. There had not been an amnesty since the Immigration Reform and Control Act 1986 (IRCA) and there had been a rapid rise in deportations during the 1990s and 2000s (Golash-Boza, 2012). Therefore, while undocumented young people had grown up into adulthood in the US, they remained unauthorised and marginalised 'non-citizens'.

DACA has often been heralded as an example of Obama's progressive and humanitarian policies. However, as Kevin, Bethzabel and Dean (activists who were involved in the movement during that period) explained, it was an undocumented young activist from DREAM Team Los Angeles (Neidi Dominguez Zamorano) who, in 2011, first highlighted that the President had the executive authority to grant administrative relief. Obama issued DACA in June 2012 following lobbying, protests and civil disobedience undertaken by undocumented youths, which intensified in the run up to the 2012 presidential election (Nicholls, 2013). DACA gave eligible undocumented young applicants a two-year renewable stay of deportation and a social security number which enabled them to work legally.

The undocumented youth movement had first emerged in the early 2000s to campaign for the passage of the federal Development, Relief, and Education for Alien Minors (DREAM) Act, which would have provided a pathway to citizenship for some eligible undocumented young people – who became referred to as 'Dreamers'. From the outset, storytelling played a pivotal role in the movement's campaign strategy because of its power in engaging people's emotions (Nicholls, 2013; Swerts, 2015). Since the early years of the movement, storytelling has been used in outward-facing claims-making. In those early years, testimonies were constructed to be understood and empathised with by US citizens and the political establishment. However, from 2010 onwards, and especially after the introduction of DACA in 2012, storytelling was also increasingly used by young activists to explore and come to terms with their identities as undocumented young people, and to build and express solidarity with their wider communities.

'Our kids': All American Dreamers

The DREAM Act campaign began in the context of a wider debate about comprehensive immigration reform. Due to increased enforcement measures introduced in the 1990s, questions arose about how to allocate limited resources. Meanwhile, there was a sense among the public that not all undocumented immigrants constituted a 'threat' (Nicholls, 2013). Therefore, despite increased immigration enforcement, 'niche openings' (Nicholls, 2013:10) appeared for some undocumented immigrants – such as educated, law-abiding young people – who could present themselves as innocent, non-threatening, assimilating and making a valued contribution to US society. These characteristics are key criteria in judgements of social worth (Sirriyeh, 2014), which in turn is a basis for membership in the nation-state that is imagined as a 'community of value' (Anderson, 2013).

In this context, some politicians and immigrant rights organisations saw an opportunity to advocate for a pathway to citizenship for *some* undocumented young people who had access to the resources to assert their social worth and enact the conditionalities of 'deservingness' within this hegemonic discourse of US citizenship. To be eligible for citizenship via the proposed DREAM Act, applicants had to have arrived in the US when they were under the age of 16, have lived there for at least 5 years, and have graduated from a US high school. They had to demonstrate 'good moral character' and have no criminal record (Nicholls, 2013).

The DREAM Act was originally introduced by Senators Dick Durbin and Orrin Hatch and the campaign was primarily led by national immigration rights organisations. In 2007, these organisations helped to establish the United We Dream coalition at a federal level through which immigrant rights organisations and undocumented young people worked together to campaign for the DREAM Act. Similar networks of youth groups were also established at state level, such as the California Dream Network.

Storytelling became a central strategy and practice in the movement from 2010 as it became increasingly youth-led and critical of the discourse that had characterised the early years of campaign messaging (Swerts, 2015). However, from the outset, storytelling was a feature of the DREAM Act campaign. Young people who would be eligible for citizenship through the Act were presented as the epitome of the 'American Dream'.

Exceptional young people who fitted this profile and had compelling stories were recruited to be the face of the campaign and to tell their stories to lobby politicians and the media, including speaking at political conventions and giving testimony to the House Judiciary Committee (Nicholls, 2013).

The rise of the 'perfect Dreamer'

Lauby (2016:376) observes that 'narratives provide explanations for events, especially those that are unusual or disturbing, and can be particularly useful for disadvantaged groups'. These narratives make use of frames 'which are persuasive devices and familiar cultural stock developed by activists to help us interpret events, seek outside support, mobilize others, and demobilize the opposition' (Lauby, 2016:376). As has been contended throughout this book, emotions are a central feature of these frames (Polleta, 1998). Emotions are social and relational, produced in patterns of relationships with people and objects that the embodied individual engages in over time in the social world in particular times and places (Burkitt, 2014). Therefore, how stories are interpreted and how emotions develop and operate through stories depends on the audience as well as the person giving testimony and the cultural location in which it is produced.

Nicholls (2013:52) quotes an activist who states that during the early years of the campaign for the DREAM Act, it was understood that the most effective campaign strategy was to focus on 'the most easily understood story, the most emotionally convincing story'; that is the story that was most convincing for politicians, the media and the wider US public in a context of widespread hostility toward undocumented immigration. This meant that some stories were more likely to be told than others, while even in these stories, certain aspects were obscured or underplayed if they did not fit with the campaign message being promoted.

Nussbaum's (2013) model of compassion is evident in the early Dreamer testimonies that sought to engage emotions in ways that leveraged the young people into the 'niche openings' available at the time. One aim of storytelling, in the outward-facing actions of social movements, is to legitimise their grievances and make moral appeals to the public. Young activists were trained in storytelling to ensure they engaged with morality, humanity and feelings of empathy in their audiences – to enable 'emotional transfer' between themselves and the audiences (Swerts, 2015). During the DREAM Act campaign in the 2000s, they were taught how to blend personal compelling life stories with the core narrative of 'the Dreamers' that drove the messaging of the DREAM Act campaign (Nicholls, 2013).

Extracts of Dreamer testimony from this period are now examined to identify and discuss the central tropes of the Dreamer narrative. It is argued that this appealed to a sense of compassion by drawing on the emotional regimes of childhood and US national identity to demonstrate the serious suffering and innocence of 'Dreamers' and how they belonged within US citizens' circle of concern (Nussbaum, 2013).

Young children are at the pinnacle of the 'hierarchy of innocence' (Moeller, 2002) in cultural and political discourse. However, teenagers and young adults are often viewed as risky, walking a tightrope between being viewed as 'vulnerable' and 'threatening' (Brown, 2015). Their identity as both 'undesired' immigrant and young person meant that undocumented young people could be subject to the policies of control faced by both these populations. They were positioned at a cross-section of contradictory policies and political discourses that simultaneously produced trajectories towards and away from citizenship. On the one hand state policies purport to protect and include children and young people, while on the other hand the undesired immigrant is deemed a stranger, burden and threat and is, therefore, excluded (Sirriyeh, 2014). The Dreamer narrative resolved this paradox by foregrounding the youthful stories of young 'Dreamers' while cleansing them of the undesirable immigrant identity. In doing so, they became not only deserving kids, but 'our' 'All American' kids. In the case of Alan Kurdi the visual imagery of his vulnerable and harmed child's body enabled his identity as innocent child to eclipse his identity as undesired refugee. However, sometimes more context is needed to challenge stigmatisation and exclusion, particularly for migrants and refugees (such as young men of colour) whose physical appearance itself is often understood as threatening and associated with violence and criminality.

Karen, an undocumented young activist, discussed the moral quandary that she faced. She placed a high value on 'doing the right thing' and being morally upstanding. However, she felt there was a contradiction because she had crossed the border the 'wrong way', when she arrived in the US with her parents without a visa as a one-year-old. In telling their stories, many young 'Dreamers' could point to their morally upstanding character and outstanding academic records. However, they were confronted with how to negotiate this primary transgression that was so central to their labelling as 'illegal' and jeopardised their good Dreamer image. As discussed later, Karen and others have since found alternative ways to negotiate this dilemma. However, during the campaign for the DREAM Act, the Dreamer narrative achieved this in two ways. First, Dreamers engaged with the testimony of *early* childhood, deploying the innocent child discourse to narrate their story of arrival and presence in the US. Audiences were reminded of the very young age at which they had arrived.

'My history in the United States began at the *age of four* when I was *brought* across the border. It has been full of both difficulties and joy. Throughout my childhood and now as an adult, *I have considered the United States my home.*' (UCLA Labor Centre, 2008) [italics added]

The age at which they crossed and the phrase 'brought' were commonly used in these stories. They had been *young* children *brought* by their parents. They could also be presented as 'innocent' because, as children, they were seen as having less agency in migration decisions. While young people explained why their parents decided to relocate to the US, the phrase 'brought' was often picked up on by politicians and the media to make the case for the Dream Act by highlighting the young people's innocence in contrast to their parents' guilt. For example, Democrat Senator Richard Durbin (the sponsor of the 2007 DREAM Act) stated, 'It's unfair to make these young people pay for the sins of their parents' (Preston, 2007). Meanwhile, in announcing DACA, Obama (2012) justified it through this same discourse: 'they were *brought* to this country by their parents – sometimes even as *infants* – and often have *no idea* that they're undocumented until they apply for a job or a driver's license, or a college scholarship.' [italics added].

Second, while the teenage refugees in Calais were held in limbo at the border, waiting to cross, the Dreamers were already embedded in neighbourhoods where they lived in the US; they attended school and participated in everyday life there. This gave them the resources to tell a positive story of innocent and hard-working '*All American*' youth,[1] through emphasising educational achievements in a narrative that would be familiar and appealing to US audiences raised on the cultural narrative of the American Dream. The young people selected as spokespeople for the campaign were all achieving excellent grades in school, or attending university. In their stories, they mentioned their high-grade point average, their career ambitions, and their determination to work hard and persevere with their education despite the struggles they faced because of their undocumented status. As one young person said, giving testimony to the House Judiciary Committee in 2007:

'We sought to live the "American Dream" – the promise of a better education, a better life, and all together a better future – what any parent would for their child. Strong values and good morals have been instilled in me from a very young age. As long as I can remember my parents have worked very hard for every dollar they've earned, and in the process have taught me that life is not easy and that I must work hard and honorably for what I want in life.' (AILA, 2007)

Young people staged mock graduations during which they gathered together in public wearing graduation caps and gowns, and 'valedictorians' told their stories of being undocumented. While images of young people may not have the same emotional pull as those of young children like Alan Kurdi, the images from these mock graduations sent a powerful message. Unlike the worn and desperate-looking young people in Calais, this visual imagery of the Dreamers was embedded in familiar American youthful cultural institutions and rites, which many US audiences themselves would have experienced.

The fact that these young people had been in the US education system and had academic and professional aspirations helped to emphasise their youthful innocence, but also demonstrated their assimilation and attachment to the professed American values and culture of hard-work epitomised in the American Dream. In connection to statements that they were 'brought' here, young people often remarked that because they had arrived in the US at a young age, they had no memories of, or attachment to, their countries of origin (Nicholls, 2013). The US was the only place they knew and loved.

Obama (2012) drew on this narrative in his DACA announcement. He asked the US public to imagine what it was like to be one of these young people and to *feel* the inherent injustice in their position. He invited US citizens to, 'put yourself in their shoes. Imagine you've done everything right your entire life – studied hard, worked hard, maybe even graduated at the top of your class – only to suddenly face the threat of deportation to a country that you know nothing about, with a language that you may not even speak' (Obama, 2012). In Aristotelian terms, they were asked to imagine the other's possibilities as their own (Nussbaum, 1996). However, the power of this message was not in the invocation of the universal innocent child, but in a specifically *'American'* child or young person. They were not *like* 'us', they *were* 'us', or 'our' American kids, in body, heart and soul. As Obama said, 'These are young people who study in our schools, they play in our neighborhoods, they're friends with our kids, they pledge allegiance to our flag. *They are Americans in their heart, in their minds, in every single way but one: on paper'* [italics added]. In a speech, two years later, announcing the (short-lived) expansion of DACA (Obama, 2014b), he compared undocumented students with his own children: 'I've seen the courage of students who, except for the circumstances of their birth, are as American as Malia or Sasha; students who bravely come out as undocumented in hopes they could make a difference in the country they love'. These sentiments reflect the definition of compassion as 'suffering together' (Garber, 2004); we feel their pain because it is our pain. Social distance is eradicated as they become us.

The 'All American' Dreamer narrative helped to bring home the pain and virtue of the undocumented youth struggle by articulating this within a familiar American cultural story of struggle that US audiences would understand and identify with. The story of vulnerable and dependent young children like Alan Kurdi had tapped into the British national stories of 'child saving' and humanitarianism, while also warning of the potential shame the country faced if it failed to live up to this reputation. In the US, the national story engaged with through the Dreamer narrative was less about shame and more about hope. The stories drew on pain, but placed this within a hopeful and aspirational journey; pain would be overcome to 'succeed' as part of the American Dream, and the US was loved and desired rather than blamed directly for their current plight. They were potentially US human beings in the making and young people who represented the country's future (Moeller, 2002). As hard working, culturally assimilated 'all American kids' they were the perfect immigrant since they were barely an immigrant at all; formal citizenship was a matter of signing off on paper what was already being practiced by these young people. Meanwhile, to deny citizenship would effectively be citizenship *loss* for these young people who had grown up American.

However, while the Dreamer messaging campaign was highly persuasive and successful in gaining political and public support and sympathy, undocumented young people's testimonies were only partially voiced and heard. Meanwhile, in facilitating the partial and conditional inclusion of some undocumented young people, the campaign discourse also reinforced the exclusion of other undocumented people who could not enact these conditionalities. Although these young people were brought back to social life, the category of illegal remained as did the social death that accompanied it (Cacho, 2012). In stating that they were innocent because they were 'brought', attention turned to those who brought them. As Jose reflected, this suggested that 'our parents are the criminals' because they 'were the ones who brought us here'. This did not fit comfortably with Jose's values and understandings of his experience. He observed, 'the original dreamer I like to think was my mum. My mum was the original dreamer because she came here to have a dream that we were all going to have that white picket fence house. So, they should have been the original dreamers, but I think we have forgotten about them'.

Waking up from the Dreamer narrative

The Dreamer testimony proved to be effective for gaining political and public support for undocumented young people, and significant material gains through the introduction of DACA in 2012 (Gonzalez et al, 2014). However, by the end of the 2000s there was growing dissatisfaction among young activists about the movement's messaging and campaign tactics. Despite significant support from politicians in both major political parties, favourable coverage in the media, and support among the electorate, the DREAM Act failed to pass each time it was introduced in the legislature. The Dreamer narrative was also a point of contention because while some young activists found it to be an empowering and positive identity (and many young people still do), some young activists felt it was out of step with what they saw as the more authentic story of their identity, values and goals. Jonathan explained that for him and other 'hood' activists, many of whom had not attended university and who centred class and race politics in their activism, the Dreamer messaging – focused on the academic success of exceptional students – did not sit comfortably with their values and priorities. Meanwhile, as Edna observed, 'not everyone came at a young age. I came at 12 so I don't identify with the whole "Oh I don't know my home country" because I went back. I had the opportunity to visit after 14 years through DACA.' The Dreamer narrative excluded the wider undocumented population, including the families and communities that young activists were embedded in. Edna said that activists had reflected on their exclusionary language, 'with recognising the problematic stuff we said, like 'I was brought through no fault of our own', so blaming our parents. Also criminalising others because we are saying I'm not a criminal, I'm a student. That is also very anti-black language because if we are not the criminals then who is the criminal?'

One of the challenges in giving testimony is that to be read by audiences as a compelling and deserving story, and to identify a relationship between the testifier and the audience, testimony is often highly selective and tailored to what the audience is likely to understand and respond positively towards. As discussed in Chapter Four, in these circumstances audiences are listening for what they already know and recognise, instead of listening for what they do not know, what might be unexpected and surprising, and the particularities of the testimony giver's story (Whitlock, 2007; Oliver, 2015; Bassel, 2017). The Dreamer narrative drew on a combination of an abstract and idealised humanity (Hoggett, 2006) and a hegemonic US narrative of deserving citizenship based on neoliberal and racist ideology. Therefore, audiences were not invited to listen to and respond with compassion to the storyteller as their complete and authentic selves; in this sense, there was a 'denial of voice and of narratable selves' because many young people were heard differently from how they wanted to be (Bassel, 2017:8). This curtailed their ability as testifiers to truly speak and respond, which is a key element of bearing witness.

In 2010, the narratives of undocumented youth testimonies began to change, as did their political strategies. This journey in narratives and organising strategy continued into the post-DACA era from 2012 onwards. In doing so, undocumented young activists shifted their focus to foreground their address to themselves, each other and their undocumented communities. This also became the basis of much of their outward-facing testimony to other audiences, which decentred the Dreamer narrative. In these testimonies, their claims become less about gratitude and a plea for compassion to the US government and public; the emotion engaged with became more akin to a model of compassion grounded in solidarity and co-suffering. This drove expressions of outrage in which the root causes of suffering were named, and restitution was demanded and claimed. The following section examines the changes that took place in the movement's organising and messaging.

Undocumented, unafraid, unapologetic

The final attempt to pass the DREAM Act was in December 2010 (until it was re-introduced in 2017) (Nicholls, 2013). However, even before this date, disillusionment and frustration had grown among many undocumented young activists. In 2009 in Chicago, a group of young activists came together to lead a campaign to stop the deportation of a friend (Unzueta Carrasco and Seif, 2014). In doing so they publicly shared their stories of being undocumented, stating that, like their friend, they were also at risk of being deported at any time. In 2010, they formed the Immigrant Youth Justice League (IYJL), an autonomous, youth-led immigrant rights group and in March 2010 held the first 'Coming Out of the Shadows' event (IYJL, 2011). Drawing inspiration from the LGBTQ practice of 'coming out', they publicly declared themselves to be undocumented and told their stories. This practice of 'coming out' spread across the movement to other parts of the US. Instead of emphasising their innocence because they were 'brought' by their parents, young people declared themselves to be 'Undocumented, Unafraid' (later adding in the word 'unapologetic') (Unzueta Carrasco and Seif, 2014). As IYJL members (2011) observed, this was 'the first time that the undocumented youth movement has taken ownership of our actions, our politics, our stories, and the risks that we are willing to take for the movement'.

Meanwhile, in Southern California, some young activists were growing increasingly frustrated at the campaign strategies of some immigrant rights organisations. They were growing tired of being told to wait and being cautioned against direct action. In August 2010 Dream Team LA and Orange County Dream Team held a public meeting in which they explained and discussed their frustrations with each other and allies (Dominguez Zamorano et al, 2010). In a 'declaration of independence' statement to news organisation Truthout in September 2010, they stated, 'WE DO NOT WANT IMMIGRATION 'ADVOCATES' SPEAKING FOR US ANY LONGER. WE DEMAND THE RIGHT TO REPRESENT OURSELVES'. They announced that, 'at a moment when hope seemed scarce, we forged new networks of solidarity. We declared ourselves UNDOCUMENTED AND UNAFRAID!' (Dominguez Zamorano et al, 2010).

Instead of surrendering to the fear that deportability (De Genova, 2002) is designed to induce and positioning themselves as more eligible for citizenship by distancing themselves from the stigma of 'illegality', they declared and embraced their undocumented status. They explained the conditions under which their parents migrated to the US, decoupling the 'undocumented' status from a sense of shame or guilt and from the category of 'criminality'; being undocumented was not a crime. Meanwhile, following the failure of the 2010 DREAM Act bill, they identified the administrative relief option that was available to President Obama to institute (see also Nicholls, 2013). Although initially declining to engage in a campaign for administrative relief, the national youth network, United We Dream, eventually adopted this as a campaign priority and undocumented young people across the US began to lobby and exert pressure on Obama to introduce this in the run up to the 2012 presidential election. Young activists broke with the 'good Dreamer' tactics of speaking on the invitation of politicians in the legislatures, and expressing gratitude to and love for the US. Instead, in their new incarnation they expressed *outrage* at their unjust exclusion and demanded recognition. They began engaging in civil disobedience actions such as: closing major roads; occupying politicians' offices, including Obama's campaign offices; and engaging in Civil Rights era inspired awareness-raising road trips – 'Dream Rides' – across the US (Nicholls, 2013; interviews with activists). In some of the more radical actions of this period, they no longer looked to the state as the site to grant rights, but took this into their own hands. For example, in 2011 two young activists from Los Angeles walked into an immigration detention facility in Alabama and declared that they were undocumented (Dream Activist, 2011; interviews with activists). On their arrest, they began documenting conditions and organising inside the detention facility until they were released. Meanwhile, in a series of 'self-deportation' actions, groups of undocumented young people (such as the Dream 9) travelled across the US–Mexico border and re-entered through the official border crossings, risking detention and deportation to make visible the violence of the border (Werber-Shirk, 2015). As in Nauru and Manus, a bodily performance of abjection was harnessed for resistance. In taking these actions, they turned their bodies over on their terms, arguing that this took away the power that living in a condition of deportability had held over them.

Activists I interviewed said that, post-DACA, they focused on defending their undocumented communities (not only undocumented youth) against detention and deportation. They examined their relationships and practices of care with one another, rather than just the vertical relationships of power with the state as the site that grants rights. Although DACA has served to (temporarily) protect 'DACAmented' young people from deportations, their families and wider communities have continued to be at risk. Indeed, DACA reaffirmed a notion that there were deserving 'good' immigrants who could be saved, and in doing so reinforced the justification for deporting the 'bad' criminal immigrants who did not fit these eligibility requirements. In his 2014 speech introducing Deferred Action for Parents of Americans and Lawful Permanent Residents (DAPA) and extensions to DACA, President Obama (2014b) reinforced this division when he declared:

> Even as we are a nation of immigrants we're a nation of laws. Undocumented workers broke our immigration laws, and I believe that they must be held accountable … we're going to keep focussing enforcement resources on actual threats to security. Felons not families. Criminals, not children. Gang members, not a mum who's working hard to provide for her kids.

As in the case of maritime arrivals in Australia, the irregular route of entry become the primary justification for excluding and criminalising undocumented people. Even those DAPA-eligible parents were effectively asked to repent for their 'sins' and seek forgiveness as a condition for receiving this compassionate gesture. Yet, aside from wider concerns about justice and exclusion, this highly individualised notion of deservingness did not even recognise young people's own sense of identity and belonging. As Edna asserted, there could be no easy divide between 'felons' and 'family' because 'felons are our family'. Meanwhile, Set observed that:

> My experience as an undocumented person isn't just based on
> going to school but also on being able to live with my family
> … if something happens to your family what good does your
> going to school do for you if like the people you are striving
> for are endangered … I feel like looking at my experience just
> through the lens of education is narrow minded.

Since the introduction of DACA, activists have continued to focus
on community-building and making the movement more inclusive.
The struggles against deportations and the heightened attacks on their
communities in the first few months of the Trump presidency have taken
a toll on the emotional well-being of many activists, while also reinforcing
their commitment to resistance. The final section of this chapter explores
how these experiences and practices have engaged with compassion as
co-suffering, while engendering solidarity through attending carefully to
the politics of listening (Bassel, 2017) and bearing witness.

Self-care, suffering together and the politics of listening

The shift in the movement's messaging had important implications for
the youth movement's outward-facing claims-making. Attention shifted
from demands for citizenship to the defence of the most vulnerable people
in their communities at risk of detention and deportation. Related to
this, there has also been significant investment in community organising
and relationship-building within the movement, and more broadly in
the undocumented community. This has supported young people and
others in the undocumented community to speak out and to inform the
movement's aims and strategies.

From the beginning, youth organisations aligned to the movement set
out to establish safe and supportive environments in which undocumented
young people could come together with others who were in similar
circumstances to themselves and provide each other with support. Lily
recalled that becoming involved in one of these groups was a 'life-changing
moment' because 'I met another group of people who were going through
the same situation as me and I found comfort, I found guidance, I found
hope'.

Many of the young people I interviewed described how they had
felt alone before becoming involved. Set said, 'I first thought I was the
only undocumented person'. Jose described how as his school friends,
who were not undocumented, gained their driving licences and began

applying to universities and jobs, he felt less able to relate to them. On joining an undocumented youth group, he made friends with people he felt he had more in common with. For many young people, speaking in these group meetings was the first time they had publicly declared themselves to be undocumented. They could talk about the challenges and suffering they had experienced to other young people who had shared similar experiences. Nicholls (2013) describes an activity that was often used called 'step up to the line' where a statement would be made, and young people were asked to step up to the line if this statement applied to them. In doing so they had shared experiences and their testimony was heard, understood and felt by others who knew what it was like to be undocumented. In this context of co-suffering their testimonies were acknowledged and responded to with care by those who knew what it was to feel this pain, and they could respond in return. Meanwhile, whereas in wider society being undocumented was a highly stigmatised identity, these groups provided a space to speak and in which their identities were validated. As Ernesto explained:

> Being most authentically ourselves is hard particularly in a place where being authentically yourself and being an immigrant that does not have legal status, in the United States it carries with it a social stigma. It also carries with it actual recourses in terms of detention, deportation, forced removals. ... That is very difficult for anyone to not be able to fully express who they are much less to not be who they are under penalty of significant violence. It's a state of terror. ... Then with agency any oppressive system means to remove as much agency as possible. It's really hard to oppress a group of folks who are fully able to connect to their own agency and have people believe that they are not able to change their circumstances.

Young people described storytelling as an intensely emotional experience in which they could address themselves and others who were in similar circumstances and receive a validating response that enabled them to speak as their authentic self. Swerts (2015) has documented the central role of storytelling in building the movement as a community by addressing feelings of shame, stigma and fear, building confidence, and witnessing stories of shared experiences. He observes how intensive this experience is as young people are encouraged to really feel and craft their story with other young people.

Storytelling helps to mobilise support for the cause and is used in claims-making through the 'collectivisation of personal experiences' so that the 'story of me' (as an individual) becomes the 'story of us' (a community) and eventually the 'story of us all' (wider outward claims-making) (Swerts, 2015:350). Yet, in this process of collectivisation some activists, such as LGBTQ young people, found that important elements of their identities and stories were marginalised or silenced.

As the centralised Dreamer grip on the narrative loosened, particularly from 2012 onwards, and central tenants of the narrative were critiqued, storytelling evolved to reflect intersectional understandings of identity and more nuanced accounts of belonging. Lily, an indigenous working class young woman from South Central LA, explained that her pathway through the movement and engagement with the opening-up of these spaces of critique had let to her shifting story of self. This story had had several iterations – from 'American' to 'Mexican American', to 'AB540' and 'undocumented', to 'indigenous'; this reflected her emotional journey through her relationship to identity, place and belonging. As a teenager she used to identify as American to assert that she was raised in the US and therefore should rightfully have the same status as US citizens. Later, in the early days of the undocumented movement she said, 'a lot of us were identifying ourselves as AB540[2] students and then Dreamers'. After the introduction of DACA she decided, 'that's a law [AB540]. You cannot be identifying yourself as a legislation! I'm not going to let legislation or immigration laws determine my identity or who I am'. Lily explained that while her student identity had been a legitimised status, she had faced discrimination because she was an Indigenous woman and from South Central (a working class and predominantly Black and Latino neighbourhood). This had affected her mental health and self-esteem. She increasingly felt ill at ease with the Dreamer identity, the classed and raced discourse it deployed, and the plea for citizenship. She said, 'I came to terms with I don't want it. I don't need a residency or citizenship to validate me as a human being, to validate all the work that I have done in my community'. Instead, since beginning to identify as Indigenous, she was planning for her return to Mexico 'on my own terms'. She said, 'I started to think more about my Indigenous routes in Mexico. I started to think about wanting to reconnect with my Indigenous routes so for the past two years I've been identifying myself as Indigenous'. Engaging with assertions that the Dreamer discourse on criminality is anti-black, and her experiences in neighbourhood activism with Black and Latino communities in South Central, she identified proudly as being 'from South Central', saying, 'I grew up in South Central. If I were to answer now what is my culture I would definitely say South Central'.

Ahmed (2014) argues that there is a sociality in pain. We seek witnesses to our pain to recognise it and grant it the status of an event, bringing it into being as a known event. The trauma of an event is not truly witnessed until testifiers are able to give a narrative of the event that is listened to and heard (Laub, 1992). A key task of witnessing is enabling 'response-ability' whereby testifiers can maintain or restore their subjective agency (Oliver, 2015). This sociality in pain was visible at a protest I observed in Los Angeles in April 2017. On 24 April Teresa de Jesus Vidal Jaime, an undocumented Mexican woman, was placed in immigration detention following a raid on her apartment complex in the Boyle Heights neighbourhood. Teresa had been in the US since 2001 and had two children, one of whom was the 21-year-old undocumented activist, Claudia Rueda. Teresa was taken to the Chula Vista detention centre and transferred a few hours later to a detention centre in San Diego closer to the US–Mexico border. The following day activists organised a rally outside the Los Angeles County Sheriff Department. On the way to the rally I spoke to Betty who is herself an undocumented activist and the mother of a young activist. She explained that she felt afraid and had apprehensions about attending the rally. She began to cry. As an undocumented mother, Teresa's experience hit very close to home for Betty who voiced her fears of being separated from her children (one of whom was a US citizen). However, she also felt a strong duty to attend out of solidarity, and was angry about the policies that generated the fear she felt. When we got to the rally she was greeted and embraced by several young protestors whom she knew. Claudia addressed the crowd and told the story of what had happened to her mother; she was comforted by a friend when she cried. As the speeches ended, music played, and the crowds continued to chant protests and wave their placards on the steps of the Sheriff's Department. At this point I glanced to my left and saw Betty smiling and dancing to the music with her placard. At a meeting after the protest she said she was glad she had gone. She told the group about the feelings of fear and anger she had expressed to me earlier and the care displayed to her by other protestors who had been present. Another person at the meeting responded that they too felt this fear, while someone else spoke about how Teresa's arrest had made them fear for the safety of their own mother. Claudia continued to lead a campaign to free her mother who was released a few weeks later.

On 18 May, Claudia was herself detained by Border Patrol officers while moving her car outside her apartment. She was taken to the Chula Vista detention centre. Claudia, a university student, was eligible for DACA but lacked the funds to apply. As in Teresa's case, undocumented young activists rallied together to campaign for her release. I attended a rally in support of Claudia in Los Angeles. To mark the start of the rally, a young woman invited people to take part in a spiritual ceremony to 'hold space' in recognition of the pain that many were experiencing. She brought us into a circle around some lit candles and began drumming as she led us in a meditation and addressed our ancestors. Space was then given to Claudia's friends and others to address the audience in Spanish and English. The campaign continued for several weeks until Claudia was released on 9 June.

In these protest actions, outrage was expressed, and demands were addressed to those in power. Yet, these gatherings also served as outlets for feelings of pain, fear, outrage and love in the community which were important for building and maintaining social relationships of care and solidarity in the movement. The protestors present not only felt for Teresa and Claudia because of the violence they had experienced; these feelings were intensified because they understood personally what this violence felt like. This shared pain enabled them to speak because they knew they were listened to by those who understood, and their pain would be witnessed. The detention and deportation process may hide and remove individual suffering bodies from sight, but in a context of interdependent relationships of suffering and care they cannot be made invisible as others step in to hold their place and mark and reveal their absence.

The Dreamer narrative primarily addressed young people's identities in terms of their individual relationship to the state – demanding citizenship. However, as these actions demonstrate, young people were embedded in interdependent relationships and networks of care. As Set said, simply being able to attend college was not enough if he could not live with his family and if they suffered. A key division sown through the Dreamer narrative was the construction of the innocent child through the criminalising of the parent who 'brought' them. While unhappy with the criminalisation of their parents, some young people also acknowledged they had felt a sense of ambivalence about their parents' decisions, while some parents also held reservations about their children's activism. This chapter ends by drawing on Set's story of their relationship with their family to explore how a politics of listening was engaged with in this context to elicit understanding and compassion for one another.

To date several films have been produced by young people about their undocumented experiences. As Set said, most films:

> Were about these students that were having a hard time going to college, but no one was talking about the families. In my family, I was the only one going to college, so I didn't see my siblings and my parents in the narratives that were being told you know. Often there was also this narrative that we were brought here as children inevitably criminalising or

incriminating our parents in why we became undocumented, putting the blame on them as if they are not also victims or survivors of this experience.

Set made a film about their family which provided them with an opportunity to talk about being undocumented. Set explained:

> We all knew we didn't have immigration status, but it was like the elephant in the room that no one addressed so when I made this documentary about my family it was the first time they were talking about being undocumented and it was a really healing process in a way because it was the first time I had heard about what it means for my mum to be undocumented or even an immigrant and my siblings.

As other young people also became used to talking about their stories, they also spoke with their parents about being undocumented. Karen, who, as mentioned earlier, had felt some contradiction in her claims to be law abiding when she had crossed the border irregularly, said that as she became active in the movement she began to wonder about her parents' story. She said:

> I remember saying [to her mother] tell me about our story. How did we get here? How did this happen? I also questioned her why did we do this illegally. And you know she brought up really good points. There were no resources in Mexico that could help them. they were escaping poverty. They didn't have room for us to live. They were trying to provide a better future for us. For me it's such an amazing thing to leave behind everything for the future. That to me blows my mind.

Just as Set's family spoke with him about their undocumented experiences, in turn Set spoke with their family about activism and took them to events. Through these conversations, Set's family began to engage in activism and organising. Their mother began delivering workshops for other undocumented parents. Set explained how Set's activism had been a point of tension with their mother who feared for Set's safety and did not understand why they did it. In turn, Set had felt frustration at their mother's unwillingness to engage and the lack of understanding expressed. However, family discussions and Set's family's divergent pathways through activism had influenced Set's own decisions about how to be active in the movement, and had shifted Set's perspectives about the undocumented population. Set said:

> I think it is important that we are not just talking about the experiences of the youth and that the youth are not speaking on behalf of their parents, but really allowing parents to feel empowered to organise in their own terms and when they are ready. Not like this 'come out, because it's like the greatest thing!' I feel like fear is a valid experience. Often we invalidate fear and say 'you must come out!' or whatever, or really discrediting that fear is an emotional experience and I think for our parents those traumas are left unspoken of and I think we need to realise that if people get involved it should be in their own terms and at their own pace.

In contrast to the idealisation inherent in socially distant relationships, a relationship of compassion structured along the model of political listening and solidarity accepts the full humanness and complexity of the sufferer and, as such, it is a more enduring and genuine commitment (Hoggett, 2006). 'Solidarity' is understood as 'standing together' – because of pragmatic shared interests and/or shared values (Dawson and Verweij, 2012). In either sense, there is an understanding of our lives as connected and interdependent. This notion of compassion as solidarity connects to the feminist ethics of care which recognises that humans are interdependent rather than autonomous (Tronto, 1995). We all need care and we all give care. This approach addresses those who are suffering as subjects rather than objects and is based on a more nuanced and less idealised notion of the human.

Conclusion

To enable their testimonies to be heard, people who experience suffering and those who advocate for them often deploy narratives that appeal to the values and emotions of their audiences, usually imagined as, to vary degrees, distant others. While the undocumented youth movement used to be primarily focused on demanding a pathway to citizenship for undocumented young people, priorities have shifted towards campaigning against the criminalisation of the wider undocumented population. In doing so, there has been a move away from an emphasis on an outward-facing appeal for the innocent and deserving subject of compassion, towards a prioritisation of community organising driven by a compassion for one another in the undocumented community and grounded in solidarity.

Notes

[1] This is unlike the more recently arrived unaccompanied young people from Central America (Perez-Huber, 2015).

[2] AB540 is a Californian law that enables undocumented students to qualify for in-state university tuition fees.

9

Conclusion

Threatening bodies

During Refugee Week 2017, a 20-foot-tall man sailed into Melbourne crouched on a wooden boat. *Inflatable Refugee* is a sculpture made by Belgian art collective (Schellekens, 2017). The sculpture was initially exhibited in Venice in 2015 to highlight and comment on the plight of people journeying across the Mediterranean during the refugee crisis, and some of the problematic responses with which they had been met. The size of the sculpture was a critical commentary on the construction of refugees as a menacing and overwhelming presence advancing on Europe.

While there are differences in local contexts and encounters between refugees, migrants and populations in receiving societies, at a global level the response from governments in societies that have received them has been characterised to a significant degree by hostility and exclusion. These responses have been particularly pronounced in the states discussed in this book, drawing on some of the discursive and emotional legacies of earlier colonial encounters which were so central in the formations of these states. In his last few months in office, President Obama spoke at the 2016 UN Summit for Refugees and Migrants. He entreated to the audience, 'This crisis is a test of our common humanity – whether we give in to suspicion and fear and build walls, or whether we see ourselves in another' (Kenny and Koziol, 2016). Two months later, the 45th President of the US was elected on an anti-immigrant platform following a campaign defined by the chants of 'build the wall'. In Autumn 2016 in Calais, as refugee camps were bulldozed, a £2.3 million British-funded border wall was erected in just two months. A few months later, in February 2017, the Dubs programme to resettle unaccompanied refugee children in the UK (discussed in Chapter Four) was brought to a premature end, having at that point assisted only 200 children. Across Europe too, border fences have been erected to prevent a repeat of the 2015 refugee exodus when people crossed the continent in search of safety, while in the summer of 2017 it was announced that some Italian ports might soon turn away humanitarian rescue boats (Wintour, 2017). The Australian government continues to maintain offshore detention facilities on the Pacific island of Nauru, despite the revelations of endemic and wide-scale abuse at the centre. The Manus detention centre closed in October 2017, following the PNG court decision declaring it to be illegal. Yet, the men detained there face no reprieve after four years of suffering and, at the time of writing, many are refusing to leave the site having been offered no safe and viable resettlement options. As the centre has been dismantled, their shelter, drinking water and other services have been removed, and the Australian government resolutely insists that no detainees will be transferred to Australia (Doherty, 2017).

Migrants and refugees are not only being met by bureaucratic and physical walls, and by abandonment. These people fleeing violence and poverty, in search of a better future for themselves and their families, are being treated as if they are an invading army. Military equipment and resources have been used in border operations by each of the nation-states discussed (Golash-Boza, 2012; Crawley et al, 2016; McKay et al, 2017). Following the EU's ongoing discrediting of humanitarian crews saving lives in the Mediterranean, in 2016 news emerged of a far-right organisation that was preparing to attack these vessels as they rescued people (Bulman, 2016). Cohen (2001:10) asserted that sometimes in relation to certain instances of social suffering, 'whole societies may slip into collective modes of denial'. This certainly appears to be the case in response to the plight of refugees and undocumented migrants who have been categorised and responded to as 'undesirables'. However, as this book has highlighted, there have been moments of interruption to this discourse.

In debates on the entrenchment of these responses, emotion has often been presented as a factor that has complicated and hindered sensible discussions. It has been treated as a layer that needs to be peeled away to get to the truth. As discussed in Chapter Two, critiques of policies and attitudes have often challenged what are perceived to be irrational negative perspectives on immigration and asylum by engaging in myth-busting to present counter-facts about the benefits that immigration offers. While this is necessary and valuable work, as one campaigner interviewed for this project stated, fear will always beat facts. Facts alone will not transform policy and public opinion.

This book has made a case for the importance of engaging with emotions in social science analysis of immigration and asylum policy discourses. As Nussbaum (2013) argues, people may be convinced and moved by political principles and arguments, but an engagement with emotions ensures enduring support. Emotions inform and guide our moral judgements; these are produced through cognitive and emotional reasoning. Our judgement about whether something is good or not depends on how we feel affected by it (Ahmed, 2014). There is a prevalent discourse that societies receiving migrants and refugees are negatively affected by their arrival. Writing about the politics of race, Ioanide (2015:2) has argued that, 'emotions function much like economies; they have mechanisms of circulation, accumulation, expression, and exchange that give them social currency, cultural legibility, and political power'. She asserts that the 'emotional economies that are attached to race ... have the unique ability to foreclose people's cognitive judgement' (Ioanide, 2015:2). Research studies have mapped and explored accounts of hostility among populations in societies receiving migrants and refugees, but also how emotion has been engaged with in governance which works to respond to, manage or even mobilise and direct fears and passions (Gest, 2016; Jones et al, 2017).

This book has examined how people are placed within and outside of 'circles of concern' in contested immigration and asylum policy discourse. All too often, refugees and undocumented migrants have been categorised as undesired because they are deemed to constitute a threat. Societies receiving migrants and refugees have frequently been referred to as 'host' societies. Derrida (2000) wrote of the inherent tension in the relationship of hospitality. Hosting implies an offer of hospitality from those who control territory to the strangers who crosses the threshold into that territory. Yet, as Derrida (2000) observed, opening their home to the uninvited and unknown stranger can induce anxieties for the host who fears that the stranger may do them harm. People arriving independently to seek asylum, rather than through organised programmes, are effectively unknown strangers. 'Queue jumping' undocumented migrants, or in the case of Australia, 'irregular maritime arrivals' are also portrayed as potentially harming citizens. As Obama's (2014b) reprimand to undocumented parents illustrates, there is a notion that these people are not playing fair and are claiming unearned rewards at the citizen's expense, 'We expect people who live in this country to play by the rules. We expect those who cut the line will not be unfairly rewarded'. Meanwhile, there is also a perceived security risk and challenge to the privileged status of the citizen. When he first introduced the Pacific Solution in 2001, the then Australian Prime Minister John Howard (2001) declared that:

This campaign more than any other that I have been involved in, is very much about the future of the Australia we know and the Australia we love so much ... It's about this nation saying to the world we are a generous open-hearted people taking more refugees on a per capita basis than any country except Canada. We have a proud record of welcoming people from 140 different nations. *But we will decide who comes to this country and the circumstances in which they come* [italics added].

It was love for Australia which allegedly drove his actions to protect it (1). The tough actions emanated not from the emotion of hostility as is often assumed, but out of love. As Ahmed (2014) has observed, this discourse has also appeared in some far-right justifications for their desire to restrict immigration. Australia has a 'generous open-hearted people' and a proud history of welcoming refugees. However, posited as a gift offered by a welcoming host, those who do not wait for the door to be opened, and instead attempt to enter clandestinely through the window, were disrespecting the hosts. This was felt as an affront as these people had refused to accept the hierarchical relationship of compassion. The infamous phrase 'we will decide who comes to this country and the circumstances in which they come', has been repeated regularly by prime ministers and immigration ministers since Howard and has become a defining catchphrase for the Pacific Solution (Peterie, 2017).

Johnson (2015) has explored why images of people in camps in the Middle East and North Africa can inspire humanitarianism, but those same people become framed as security risks once they arrive in Europe, Australia or North America. She suggests this is because they are: 1) people who are mobile taking control, and 2) because these mobile people are now here, in 'our' space. Boltanski (1999:13) has also remarked that, 'when they come together in person to invade the space of those more fortunate than they and the desire to mix with them, to live in the same places and to share the same objects, then they no longer appear as unfortunates'. Peterie (2017:1) asserts that in contrast to the weak and passive ideal subject of compassion (the suffering victim face of the Other [Douzinas, 2007]), strong and agentic irregular maritime arrivals may be understood as having 'similar possibilities' to Australians; thus, they pose a threat which speaks to the 'fears and insecurities of the Australian people'.

As Ahmed (2014:211) writes, 'there can be nothing more dangerous to a body than the social agreement that *that* body is dangerous'. Preoccupation with 'queue jumping' and the threatening figure of the stranger also emerged out of histories of previous encounters in the establishment and development of immigration regimes, and in colonial narratives of civility and savagery. As Ahmed (2014:212) has argued, some bodies are 'perceived as dangerous *in advance of their arrival*'; 'the immediacy of bodily reactions is mediated by histories that come before subjects and which are at stake in how the very arrival of some bodies is noticeable in the first place'.

Vulnerability and compassion

In the context of decades of restrictive immigration legislation and policies, negative media reporting on migrants and refugees, and seemingly entrenched public opposition to many forms of immigration, the events of the autumn of 2015 seemed to signal a significant and surprising shift in the emotional scripts of public debate on asylum. The images of the dead body of 3-year-old Alan Kurdi sent shockwaves across the globe and were a catalyst for unprecedented outpourings of sentiments of compassion which were mobilised into action as ordinary people took over where states had failed to act. Although embedded in differing local policy debates and histories, interruptions have also been witnessed in US and Australian migration and asylum debates, centred primarily on the reception of children and young people.

The 'Inflatable Refugee' sculpture is made of the same materials as the flimsy boats used by refugees to cross the Mediterranean. The accoutrements of these journeys – lifejackets and rubber dinghies – were used in several art works produced in response to the refugee crisis. These appeared to signify both the desperation of people who set forth on these precarious journeys, and their vulnerability. As Brown (2014) has argued, vulnerability has become a zeitgeist term in social policy, used to mobilise access to increasingly scarce and conditional resources, but it has also been used as a justification for the withholding of these resources, and for the conditionalities and control that characterise the terms under which they are offered.

In examining the drivers of these 'compassionate turns', this book has explored the different forms of testimony – visual, verbal, bodily – that have been produced and engaged with in processes of bearing witness, and the successes and challenges that have been faced in doing so. It has been argued that compassionate turns often occurred because of the way the stories of these children and young people were encountered and narrated, engaging an audience through the emotional regimes of childhood and national identity. These narratives mapped onto the framework of compassion outlined by Nussbaum (2013) (see Chapter Two) as based on the criteria of serious suffering, innocence and eudaimonistic judgement. In doing so, they interrupted the hostile emotional regime of asylum and immigration. While engaging with a discourse of compassion has led to some success, it has also been problematic when the model of compassion that is engaged with has engendered exclusions, has inhibited the response-ability of those migrants and refugees giving testimony, and when it has been depoliticised. In its logic, the model and structure of compassion that has been engaged with by politicians and other actors, has also implied and often inevitably led to restrictive outcomes. In this book, it has been argued that compassion has been mobilised in various ways that have reinforced exclusion and suffering, or at least inhibited or created challenges for securing pathways to social justice. Not only have people been refused compassion, but exclusions and violence have been legitimated through recourse to a discourse of compassion leading to what are in effect 'compassionate' refusals.

Compassion as solidarity

Immigration and asylum policies in the nation–states examined in this book continue to enact the violent exclusion of those who have been deemed 'undesirable'. As Gill (2016) has argued, pleas for compassion have often been made as a last resort against seemingly intractable walls of hostility, and when other attempts at resistance and critique have failed to produce shifts in policy. Meanwhile, as the case studies explored in this book have illustrated, rather than being opposite to hostility, compassion has also formed a significant constitutive element of a politics of refusal. It has been argued in this book that, while compassion has produced moments of hope and slight shifts or openings in government policies, there are also real problems for mobilising compassion as a route to social justice.

However, the pursuit and implementation of alternative models of compassion that are centrally grounded in solidarity, and not in hierarchical power relations, offers more promising prospects for social justice. The basis of eudaimonistic judgement may differ according to the degree of social distance or proximity that is perceived to exist between the person suffering and the person who might feel compassion. As discussed earlier, there were two original meanings to the term compassion. The first, *'suffering together with one another,* or "fellow feeling"' (Garber, 2004:20), intimated a high degree of proximity between the sufferer and the person responding. The other's pain was felt as their own. The second meaning described an emotion that was felt at a distance from a spectator towards a sufferer, rather than between equals (Garber, 2004).

It is proposed that a notion of compassion based on proximity and solidarity rather than distance and pity is more conducive to the realisation of social justice. In contrast to the idealisation inherent in socially distant relationships, a relationship of compassion structured along a model of solidarity accepts the full humanness and complexity of the sufferer and, as such, is likely to be a more enduring and genuine commitment (Hoggett, 2006). Practices, such as those in the undocumented youth movement that facilitate emotional sustenance, solidarity and a fight for the most affected rather than those most likely to succeed (Schweirtz, 2016), enable the care and support of all. In a context where a discourse of compassion has been appropriated to justify oppressive measures, the cases explored in Chapters Seven and Eight present examples of how activists have worked to identify and refocus the locus of action, linking compassion with outrage to address the causes of suffering and alleviate it in the long term. In this way, compassion can be understood as a catalyst emotion rather than simply an end in itself.

References

6, P., Squire, C., Treacher, A. and Radstone, S. (2007) 'Introduction', in P. 6, S. Radstone, C. Squire, and A. Treacher (eds) *Public emotions*. Basingstoke: Palgrave, pp. 1-34.

Abbott, T. (2014) 'Abbott likens campaign against people smugglers to war'. *Transcript of interview with ABC Channel 10 News*. 1 October. Hansard Parlinfo.

Achilli, L. (2015) *The smuggler: hero or villain?* Florence: Migration Policy Centre, European University Institute. Available at: cadmus.eui.eu/bitstream/handle/1814/36296/MPC_2015_10_PB.pdf?sequence=1&isAllowed=y.

Addley, E. and Gani, A. (2015) "Completely inundated': Britons take refugees' aid into their own hands', *The Guardian* [Online]. 5 September. Available at: www.theguardian.com/world/2015/sep/04/completely-inundated-the-britons-taking-aid-for-calais-refugees-into-their-own-hands.

Agencies in Budapest and Vienna (2015) 'Packed trains reach Germany as refugee visa checks are waived', *The Guardian* [Online]. 1 September. Available at: www.theguardian.com/world/2015/sep/01/trains-of-refugees-reach-germany-as-eu-asylum-checks-collapse.

Ahmed, S. (2014) *The cultural politics of emotion*, Edinburgh: Edinburgh University Press.

Allsop, J. (2015) 'The refugee crisis: demilitarising masculinities', *Open Democracy* [Online]. 17 September. Available at: www.opendemocracy.net/5050/jennifer-allsopp/refugee-crisis-demilitarising-masculinities.

Alsultany, E. (2007) 'Selling American diversity and Muslim American identity through non-profit advertising post-9/11', *American Quarterly*, 59(3): 593-622.

American Immigration Lawyers Association (AILA) (2007) Testimony on undocumented students before the House Immigration Subcommittee, *AILA Doc. No. 07072463* [Online]. 18 May. Available at: www.aila.org/infonet/testimony-on-undocumented-students.

Amin, A. (2013) 'Land of Strangers', *Identities: global studies in culture and power,* 20(1): 1-8.

Amnesty International (2015) *Europe: drastic change in response needed to tackle refugee crisis*. Available at: www.amnesty.org/en/latest/news/2015/09/europe-drastic-change-in-response-needed-to-tackle-refugee-crisis/.

Anderson, B. (2013) *Us and them? the dangerous politics of immigration control*. Oxford: Oxford University Press.

Anderson, B. and De Noronha, L. (2015) 'Interview: Bridget Anderson on Europe's 'violent humanitarianism' in the Mediterranean', *Ceasefire* [Online]. Available at: ceasefiremagazine.co.uk/interview-bridget-anderson/.

(Anon) (2015) 'Aylan's photo has changed everything', *Sun*, [Unavailable online]. 5 September. NexisUK.

Anthony, A. (2016) 'Accidental activists: the British women on the front line of the refugee crisis', *The Guardian* [Online]. 12 June. Available at: www.theguardian.com/world/2016/jun/12/help-refugees-calais-accidental-activists.

Arendt, H. (1977) *On revolution*. New York: Penguin.

Arneil, B. (1996) *John Lock and America: the defence of English colonialism*, Oxford: Clarendon Press.

Austen, I. (2017) 'In Canada, Justin Trudeau says refugees are welcome', *New York Times* [Online]. 28 January. Available at: www.nytimes.com/2017/01/28/world/canada/justin-trudeau-trump-refugee-ban.html.

The Australian (2016a) 'Australian border protection best in the world: Turnbull', [Online]. 18 September. Available at: www.theaustralian.com.au/news/australian-border-protection-best-in-the-world-turnbull/news-story/42329abe83b700e0d67eaf2f2f378834.

The Australian (2016b) 'Protestors force suspension of Question Time'. [Online]. 30 November. Available at: http://www.theaustralian.com.au/national-affairs/protesters-force-suspension-of-question-time/news-story/3a9ffa92f44b2166580e022a828bc789.

Barbalet, J. M. (1998) *Emotion, social theory and social structure: a macrosociological approach*. Cambridge: Cambridge University Press.

Barker, C. (2013) *The people smugglers' business model*. Foreign Affairs, Defence and Security Section, Department of Parliamentary Affairs. Research paper no. 2. Available at: apo.org.au/system/files/33034/apo-nid33034-74366.pdf.

Barr, C. (2016) 'The areas and demographics where Brexit was won', *The Guardian* [Online]. 24 June. Available at: www.theguardian.com/news/datablog/2016/jun/24/the-areas-and-demographics-where-the-brexit-vote-was-won.

Bashford, A. and McAdam, J. (2014) 'The right to asylum: Britain's 1905 Aliens Act and the evolution of refugee law', *Law and history review*, 32(2): 309-350.

Bassel, L. (2017) *The politics of listening*. Basingstoke: Palgrave Macmillan.

Bauman, Z. (2004) *Wasted lives: modernity and its outcasts*, Cambridge: Polity Press.

Belot, H. (2016) 'Question Time suspended as pro-refugee protestors call to 'close the camps' and bring them here', *ABC News* [Online]. 30 November. Available at: www.abc.net.au/news/2016-11-30/protesters-disrupt-question-time/8079674.

Ben-Ze'ev, A. (2000) *The subtlety of emotions*, Massachusetts: Massachusetts Institute of Technology Press.

Berlant, L. (2004) 'Compassion (and withholding)', in L. Berlant (ed) *Compassion: the culture and politics of an emotion*, New York: Routledge, pp. 1-14.

Berlant, L. (2005) 'The epistemology of state emotion', in A. Sarat, A. (ed) *Dissent in Dangerous Times*, Ann Arbour: University of Michigan Press, pp. 46-80.

Bhambra, G. (2017) 'Brexit, Trump, and 'Methodological Whiteness': On the Misrecognition of Race and Class,' *British Journal of Sociology*, special issue on The Trump/Brexit Moment: Causes and Consequences 68 (S1): 214–232.

Bishop, J. (2015) '*The Syrian and Iraqi humanitarian crisis*', Media press release. 9 September. Hansard Parlinfo.

Bleiker, R., Campbell, D., Hutchinson, E. and Nicholson, X. (2013) 'The visual dehumanisation of refugees', *Australian Journal of Political Science*, 48(4): 38-416.

Blinder, S. (2016) *Migration to the UK: asylum*. Migration Observatory, Oxford University. Available at: www.migrationobservatory.ox.ac.uk/resources/briefings/migration-to-the-uk-asylum/.

Bloch, A. (2014) 'Living in fear: rejected asylum seekers living as irregular migrants in England', *Journal of Ethnic and Migration Studies*, 40(10): 1507-1525.

Bloch, A. and Schuster, L. (2002) 'Asylum and welfare: contemporary debates', *Critical Social Policy*, 22(3): 393-414.

Boltanski, L. (1999) *Distant suffering: morality, media and politics*. Cambridge: Cambridge University Press.

Boochani, B. (2016) 'For refugees kidnapped and exiled to the Manus prison, hope is our secret weapon', *The Guardian* [Online]. 3 October. Available at: www.theguardian.com/australia-news/2016/oct/03/for-refugees-kidnapped-and-exiled-to-the-manus-prison-hope-is-our-secret-weapon.

Boochani, B. (2017) 'A kyriarchal system: new colonial experiments/ new decolonial resistance', *9th International maroon conference magazine.* Charles Town, Jamaica: Charles Town Maroon Council, pp. 20-22. Available at: maroons-jamaica.com/conference2017/modules/ mod_flipbook_3/tmpl/mobile/index.html.

Boochani, B. (2018) *No friend but the mountains. Writing from Manus Prison.* Sydney: Picador-Pan Macmillan.

Bosworth, M. (2014) *Inside immigration detention: foreigners in a carceral age.* Oxford: Oxford University Press.

Brokenshire, J. (Minister of State for Immigration) (2016) *Refugees and resettlement: written statement – HCWS687* [Online]. 21 April. Available at: www.parliament.uk/business/publications/written-questions-answers-statements/written-statement/Commons/2016-04-21/ HCWS687.

Brown, K. (2014) 'Questioning the vulnerability zeitgeist: care and control practices with 'vulnerable' young people', *Social Policy and Society,* 13(3): 371-387.

Brown, K. (2015) *Vulnerability and young people: care and social control in policy and practice.* Bristol: Policy Press.

Bulman, M. (2016) 'Far-right group sends ship to confront boats rescuing refugees in Mediterranean 'and take them back to Africa'', *Independent* [Online]. 13 July. Available at: www.independent.co.uk/ news/world/europe/anti-immigrant-ship-mediterranean-ngo-ships-refugee-crisis-migrant-boats-people-smugglers-defend-a7838731. html.

Burkitt, I. (2005) 'Powerful emotions: power, government and opposition in the 'war on terror'', *Sociology,* 39(4): 679-695.

Burkitt, I. (2014) *Emotions and social relations.* London: Sage.

Burrows, T. (2015) 'Just days after pictures of Aylan's body shocked the world, a desperate father carries his baby boy through the water as 34 refugees die off Greek island' *Daily Mail,* 13 September. Available at: www.dailymail.co.uk/news/ article-3232816/Not-two-weeks-pictures-little-migrant-Aylan-s-body-shocked-world-desperate-father-carries-two-month-old-baby-boy-water-rubber-ring-day-28-refugees-die-Greek-island.html.

Butler, J. (2009) *Frames of war, when is life grievable?* New York: Verso.

Butler, J. (2016) 'Asylum seekers on Nauru protest for fourth day, after 1000 days in detention', *Huffington Post* [Online]. 23 March. www.huffingtonpost.com.au/2016/03/23/nauru-protest-asylum-seeker_n_9537394.html.

Cacho, L. M. (2012) *Social death: racialised rightlessness and the criminalisation of the unprotected.* New York: New York University Press.

Canas, T. (2016) *On experiential-based refugee campaigns and the performance of humanitarianism*, Melbourne: RISE. Available at: riserefugee.org/on-experiential-based-refugee-campaigns-the-performance-of-humanitarianism/.

Canizales, S. L. (2015) *Unaccompanied migrant children: a humanitarian crisis at the U.S. border and beyond*. Davis: UC Davis Center for Poverty Research.

Carrera, S. and Guild, E. (2016) (eds) *Irregular migration, trafficking and smuggling of human beings: policy dilemmas in the EU*. Brussels: Centre for European Policy Studies.

Centre for Political Beauty (2015) *The dead are coming*. Available at: www.politicalbeauty.com/dead.html.

Centre for Research on Migration, Refugees and Belonging (CRMRB) (2015) *Everyday Borders*. London: University of East London. Available at: vimeo.com/126315982.

Charteris-Black, J. (2006) 'Britain as a container: immigration metaphors in the 2005 election campaign', *Discourse and Society*, 17(5): 563–581.

Chavez, L. (2013) *The Latino threat: constructing immigrants, citizens and the nation*, second edition. Redwood City, CA: Stanford University Press.

Chebel D'Appollonia, A. (2015) *Frontiers of fear: immigration and insecurity in the United States*. Ithaca: Cornell University Press.

Chouliaraki, L. (2010) 'Post-humanitarianism: humanitarian communication beyond a politics of pity', *International Journal of Cultural Studies*, 13(2): 107-126.

Chu, H. (2015) 'Europe's refugee crisis is darkened by the shadows of WWII', *LA Times* [Online]. 5 September. Available at: www.latimes.com/world/europe/la-fg-refugee-crisis-shadows-of-wwii-20150905-story.html.

Clarke, S., Hoggett P. and Thompson, S. (2006), 'The study of emotion: an introduction', in S. Clarke, P. Thompson, and P. Hoggett (eds), *Emotion, politics and society*, Basingstoke: Palgrave Macmillan, pp. 3-13.

CNN (2016) 'Here's the full text of Donald Trump's victory speech', *CNN* [Online]. 9 November. Available at: edition.cnn.com/2016/11/09/politics/donald-trump-victory-speech/index.html.

CNN International (2016) 'We are dead souls in living bodies: Australia accused of abusing refugees', [Online]. Available at: twitter.com/cnni/status/760709535975763968.

Cohen, S. (2001) *States of denial: knowing about atrocities and suffering*. Cambridge: Polity Press.

Cohen, N. (2017) 'Trump's lies are not the problem. It's the millions who swallow them who really matter', *The Guardian* [Online]. 5 February. Available at: www.theguardian.com/commentisfree/2017/feb/05/donald-trump-lies-belief-totalitarianism.

Connolly, K. (2015) 'Germany greets refugees with help and kindness at Munich central station, *The Guardian* [Online]. 3 September. Available at: www.theguardian.com/world/2015/sep/03/germany-refugees-munich-central-station.

Cooper, Y. (2015) 'Speech on the European refugee crisis by Yvette Cooper, Shadow Home Secretary', *Centre for European Reform* [Online]. 1 September. Available at: www.cer.eu/in-the-press/speech-european-refugee-crisis-yvette-cooper-shadow-home-secretary.

Crawley, H. (2007) *When is a child not a child? asylum, age disputes and the process of age assessment.* London: ILPA.

Crawley, H., Düvell, F., Jones, K., McMahon, S. and Sigona, N. (2016) *Destination Europe? Understanding the dynamics and drivers of Mediterranean migration in 2015*, Unravelling the Mediterranean Migration Crisis (MEDMIG) Final Report. Available at: www.medmig.info/wp-content/uploads/2016/12/research-brief-destination-europe.pdf.

Danewid, I. (2017) 'White innocence in the Black Mediterranean: hospitality and the erasure of history', *Third World Quarterly*, 38(7): 1674-1689.

Davidov, E. and Meuleman, B. (2012) 'Explaining attitudes towards immigration policies in European countries: the role of human values', *Journal of Ethnic and Migration Studies,* 38(5): 757-775.

Davidson, J., Bondi, L. and Smith, M. (2005) *Emotional geographies.* Abingdon: Routledge.

Davidson, H. and Doherty, B. (2016) Nauru files: widespread condemnation of Australian government by UN and others, *The Guardian* [Online]. 10 August. Available at: www.theguardian.com/australia-news/2016/aug/10/nauru-files-widespread-condemnation-of-australian-government-by-un-and-others.

Davis, D. B. (2014) *The problem of slavery in the age of emancipation.* New York: Alfred A. Knopf.

Davis, W. (2016) 'The age of post-truth politics', *New York Times* [Online]. 24 August. Available at: www.nytimes.com/2016/08/24/opinion/campaign-stops/the-age-of-post-truth-politics.html.

Dawson, A. and Verweij, M. (2012) 'Solidarity: a moral concept in need of clarification' *Public Health Ethics*, 5(1):1-5.

De Genova, N. (2002) 'Migrant "illegality" and deportability in everyday life', *Annual Review of Anthropology*, 31: 419-447.

De Genova, N. and Tazzioli, M. (eds) (2016) *Europe / crisis: introducing new keywords of "the crisis" in and of "Europe"*. Available at: nearfuturesonline.org/europecrisis-new-keywords-of-crisis-in-and-of-europe/.

Department of Immigration and Border Protection (2012) *Safety gear*. Available at: www.youtube.com/watch?v=ja7DOO8YbWM.

Department of Immigration and Border Protection (2014a) *You won't be settled*. Available at: www.youtube.com/watch?v=bvz3U-JOvOU.

Department of Immigration and Border Protection (2014b) *No way*. Available at: https://www.youtube.com/watch?v=rT12WH4a92w.

Department of Immigration and Border Protection (2016) *Fact sheet: Australia's response to the Syrian and Iraqi humanitarian crisis*. [Online]. Available at: www.homeaffairs.gov.au/trav/refu/response-syrian-humanitarian-crisis.

Derrida, J. (2000) Hostipitality. *Angelaki*, 5 (3), 3–18.

Doherty, B. (2015) 'Manus island asylum seekers declare end to two-week long hunger strike', *The Guardian* [Online]. 27 January. Available at: www.theguardian.com/australia-news/2015/jan/27/manus-island-asylum-seekers-end-hunger-strike.

Doherty, B. (2016a) 'Doctors refuse to discharge 'Baby Asha' because of fears for safety on Nauru', *The Guardian* [Online]. 12 February. Available at: www.theguardian.com/australia-news/2016/feb/12/doctors-refuse-to-discharge-baby-asha-because-of-fears-for-safety-on-nauru.

Doherty, B. (2016b) "Let them stay': backlash in Australia against plans to send asylum seekers to detention camps', *The Guardian* [Online]. 10 February. Available at: www.theguardian.com/australia-news/2016/feb/10/let-them-stay-australia-backlash-267-asylum-seekers-island-detention-camps.

Doherty, B. (2016c) 'Baby Asha discharged from hospital into community detention', *The Guardian* [Online]. 21 February. Available at: www.theguardian.com/australia-news/2016/feb/22/baby-asha-reportedly-discharged-from-hospital-into-community-detention.

Doherty, B. (2017) 'Manus Island detention centre closing down with refugees still inside', *The Guardian* [Online]. 5 July. Available at: www.theguardian.com/australia-news/2017/jul/05/manus-island-detention-centre-closing-down-with-refugees-still-inside.

Doherty, B. and Davidson, H. (2016) 'Somali refugee in critical condition after setting herself alight on Nauru', *The Guardian* [Online], 2 May. Available at: www.theguardian.com/australia-news/2016/may/03/somali-refugee-in-critical-condition-after-setting-herself-alight-on-nauru.

Dominguez Zamorano, N., Perez, J., Meza, N. and Guitierrez, J. (2010) 'DREAM Activists: Rejecting the Passivity of the Nonprofit Industrial Complex', *Truthout* [Online]. 21 September. Available at: truth-out.org/archive/component/k2/item/91877:dream-activists-rejecting-the-passivity-of-the-nonprofit-industrial-complex.

D'Orazio, F. (2015) 'Journey of an image: from a beach in Bodrum to twenty million screens across the world', in *The iconic image on social media: a rapid research response to the death of Aylan Kurdi*. Available at: http://visualsocialmedialab.org/projects/the-iconic-image-on-social-media, pp. 11-18.

Dorling, D. (2017) 'Brexit, the NHS and the elderly middle class', *Soundings*, 64: 50-53.

Douzinas, C. (2007) *Human rights and empire: the political philosophy of cosmopolitanism*. Abingdon: Routledge.

Dream Activist (2011) *Undocumented Youth vs. Border Patrol Round 1 – Mobile, Alabama*. Available at: www.youtube.com/watch?v=iA54ErBfZ8E.

Dustmann, C. and Frattini, T. (2013) *The fiscal effects of immigration to the UK*. London: Centre for Research and Analysis of Migration.

Dutton, P. (2015a) 'Operation Sovereign Borders delivers six months without a successful people smuggling venture'. *Media releases for Peter Dutton*. 28 January. Minister for Immigration and Border Protection. Available at: www.minister.border.gov.au/peterdutton/2015/Pages/Operation-Sovereign-Borders-delivers-six-months-without-a-successful-people-smuggling-venture.aspx.

Dutton, P. (2015b) 'Restoring integrity to refugee intake'. *Media releases for Peter Dutton*. 12 May. Minister for Immigration and Border Protection. Available at: http://minister.homeaffairs.gov.au/peterdutton/2015/Pages/restoring-integrity-to-refugee-intake.aspx.

Dutton, P. (2016a) 'Regional agreement to combat people smuggling and human trafficking', *Media releases for Peter Dutton* [Online]. 23 March. Minister for Immigration and Border Protection. Available at: www.minister.border.gov.au/peterdutton/2016/Pages/regional-agreement-combat-people-smuggling.aspx.

Dutton, P. (2016b) 'Interview with Ross Greenwood, Money News Radio 2GB'. *Media releases for Peter Dutton* [Online]. 15 November. Minister for Immigration and Border Protection. Available at: http://minister.homeaffairs.gov.au/peterdutton/2016/Pages/interview-ross-greenwood-money-news-radio-2gb.aspx.

Dutton, P. (2016c) 'Recent incidents in Nauru'. *Media releases for Peter Dutton* [Online]. 3 May. Minister for Immigration and Border Protection. Available at: www.minister.border.gov.au/peterdutton/2016/Pages/recent-incidents-in-nauru.aspx.

Edwards, D. and Fasulo, A. (2006) '"To be honest": sequential uses of honesty phrases in talk-in-interaction', *Research on Language and Social Interaction,* 39(4): 343-376.

El-Enany, N. and Keenan, S. (2016) '#NauruFilesReading: Articulating the Violence of Australia's Refugee Policy', *Critical Legal Thinking* [Online]. Available at: criticallegalthinking.com/2016/10/25/nauru-files-reading/.

El-Enany, N. (2016) 'AylanKurdi: the human refugee', *Law and Critique,* 27(1): 13-15.

Emejulu, A. (2016) 'The centre of a whirlwind: watching whiteness work'. *Verso Blog* [Online]. 10 November. Available at: www.versobooks.com/blogs/2934-the-centre-of-a-whirlwind-watching-whiteness-work.

European Journalism Observatory (2015) *Research: how Europe's newspapers reported the migration crisis.* Available at: en.ejo.ch/research/research-how-europes-newspapers-reported-the-migration-crisis.

European Commission (EC) (2016) *EU operations in the Mediterranean Sea.* European Commission [Online]. Available at: ec.europa.eu/home-affairs/sites/homeaffairs/files/what-we-do/policies/securing-eu-borders/fact-sheets/docs/20161006/eu_operations_in_the_mediterranean_sea_en.pdf.

European Union (EU) (2016) *European Union naval force: Mediterranean Operation Sophia Fact sheet* [Online]. Available at: eeas.europa.eu/archives/docs/csdp/missions-and-operations/eunavfor-med/pdf/factsheet_eunavfor_med_en.pdf.

Europol-INTERPOL (2016) *Migrant smuggling networks: executive summary.* Available at: www.europol.europa.eu/sites/default/files/documents/ep-ip_report_executive_summary.pdf.

Eurostat (2015) 'More than 410 000 first time asylum seekers registered in the third quarter of 2015', *Eurostat news release* [Online]. 10 December. Available at: http://ec.europa.eu/eurostat/documents/2995521/7105334/3-10122015-AP-EN.pdf/04886524-58f2-40e9-995d-d97520e62a0e.

Evans, B. (2013) *Liberal terror.* Cambridge: Polity.

Evans, B. (2017) Dead in the waters', in A. Baldwin and G. Bettini [eds] *Life adrift: critical reflections on climate change and migration.* Maryland, Rowman & Littlefield, pp. 59-78.

Evans, B. and Giroux, H. (2014) *Disposable futures: the seduction of violence in the age of spectacle.* San Francisco: City Lights Books.

Evans, B. and Bauman, Z. (2016) 'The refugee crisis is humanity's crisis', *New York Times* [Online]. 2 May. Available at: www.nytimes.com/2016/05/02/opinion/the-refugee-crisis-is-humanitys-crisis.html.

Every, D. and Agoustinos, M. (2008) 'Constructions of Australia in pro- and anti-asylum seeker political discourse', *Nations and Nationalism,* 14(3): 562-580.

Ewing, W. (2015) *How much do undocumented immigrants pay in state and local taxes?* Available at: immigrationimpact.com/2015/04/21/how-much-do-undocumented-immigrants-pay-in-state-and-local-taxes/.

Farrell, P., Evershed, E. and Davidson, H. (2016) 'The Nauru files: cache of 2,000 leaked reports reveal scale of abuse of children in Australian offshore detention', *The Guardian* [Online]. 10 August. Available at: www.theguardian.com/australia-news/2016/aug/10/the-nauru-files-2000-leaked-reports-reveal-scale-of-abuse-of-children-in-australian-offshore-detention.

Farrell, P. and Karp, P. (2016) 'Peter Dutton attacks Guardian and ABC over reporting of Nauru files', *The Guardian* [Online]. 18 August. Available at: www.theguardian.com/australia-news/2016/aug/18/peter-dutton-says-he-wont-be-defamed-by-guardian-and-abc-over-nauru-files.

Farrier, D. (2011) *Postcolonial asylum: seeking sanctuary before the law.* Oxford: Oxford University Press.

Farris, S. (2017) *In the name of women's rights: The rise of femonationalism.* Durham: Duke University Press.

Fasenfest, D. (2016) 'Class, politics and the reactionary electorate', *Critical Sociology,* 42(1): 3-5.

Fassin, D. (2005) 'Compassion and repression: the moral economy of immigration policies in France', *Cultural Anthropology,* 20(3): 362-387.

Fassin, D. (2012) *Humanitarian reason: a moral history of the present times.* Berkeley and Los Angeles: University of California Press.

Fernando, N. (2017) The discursive violence of postcolonial asylum in the Irish Republic, *Postcolonial Studies,* 19(4): 393-408.

Field, K. and Field, B. (2014) *Racecraft,* New York: Verso.

Fitzgerald, D. and Cook-Martin, D. (2014) *Culling the masses: the democratic origins of immigration policy in the Americas,* Cambridge, MA: Harvard University Press.

Follis, K. (2017) 'Reflections on post-humanitarianism in dark times', *Open Democracy* [Online]. 21 April. Available at: www.opendemocracy.net/5050/karolina-follis/reflections-on-post-humanitarianism-in-dark-times.

Forkert, K., Jackson, E. and Jones, H. (2016) 'Whose feelings count? Performance politics, emotion and government immigration control', in E. Jupp, J. Pykett, and F. Smith (eds) *Emotional States: sites and spaces of affective governance*. Abingdon: Routledge, pp. 177-190.

Franko Aas, K. and Gundhus, H. (2015) 'Policing humanitarian borderlands: Frontex, human rights and the precariousness of life', *British Journal of Criminology*, 55(1): 1-18.

Freedland, J. (2015) 'Aylan Kurdi: this one small life has shown us the way to tackle the refugee crisis', *The Guardian* [Online]. 4 September. Available at: www.theguardian.com/commentisfree/2015/sep/04/aylan-kurdi-refugee-crisis.

Gale, P (2004) 'The refugee crisis and fear: populist politics and media discourse', *Journal of Sociology*, 40(4): 321-340.

Gale, P. (2005) *The politics of fear: lighting the wik*, Frenchs Forest, NSW: Pearson Education.

Garber, M. (2004) 'Compassion', in L. Berlant (ed) *Compassion: the culture and politics of an emotion*, New York: Routledge, pp. 15-28.

Gelber, K. (2003) 'A fair queue? Australian public discourse on refugees and immigration', *Journal of Australian Studies*, 27(77): 23-30.

Gest, J. (2016) *The new minority*. Oxford: Oxford University Press.

Get Up (2016) *Let them stay*. Available at: www.getup.org.au/campaigns/refugees/refugee-x/let-them-stay.

Gill, N. (2016) *Nothing personal? geographies of governing and activism in the British asylum system*, Oxford: Wiley-Blackwell.

Gillard, J. (2010) *Christmas Island boat tragedy: transcript of Prime Minister's press conference speech, Sydney*. 16 December. Hansard Parlinfo.

Gilligan, C. (2015) The public and the politics of immigration controls, *Journal of Ethnic and Migration Studies*, 41(9): 1373-1390.

Gilligan, C. (2016) The immigration debate, what debate? *GRAMNet* [Online]. 11 February. Available at: gramnet.wordpress.com/2016/02/11/the-immigration-debate-what-debate/.

Giroux, H. (2002) 'Terrorism: community, fear, and the suppression of dissent', *Cultural Studies: Critical Methodologies*, 2(3): 334-342.

Gleeson, M. (2016) *Offshore: behind the wire on Manus and Nauru*, Sydney: New South Books.

Goffman, E. (1986) *Frame analysis. an essay on the organization of experience*. Boston, MA: Northeastern University Press.

Golash-Boza, T. (2012) *Immigration nation: raids, detentions and deportations in post-9/11 America*, New York: Routledge.

Gonzales, R., Terriquez, V. and Ruszczyk, S. (2014) 'Becoming DACAmented: assessing the short-term benefits of Deferred Action for Childhood Arrivals (DACA)', *American Behavioural Scientist*, 58(14): 1852-1872.

Goodman, S. and Burke, S. (2010) '"Oh you don't want asylum seekers, oh you're just racist": A discursive analysis of discussions about whether it's racist to oppose asylum seeking', *Discourse and Society*, 21(3): 325-340.

Goodman, S., Sirriyeh, A. and McMahon, S. (2017) 'The evolving (re) categorisations of refugees throughout the 'Refugee/Migrant crisis'', *Journal of Community and Applied Social Psychology*, 27(2): 105-114.

Gower, M. and Cromarty, H. (2016) 'Syrian refugees and the UK'. Briefing paper no 06805'. House of Commons [Online]. 21 January. Available at: www.rcpsych.ac.uk/pdf/Syrian%20Refugees%20 and%20The%20UK.pdf.

Graham-Harrison, E. and Davies, L. (2015) '"Refugees welcome here': UK marchers take to streets with message of support', *The Guardian* [Online]. 12 September. Available at: www.theguardian. com/world/2015/sep/12/refugees-welcome-uk-marchers-un-warns-war-syria-million-displaced.

Greening, J. (then Secretary of State for International Development) (2015) 'Every British person can be proud of the help we have given, says Justine Greening', *Express*. 6 September. Available at: www. express.co.uk/comment/expresscomment/603283/Every-British-person-proud-help-we-have-given-Justine-Greening.

Greenslade, R. (2015) 'Will the image of a lifeless boy on a beach change the refugee debate?', *The Guardian* [Online]. 3 September. Available at: www.theguardian.com/media/greenslade/2015/sep/03/ will-the-image-of-a-lifeless-boy-on-a-beach-change-the-refugee-debate.

Grewcock, M. (2013) 'People smuggling and state crime', in K. Carrington, M. Ball, E, O'Brien and J. Tauri (eds) *Crime, justice and social democracy: critical criminological perspectives.* Basingstoke: Palgrave, p.327-343.

Griffiths, M. (2012) 'Vile liars and truth distorters'; truth, trust and the asylum system, *Anthropology Today*, 28(5): 8-12.

Griffiths, M. (2015) '"Here, man is nothing!", gender and policy in an asylum context', *Men and Masculinities*, 18(4): 468-488.

Hall, B. (2016) '"A huge win for doctors": Turnbull government backs down on gag laws for doctors on Nauru and Manus', *Sydney Morning Herald* [Online]. 20 October. Available at: www.smh.com.au/federal-politics/political-news/a-huge-win-for-doctors-turnbull-government-backs-down-on-gag-laws-for-doctors-on-nauru-and-manus-20161019-gs6ecs.html.

Hall, J. and Macfarlan. T. (2015) 'Humanity washed ashore: Outpouring of grief continues for Syrian toddler Aylan, three, after images of his dead body on a Turkish shoreline shocked the world', *Daily Mail* [Online]. 4 September. Available at: www.dailymail.co.uk/news/article-3222829/Outpouring-grief-continues-images-Syrian-toddler-Aylan-Kurdi-s-dead-body-Turkey.html.

Halliday, J. (2017) 'Man who tried to smuggle child refugee into UK: "I'd never do it again. Well...", *The Guardian* [Online]. 2 January. Available at: www.theguardian.com/world/2017/jan/02/man-who-tried-to-smuggle-child-refugee-into-uk-id-never-do-it-again-well-.

Harding, L. (2015) 'Refugees welcome? How UK and Germany compare on migration', *The Guardian*, 2 September. Available at: www.theguardian.com/world/2015/sep/02/refugees-welcome-uk-germany-compare-migration.

Hariman, R. and Lucaites, J. L. (2010) 'Public identity and collective memory in U.S. iconic photography: the image of "Accidental Napalm"', *Critical Studies in Media Communication,* (20)1: 35-66.

Harrison, M. and Sanders, T. (eds.) (2014) *Social policies and social control: New perspectives on the not-so-big society.* Bristol: Policy Press.

Harvey, D. (2007) *A brief history of neoliberalism.* New York: Oxford University Press.

Hayter, T. (2004) *Open borders: the case against immigration controls* (2nd edn), London: Pluto Press.

Head, N. (2016) *The failure of empathy: European responses to the refugee crisis.* Available at: www.opendemocracy.net/can-europe-make-it/naomi-head/failure-of-empathy-european-responses-to-refugee-crisis.

Heller, C. Nicholas De Genova, N., Stierl, M., Tazzioli, M. and van Baar, H. (2016) 'Europe/Crisis: New Keywords of "the Crisis" in and of "Europe"', Available at: nearfuturesonline.org/europecrisis-new-keywords-of-crisis-in-and-of-europe/.

Heller, C. and Pezzani, L. (2017) 'Mourning the dead while violating the living', *Open Democracy* [Online]. 30 June. Available at: www.opendemocracy.net/5050/charles-heller-lorenzo-pezzani/mourning-dead-while-violating-living.

Henley, J., Grant, H., Elgot, J., McVeigh, K. and O'Carroll, L. (2015) 'Britons rally to help people fleeing war and terror in Middle East;', *The Guardian* [Online]. 4 September. Available at: www.theguardian. com/uk-news/2015/sep/03/britons-rally-to-help-people-fleeing-war-and-terror-in-middle-east.

Hochschild, A. (1979). 'Emotion work, feeling rules, and social structure', *American Journal of Sociology*, 85(3): 551-575.

Hochschild, A. (2002) 'Emotion management in the age of global terrorism', *Soundings,* 20: 117-126.

Hochschild, A. (2016) *Strangers in our own land,* New York: The New Press.

Hodges, K. (2015) 'Drowned Aylan's dad 'a people smuggler', *The Sun,* 12 September. Available at: www.thesun.co.uk/archives/news/80578/drowned-aylans-dad-a-people-smuggler-2/.

Hogan, J. and Haltinner, K. (2015) 'Immigration Threat Narratives and Right-Wing Populism in the USA, UK and Australia', *Journal of Intercultural Studies*, 36(5): 520-543.

Hoggett, P. (2006) 'Pity, compassion, solidarity', in S. Clarke, P. Hoggett, S. Thompson (eds.), *Emotion, politics and society*. Basingstoke: Palgrave Macmillan, pp. 3-13.

Hoggett, P. and Thompson, S. (2012) 'Introduction', in S. Thompson and P. Hoggett (eds.) *Politics and the emotions: the affective turn in contemporary political studies.* London: Continuum International Publishing Group, pp. 1-20.

Höijer, B. (2004) 'The discourse of global compassion: the audience and media reporting of human suffering', *Media, Culture and Society*, 26(4): 513-531.

Home Office (2002) *Safe borders, safe haven: integration with diversity in modern Britain.* Available at: www.gov.uk/government/uploads/system/uploads/attachment_data/file/250926/cm5387.pdf.

Home Office (2015) 'Border Force cutter in Mediterranean migrant rescue mission'. *Home Office* [Online]. 31 May. Available at: www.gov.uk/government/news/border-force-cutter-in-mediterranean-migrant-rescue-mission.

House of Lords (HL) (2015) *EU action plan against migrant smuggling*, 4th report of session 2015-2016, HL Paper 46. Available at: publications.parliament.uk/pa/ld201516/ldselect/ldeucom/46/46.pdf.

Howard, J. (2001) *Address at the Federal Liberal Party campaign launch,* Sydney. 28 October. Hansard Parlinfo.

Huang, J., Jacoby, S., Lai, R. K. K. and Strickland, M. (2016) 'Election 2016: Exit Polls', *New York Times* [Online]. 8 November. Available at: www.nytimes.com/interactive/2016/11/08/us/politics/election-exit-polls.html?_r=0.

Hunter, F. (2016) 'Prime minister Malcolm Turnbull cries during TV interview with Stan Grant', *Sydney Morning Herald* [Online]. 1 March. Available at: www.smh.com.au/federal-politics/political-news/prime-minister-malcolm-turnbull-cries-during-tv-interview-with-stan-grant-20160229-gn6e10.html.

Hurst, D. (2015) 'Tony Abbott refuses to rule out paying people smugglers to turn back boats', *The Guardian* [Online] 12 June. Available at: www.theguardian.com/australia-news/2015/jun/12/tony-abbott-refuses-to-rule-out-paying-people-smugglers-to-turn-back-boats.

Hynes, P. (2011) *The dispersal and social exclusion of asylum seekers: between liminality and belonging.* Bristol: Policy Press.

Immigrant Youth Justice League (IYJL) (2011) 'Coming out of the shadows: undocumented, unafraid, unapologetic', *Organised Communities Against Deportations,* [Online]. Available at: organizedcommunities.org/coming-out-of-the-shadows-undocumented-unafraid-unapologetic/.

Independent (2015) 'Make your voice heard: Sign The Independent's petition to welcome refugees', *Independent* [Online]. 2 September. Available at: www.independent.co.uk/voices/editorials/make-your-voice-heard-sign-the-independents-petition-to-welcome-refugees-10483488.html.

International Development Committee (IDC) (2016) 'Syria's lost refugee children – urgent Government response needed'. IDC [Online]. 5 January. Available at: www.parliament.uk/business/committees/committees-a-z/commons-select/international-development-committee/news-parliament-20151/report-published-syrian-refugee-crisis-15-16/.

International Organisation for Migration (IOM) (2015) *EU migrant, refugee arrivals by land and sea approach one million in 2015.* Press release. 18 December. Available at: www.iom.int/news/eu-migrant-refugee-arrivals-land-and-sea-approach-one-million-2015.

International Organisation for Migration (IOM) (2016) *IOM counts 3,771 migrant fatalities in Mediterranean in 2015.* Press release. 1 May. Available at: www.iom.int/news/iom-counts-3771-migrant-fatalities-mediterranean-2015.

Ioanide, P. (2015) *The emotional politics of racism: how feelings trump facts in an era of colourblindness.* Stanford: Stanford University Press.

Isin, E. (2009) 'Citizenship in Flux: The Figure of the Activist Citizen', *Subjectivity*, 29: 367-388.

Jenks, C. (1996) *Childhood*. London: Routledge.

Jenkins, B. and Warren, N. (2012) 'Concept analysis: compassion fatigue and effects upon critical care nurses', *Critical Care Nursing Quarterly*, 35(4): 388-395.

Jenson, T. and Tyler, I. (2015) 'Benefit broods': the cultural and political crafting of anti-welfare commonsense', *Critical Social Policy*, 35(4): 470-491.

Joffe, H. (2008) 'The power of visual material: persuasion, emotion and identification', *Diogenes*, 217: 84-93.

Johnson, J. (2015) "'Border granny wants you!'": grandmothers policing nation at the US – Mexico border', in N. Naples and J. Bickham Mendez (eds) *Border politics*. New York: New York University Press, pp. 35-59.

Johnston, C. and Simon, D. (2017) 'Texas government signs bill banning sanctuary cities', *CNN* [Online]. 8 May. Available at: www edition.cnn.com/2017/05/07/us/texas-bans-sanctuary-cities/index. html.

Jones, H., Gunaratnam, Y., Bhattacharyya, G., Davies, W., Dhaliwal, S., Forkert, K., Jackson, E. and Saltus, R. (2017) *Go home? The politics of immigration controversies*. Manchester: Manchester University Press.

Jones, H. and Jackson, E. (2014) *Stories of cosmopolitan belonging: emotion and location*. Abingdon: Routledge.

Jupp, J. (2007) *From white Australia to Woomera: the story of Australian immigration* (2nd edn). Cambridge: Cambridge University Press.

Karlsen, E. (2016) *Australia's offshore processing of asylum seekers in Nauru and PNG: a quick guide to statistics and resources*. Parliament of Australia. Available at: www.aph.gov.au/About_Parliament/ Parliamentary_Departments/Parliamentary_Library/pubs/rp/ rp1617/Quick_Guides/Offshore.

Kaufman, G. (1992) *Shame: the power of caring*, Vermont: Schenkman Books.

Kenny, M and Koziol, M. (2016) 'Half of all Australians want to ban Muslim immigration: poll', *Sydney Morning Herald* [Online]. 21 September. Available at: www.smh.com.au/federal-politics/political-news/half-of-all-australians-want-to-ban-muslim-immigration-poll-20160920-grkufa.html.

Kidd, R. (1997) *The way we civilise*. St. Lucia, Queensland: University of Queensland Press.

Kilby, J. and Rowland, A. (2014) 'Introduction', in J. Kilby and A. Rowland (eds.) *The future of testimony: interdisciplinary perspectives on witnessing*. Oxford: Routledge, pp. 1-16.

Kingsley, P. (2016) *The new odyssey: the story of Europe's refugee crisis*. London: Guardian Faber Publishing.

Kingston, T. (2017) 'Migrants treat Med charities like a taxi service, says EU', *Times* [Online], 28 February. Available at: www.thetimes.co.uk/article/migrants-treat-med-charities-like-a-taxi-service-says-eu-lsvqww6fk.

Kinnick, K., Krugman, D. M., and Cameron, G. (1996) Compassion fatigue: communication and burnout toward social problems', *Journalism and Mass Communication Quarterly*, 73(3): 687-707.

Klein, N. (2014) *This changes everything: capitalism vs the climate*. New York: Simon and Schuster.

Krogstad, J. (2016) *U.S. border apprehensions of families and unaccompanied children jump dramatically*. Pew Research Centre. Available at: www.pewresearch.org/fact-tank/2016/05/04/u-s-border-apprehensions-of-families-and-unaccompanied-children-jump-dramatically/.

Kronick, R. and Rousseau, C. (2015) 'Rights, compassion and invisible children: a critical discourse analysis of the parliamentary debates on the mandatory detention of migrant children in Canada', *Journal of Refugee Studies*, 28(4): 544-569.

Kumar Das, S. (2008) 'Ethnicity and democracy meet when mothers protest', in P. Banerjee (ed) *Women in peace politics*. New Dehli: Sage, pp. 54-77.

Kupeli, I. (2015) 'We spoke to the photographer behind the picture of the drowned Syrian boy', *Vice News* [Online]. 4 September. Available at: www.vice.com/en_us/article/nilfer-demir-interview-876.

Kurasawa, F. (2009) 'A message in a bottle: bearing witness as a mode of transnational practice', *Theory, Culture and Society*, 26(1): 96-111.

Landolt, P. and Goldring, L. (2016) 'Assembling noncitizenship through the work of conditionality', *Journal of Citizenship Studies*, 19(8): 853-869.

Laney, H., Lenette, C., Kellett, A. N., Smedley, C. and Karan, P. (2016) '"The most brutal immigration regime in the developed world": international media responses to Australia's asylum-seeker policy', *Refuge*, 32(3): 135-150.

Lasser, C. (2011) 'Immediatism, dissent, and gender: women and the sentimentalisation of transatlantic anti-slavery appeals', in E. Clapp and J. R. Jeffrey (eds) *Women, dissent, and anti-slavery in Britain and America, 1790-1865*. Oxford: Oxford University Press, pp. 111-131.

Laub, D. (1992) 'Bearing witness or the vicissitudes of listening' in S. Felman and D. Laub (eds) *Testimony: crises of witnessing in literature, psychoanalysis and history.* New York and London: Routledge, pp. 57-74.

Lauby, F. (2016) 'Leaving the 'perfect DREAMer' behind? Narratives and mobilization in immigration reform', *Social Movement Studies,* 15(4): 374-387.

Lauret, M (2016) 'Americanization now and then: the "Nation of Immigrants" in the early twentieth and twenty-first centuries', *Journal of American Studies,* 50(2): 419-447.

Lentin, A. and Titley, G. (2011) *The crisis of multiculturalism: racism in a neoliberal age.* London: Zed Books.

Levinas, E. (1979) *Totality and infinity: an essay on exteriority.* Boston: M. Nijhoff Publishers.

Lewis, H., Dwyer, P., Hodkinson, S. and Waite, L. (2015) *Precarious lives: forced labour, exploitation and asylum.* Bristol: Policy Press.

London, L. (2000) *Whitehall and the Jews 1933-1948: British immigration policy, Jews and the Holocaust,* Cambridge: Cambridge University Press.

Long, K. (2013) 'When refugees stopped being migrants: Movement, labour and humanitarian protection', *Migration Studies,* 1 (1): 4-26.

Love Makes a Way (2016) *Take action on #Naurufiles.* Available at: lovemakesaway.org.au/2016/08/24/take-action-on-naurufiles/.

Lowe, L. (2015) *The intimacies of four continents.* Durham and London: Duke University Press.

Lusher, A. (2016) 'First Calais jungle children with no UK links arrive in Britain', *Independent* [Online]. 23 October. Available at: www.independent.co.uk/news/uk/home-news/calais-jungle-child-refugees-age-controversy-dubs-amendment-unaccompanied-minors-migrants-a7376151.html.

Maley, P. (2008) Pacific solution sinks quickly, *The Australian* [Online]. 9 February. Available at: www.theaustralian.com.au/archive/news/pacific-solution-sinks-quietly/story-e6frg6no-1111115512067.

Malkki, L. (1996) Speechless emissaries: refugees, humanitarianism and dehistoricization, *Cultural Anthropology,* 11(3):377-404.

Manzo, K. (2008) 'Imaging humanitarianism: NGO identity and the iconography of childhood', *Antipode,* 40(4): 632-657.

Marciniak, K. and Tyler, I. (2014) *Immigrant protest: politics, aesthetics and everyday dissent,* New York: Suny Press.

Marcus, G. (2002) *The sentimental citizen: emotion in democratic politics,* University Park, Pennsylvania: Pennsylvania State University Press.

Martin, G. (2015) 'Stop the boats! moral panic in Australia over asylum seekers', *Journal of Media & Cultural Studies,* 29(3): 304-322.

Martin, P. (2014) The United States: the continuing immigration debate', in J. Hollifield, P. Martin and P. Orrenius (eds.) *Controlling immigration: a global perspective* (3rd edn). Stanford: Stanford University Press, pp. 47-77.

Martinson, J. (2016) 'Iain Duncan Smith 'wept about plight of single mother' in TV interview', *The Guardian* [Online]. 5 April. Available at: www.theguardian.com/politics/2016/apr/05/iain-duncan-smith-wept-tv-interview-ian-hislop-workers-or-shirkers.

Massoumi, N. (2015) "The Muslim woman activist': Solidarity across difference in the movement against the 'War on Terror", *Ethnicities,* 15(5): 715-741.

Massumi, B. (1987) 'Notes on the translation and acknowledgements', in G. Deleuze and F. Guttari (eds) *A thousand plateaus.* London: Continuum, pp. xvii-xx.

May, T. (2014) Oral Statement by the Home Secretary on Syrian Refugees. *Home Office* [Online]. 29 January. Available at: www.gov.uk/government/speeches/oral-statement-by-the-home-secretary-on-syrian-refugees.

May, T. (2015a) 'Home Secretary statement on illegal immigration in Calais, statement to the House of Commons', *Home Office* [Online]. 14 July. Available at: www.gov.uk/government/speeches/home-secretary-statement-on-illegal-immigration-in-calais.

May, T. (2015b) 'Theresa May's speech to the Conservative party conference – in full', *Independent* [Online]. 6 October. Available at: www.independent.co.uk/news/uk/politics/theresa-may-s-speech-to-the-conservative-party-conference-in-full-a6681901.html.

Mayblin, L. (2015) 'Politics, publics and Aylan Kurdi', in *The iconic image on social media: a rapid research response to the death of Aylan Kurdi.* Available at: visualsocialmedialab.org/projects/the-iconic-image-on-social-media, pp. 42-43.

Mayblin, L. (2017) *Asylum after empire: colonial legacies in the politics of asylum seeking,* London: Rowman and Littlefield International.

McClintock, A. (1995) *Imperial leather: race, gender and sexuality in the colonial contest.* Abingdon: Routledge.

McGrath, S. (2005) 'Compassionate refugee politics?', *M/C – A Journal of Media and Culture,* 8(6). Available at: journal.media-culture.org.au/0512/02-mcgrath.php.

McKay, F., Thomas, S. and Kneebone, S. (2011) 'It would be okay if they came through the proper channels': community perceptions and attitudes towards asylum seekers in Australia', *Journal of Refugee Studies,* 25(1): 113-133.

McKay, F., Hall, L. and Lippi, K. (2017) 'Compassionate deterrence: a Howard government legacy', *Politics and Policy*, 45(2):169-193.

McMahon, S. (2016) 'A magnificent atmosphere? Romanian immigration in the political debate of Madrid, Spain', *Ethnic and Racial Studies*, 39(11): 2022-2040.

McMaster, D. (2001) *Asylum seekers: Australia's response to refugees*. Melbourne: Melbourne University Press.

McNevin, A. (2011) *Contesting citizenship: irregular migrants and new frontiers of the political*. New York: Colombia University Press.

Merrick, J. (2017) 'Theresa May's cold, insensitive reaction to the Grenfell disaster puts her in great political danger', *The Telegraph* [Online]. 16 June. Available at: www.telegraph.co.uk/news/2017/06/16/theresa-mays-cold-insensitive-reaction-grenfell-disaster-puts/.

Merrill, J. (2015) 'Refugee aid charities see surge in donations after image of drowned Syrian toddler Aylan Kurdi moves the nation', *Independent* [Online]. 3 September. Available at: www.independent.co.uk/news/uk/home-news/refugee-aid-charities-see-surge-in-donations-after-image-of-drowned-syrian-toddler-aylan-kurdi-moves-10484953.html.

Merrill, J. (2014) 'Exclusive: A call of duty – 25 leading charities urge PM to open Britain's door to its share of Syria's most vulnerable refugees', *Independent* [Online]. 14 January. Available at: www.independent.co.uk/news/uk/politics/exclusive-a-call-of-duty-25-leading-charities-urge-pm-to-open-britain-s-door-to-its-share-of-syrias-9068475.html.

Mestrovic, S. (1997) *Postemotional society*. Thousand Oaks: Sage.

Mignolo, W. (2011) *The darker side of western modernity: global futures, decolonial options*. Durham and London: Duke University Press.

Migration Observatory (2017) *Immigration detention in the UK*. Available at: www.migrationobservatory.ox.ac.uk/resources/briefings/immigration-detention-in-the-uk/.

Moeller, S. (1999) *Compassion fatigue: how the media sell disease, famine, war and death*. New York: Routledge.

Moeller, S. D. (2002) 'A hierarchy of innocence': the media's use of children in the telling of international news', *The International Journal of Press/Politics*, 7(1): 36-56.

Morales, L., Pilet, J. and Ruedin, D. (2015) 'The gap between public preferences and policies on immigration: a comparative examination of the effect of politicisation on policy congruence', *Journal of Ethnic and Migration Studies*, 41(9): 1495-1516.

Morrison, S. (2013) *Transcript of Operation Sovereign Borders Update*. 4 October. Hansard Parlinfo.

Morrison, S. (2014) *Restoring integrity and public confidence in Immigration and Border Protection*. Transcript of speech to the National Press Club in Canberra. 10 September. Hansard Parlinfo.

Mortensen, M. and Hans-Jörg Trenz, H. J. (2016) 'Media morality and visual icons in the age of social media: Alan Kurdi and the emergence of an impromptu public of moral spectatorship', *Javnost – The Public*, 23(4): 343-362.

Mortimer, C. (2016) 'Cologne: three out of 58 men arrested over mass sex attack on New Year's Eve were refugees from Syria or Iraq', *Independent* [Online]. 15 February. Available at: www.independent.co.uk/news/world/europe/cologne-only-three-out-of-58-men-arrested-in-connection-with-mass-sex-attack-on-new-years-eve-are-a6874201.html.

Mountz, A. (2010) *Seeking asylum: human smuggling and bureaucracy at the border*. University of Minnesota Press.

Mythen, G. and Walklate, S. (2006) 'Communicating the terrorist risk: Harnessing a culture of fear?', *Crime, Media, Culture: An International Journal*, 2(2): 123-142.

Nail, T. (2016) 'A tale of two crisis: migration and terrorism after the Paris attacks', *Studies in Ethnicity and Nationalism*, 16(1): 158-167.

Nair, P. (2012) 'The body politic of dissent: the paperless and the indignant', *Citizenship Studies*, 16(5-6): 783-792.

New Matilda (2016) 'Turnbull's office disrupted by 'Mums 4 Refugees' protest', *New Matilda* [Online]. 3 June. Available at: newmatilda.com/2016/06/03/in-pictures-turnbulls-office-disrupted-by-mums-4-refugees-protest/.

Newman, C. (2002) 'A life revealed', *National Geographic*. Available at: www.nationalgeographic.com/magazine/2002/04/afghan-girl-revealed/.

Newton Dunn, T. (2015) 'Bomb IS so Aylan didn't die in vain', *Sun* [Online]. 4 September. Available at: www.thesun.co.uk/archives/news/43447/bomb-is-so-aylan-didnt-die-in-vain/

Nicholls, W. (2013) *The DREAMers: how the undocumented movement transformed the immigrant rights debate*, Stanford: Stanford University Press.

Nicholls, W., Uitermark, J. and van Harperen, S. (2016) 'The networked grassroots: how radicals outflanked reformists in the United States' immigrant rights movement', *Journal of Ethnic and Migration Studies*, 42(6): 1036-1054.

Nielsen, L. (2016) *Human trafficker: when humanity becomes criminalised.* Denmark: Refugees.dk. Available at: refugees.dk/en/focus/2016/may/human-trafficker-when-humanity-becomes-criminalized/.

Nunn, A. and Tepe-Belfrage, D. (2017) 'Disciplinary social policy and the failing promise of the new middle classes: The Troubled Families Programme', *Social Policy and Society*, Special Issue on Troubled Families Programme, 16:1: 119-129.

Nunn, H. (2004) 'Emotional death: the charity advert and photographs of childhood trauma', *Journal for Cultural Research*, 8(3): 271-292.

Nussbaum, M. (1996) 'Compassion: the basic social emotion', *Social Philosophy and Politics,* 13(1): 27-58.

Nussbaum, M. (2001) *Upheavals of thought: the intelligence of emotions.* New York: Cambridge University Press.

Nussbaum, M. (2013) *Political emotions: why love matters for justice.* Cambridge: Harvard University Press.

Nyers, P. and Rygiel, K. (2012) *Citizenship, migrant activism and the politics of movement.* London: Routledge.

Obama, B. (2012) 'Remarks by the president on immigration', *Whitehouse, Office of the Press Secretary* [Online]. 12 June. Available at: obamawhitehouse.archives.gov/the-press-office/2012/06/15/remarks-president-immigration.

Obama, B. (2014a) *Letter from the President – efforts to address the humanitarian situation in the Rio Grande Valley areas of our nation's southwest border.* Washington: Office of the Press Secretary, The White House. 30 June. Available at: obamawhitehouse.archives.gov/the-press-office/2014/06/30/letter-president-efforts-address-humanitarian-situation-rio-grande-valle.

Obama, B. (2014b) 'Remarks by the president in address to the nation on immigration', *Whitehouse, Office of the Press Secretary* [Online]. 20 November. Available at: obamawhitehouse.archives.gov/the-press-office/2014/11/20/remarks-president-address-nation-immigration.

O'Brien, A. (2015) *Philanthropy and settler colonialism.* Basingstoke: Palgrave Macmillan.

O'Dell, L. (2007) Representations of the 'damaged' child: 'child saving' in a British children's charity ad campaign, *Children and Society*, 22: 383-392.

Oldfield, J.R. (2008) 'Slavery, abolition and empire', in F. Rosen (ed.) *Empire and dissent: the United States and Latin American.* Durham and London: Duke University Press, pp. 74-89.

Oliver, K. (2015) 'Witnessing, recognition and response ethics', *Philosophy and Rhetoric,* 48(4): 473-493.

Ousey, G. C. and Kubrin, C. E. (2018) 'Immigration and crime: assessing a contentious issue', *Annual Review of Criminology*, doi.org/10.1146/annurev-criminol-032317-092026.

Pallister-Wilkins, P. (2016) 'Interrogating the Mediterranean 'migration crisis'', *Mediterranean Politics*, 21(2): 311-315.

Pasha-Robinson, L. (2016) 'Thousands of lifejackets appear outside parliament to remind MPs they are failing drowning refugees', *Independent* [Online]. 19 September. Available at: www.independent.co.uk/news/uk/home-news/life-jackets-parliament-square-london-graveyard-refugee-deaths-sea-lifejacketlondon-international-a7316096.html.

Patler, C. (2017) '"Citizens but for papers": undocumented youth organizations, anti-deportation campaigns, and the reframing of citizenship', *Social Problems*, doi: 10.1093/socpro/spw045.

Perera, S. (2013) 'Oceanic corpo-graphies, refugee bodies and the making and unmaking of waters', *Feminist Review*, 103(1): 58-79.

Perera. S. and Pugliese, J. (2016) 'A nightmare world in plain sight', *Researchers Against Pacific Black Sites*. Available at: http://rapbs.org/index.php/tag/manus-island/.

Perez Huber, L. (2015) 'Constructing "deservingness": DREAMers and Central American unaccompanied children in the national immigration debate', *Association of Mexican-American Educators* (AMAE), 9(3):22-34.

Perkowski, N. (2016) 'Deaths, interventions, humanitarianism and human rights in the Mediterranean 'migration crisis'', *Mediterranean Politics*, 21(2): 331-335.

Perugini, N. and Gordon, N. (2015) *The human right to dominate*. Oxford: Oxford University Press.

Peterie, M. (2017) 'Docility and desert: government discourses of compassion in Australia's asylum seeker debate', *Journal of Sociology*, 53(2): 351-366.

Phillips, A. (2015) 'After Aylan Al-Kurdi's tragedy we must let the refugees in and learn from them', *Mirror* [Online]. 8 September. Available at: www.mirror.co.uk/news/uk-news/after-aylan-al-kurdis-tragedy-6407578.

Philo, G., Briant, E. and Donald, P. (2013) *Bad news for refugees*. London: Pluto Press.

Piper, C. (1999) 'Moral campaigns for children's welfare in the nineteenth century', in M. King (ed.) *Moral agendas for children's welfare*. London: Routledge, pp. 33-52.

Polletta, F. (1998) 'Contending stories: narrative in social movements', *Qualitative Sociology*, 21(4): 419-446.

Porter Novelli (2011) *Malaysian public information campaign post-implementation report*. Available at: www.border.gov.au/ AccessandAccountability/Documents/FOI/2012-018673_ Document12_Released.pdf.

Potter, J. and Wetherell, M (1987) *Discourse and social psychology, beyond attitudes and behaviour*. Sage: London.

Preston, J. (2007) 'In increments, senate revisits immigration bill', *New York Times* [Online]. 3 August. Available at: www.nytimes. com/2007/08/03/washington/03immig.html.

Proctor, L. and Yamada-Rice, D. (2015) 'Shoes of childhood: exploring the emotional politics through which images become narrated on social media', in *The iconic image on social media: a rapid research response to the death of Aylan Kurdi*. Available at: visualsocialmedialab.org/ projects/the-iconic-image-on-social-media, pp. 57-60.

Prowse, H. (2015) 'Refugees need the supplies I brought. But respect is just as critical', *The Guardian*. 16 September. Available at: www. theguardian.com/commentisfree/2015/sep/16/refugees-greece-supplies-respect-treated-like-humans.

Quijano, A. (2000) 'Coloniality of power, eurocentrism and Latin America', *International Sociology*, 15(2): 215-232.

Qvortrup, J. (2007) 'Editorial: A reminder', *Childhood*, 14(4): 395.

Richards, B. (2007) *Emotional governance: politics, media and terror*, Basingstoke: Palgrave Macmillan.

RISE (2016) *Media release – sovereignty + sanctuary: a first nations/ refugee solidarity event*. 13 July. Available at: riserefugee.org/media-release-sovereignty-sanctuary-a-first-nations-refugee-solidarity-event-13072016/.

Robertson, J. (2017) 'Eaten Fish: Iranian asylum seeker and cartoonist ends Manus Island hunger strike', *The Guardian* [Online]. 19 February. Available at: www.theguardian.com/australia-news/2017/feb/19/ eaten-fish-iranian-asylum-seeker-and-cartoonist-ends-manus-island-hunger-strike.

Rose, J. (2003) *On not being able to sleep: psychoanalysis and the modern world*. London: Chatto and Windus.

Rudd, A. (2017) 'Unaccompanied Child Refugees' – HCWS23. Hansard [Online]. 9 February. Available at: hansard.parliament.uk/ Commons/2017-02-09/debates/441DB6F3-2F20-4A12-A13C-9CB86838707E/UnaccompaniedChildRefugees.

Sales, R. (2002) 'The deserving and the undeserving? Refugees, asylum seekers and welfare in Britain', *Critical Social Policy*, 22(3): 456-478.

Sanchez, G. (2017) 'Critical perspectives on clandestine migration facilitation: an overview of migrant smuggling research', *Journal of Migration and Human Security*, 5(1): 9-27.

Saucier, P. K. and Woods, T. (2014) 'Ex-aqua: the Mediterranean basin, Africans on the move and the politics of policing', *Theoria*, 61(141): 55-75.

Scheffer, P. (2011) *Immigrant Nations*, Cambridge: Polity Press.

Scheibelhofer, P. (2017) '"It won't work without ugly pictures": images of othered masculinities and the legitimisation of restrictive refugee-politics in Austria', *NORMA International Journal for Masculinity Studies, Special issue: men and migration*, 12(2): 96-111.

Schellekens, (2017) *Inflatable refugee*. Available at: www.dirkschellekens.com/inflatable-refugee/.

Schubert, M. (2007) 'Rudd gets to it, with vows and vision', *The Age* [Online]. 28 November. Available at: www.theage.com.au/news/federal-election-2007-news/rudd-gets-to-it-with-vows-and-vision/2007/11/27/1196036892888.html.

Schuster, L. (2005) 'A Sledgehammer to Crack a Nut: Deportation, Detention and Dispersal in Europe', *Social Policy and Administration*, 39(6): 606-621.

Schwiertz, H. (2016) 'Transformations of the undocumented youth movement and radical egalitarian citizenship', *Citizenship Studies*, 20(5): 610-628.

Sessions, J. (2017) Sessions: Obama's DACA program being rescinded, *CNN Politics* [online], 5 September. Available at: www.cnn.com/videos/politics/2017/09/05/jeff-sessions-daca-decision-sot.cnn.

Sevenhuijsen, S. (1998) *Citizenship and the ethics of care: feminist considerations on justice, morality and politics*. London: Routledge.

Seymour-Smith, S., Wetherell. M. and Phoenix, A. (2002) '"My Wife Ordered Me to Come!': A Discursive Analysis of Doctors' and Nurses' Accounts of Men's Use of General Practitioners'. *Journal of Health Psychology*, 7:253-267.

Sigona, N. (2016) 'There is no refugee crisis in the UK', *Postcards* [Online]. 12 April. Available at: nandosigona.info/2016/04/12/there-is-no-refugee-crisis-in-the-uk/.

Sigona, N. and Humphries, R. (2017) 'Child mobility in the EU's refugee crisis: what are the data gaps and why do they matter?', *Border Criminologies* [Online]. 23 January. Available at: www.law.ox.ac.uk/research-subject-groups/centre-criminology/centreborder-criminologies/blog/2017/01/child-mobility-eu.

Sirriyeh, A. (2014) 'Sanctuary or sanctions: children, social worth and social control in the UK asylum process', in M. Harrison and T. Sanders (eds) *Social policies and social control: New perspectives on the not-so-big society*. Bristol: Policy Press.

Skeggs, B. (1997) *Formations of class and gender*. London: Sage.

Smith, H. (2016) 'The idealists of Lesbos: volunteers at the heart of the refugee crisis', *The Guardian* [Online]. 15 April. Available at: www.theguardian.com/world/2016/apr/15/idealists-of-lesbos-volunteers-refugee-crisis-pope-francis?CMP=Share_iOSApp_Other.

Solomos, J. (2003) *Race and racism in contemporary Britain*, (3rd edn), Basingstoke: Palgrave Macmillan.

Sontag, S. (2003) *Regarding the pains of others*. London: Penguin.

Spellman, E. (1997) *Fruits of sorrow: framing our attention to suffering*, Boston: Beacon Press.

Spivak, G. C. (1988) 'Can the Subaltern Speak?', in C.Nelson and L. Grossberg (eds) *Marxism and the interpretation of culture*, Chicago: University of Illinois Press, pp. 271-316.

Stanton, J., Altin, V., Hall, J., Wells, L. and Sinmaz, E. (2015) 'The final journey of tragic little boys washed up on a Turkish beach: Mother and sons who died in sea tragedy are taken from morgue after heartbroken father says goodbye to the family he couldn't save', *Daily Mail* [Online]. 5 September. Available at: www.dailymail.co.uk/news/article-3219553/Terrible-fate-tiny-boy-symbolises-desperation-thousands-Body-drowned-Syrian-refugee-washed-Turkish-beach-family-tried-reach-Europe.html#ixzz4mWRTbe2F.

Stanton, J. (2015) 'Father of Alan Kurdi angrily hits out at Iraqi mother who accused him of being a 'people smuggler' after she lost two children on same doomed boat ship that killed his family', *Daily Mail*, 11 September. Available at: www.dailymail.co.uk/news/article-3230422/Abdullah-Kurdi-people-smuggler-migrant.html.

Stierl, M. (2016) 'Contestations in death – the role of grief in migration struggles', *Citizenship Studies*, 20(2): 173-191.

Stierl, M. (2017) 'A fleet of Mediterranean border humanitarians', *Antipode*, DOI: 10.1111/anti.12320.

Stumpf, J. (2006) 'The crimmigration crisis: immigrants, crime, and sovereign power', *American University Law Review*, 56(2): 367-419.

'Such a Human #Nauru' (2016) "Don't stop the boats by killing us in offshore" Protest in #Nauru 10-6-2016'Don't stop the boats by killing us in offshore' protest in Nauru, [Online]. 10 June. Available at: twitter.com/suchnigel/status/741260634436698112.

Suhnan, A., Pedersen, A.and Hartley, L. (2012) 'Re-examining prejudice against asylum seekers in Australia: the role of people smugglers, the perception of threat, and acceptance of false beliefs', *The Australian Community Psychologist* 24(2): 79-97.

Sykes, S. (2015) 'Tragic Aylan Kurdi's father was the PEOPLE SMUGGLER driving doomed boat, claims survivor', *Express*, 11 September. Available at: www.express.co.uk/news/world/604535/ Aylan-Kurdi-father-people-smuggler-refugee-crisis.

Swaine, J. (2016) 'White, working-class and angry: Ohio's left behind help Trump to stunning win', *The Guardian* [Online]. 9 November. Available at: www.theguardian.com/us-news/2016/nov/09/donald-trump-ohio-youngstown-voters.

Swerts, T. (2015) 'Gaining a voice: storytelling and undocumented youth activism in Chicago', *Mobilization: An International Quarterly,* 20(3): 345-360.

Taylor, D. (2001) 'Making a spectacle: the mothers of the Plaza de Mayo', *Journal of the Association of Research on Mothering*, 3(2): 97-107.

Terriquez, T. (2015) 'Dreams Delayed: Barriers to Degree Completion among Undocumented Community College Students', *Journal of Ethnic and Migration Studies*, 41(8): 1302-1323.

Thomas, N. (2006) 'The uses of Captain Cook: early exploration in the public history of Aotearoa New Zealand and Australia', in: A. E. Coombes (ed.) *Rethinking settler colonialism: history and memory in Australia, Canada, Aoteroa New Zealand and South Africa*. Manchester: Manchester University Press, pp. 140-155.

Tickle, L. (2015) 'Why we're ready to open our homes to refugees', *The Guardian* [Online]. 5 September. Available at: www.theguardian. com/world/2015/sep/05/why-were-ready-to-open-our-homes-to-refugees.

Ticktin, M. (2014) 'Transnational humanitarianism', *Annual Review of Anthropology*, 43: 273-289.

Tirman, J. (2015) *Dream chasers: immigration and the American backlash*. Cambridge, MA: MIT Press.

Townsend, M. (2015) 'Bishop says Britain has a moral duty to accept refugees from its wars', *The Guardian* [Online]. 15 April. Available at: www.theguardian.com/world/2015/apr/25/uk-moral-duty-accept-refugees-from-wars-david-walker-bishop-manchester.

Townsend, M. (2016) '10,000 refugee children are missing, says Europol', *The Guardian* [Online]. 30 January. Available at: www. theguardian.com/world/2016/jan/30/fears-for-missing-child-refugees?CMP=Share_iOSApp_Other.

Travis, A. and Chrisafis, A. (2016) 'UK immigration minister confirms work to start on £1.9 million Calais wall', *The Guardian* [Online]. 6 September. Available at: www.theguardian.com/world/2016/sep/06/uk-immigration-minister-confirms-work-will-begin-on-big-new-wall-in-calais?CMP=share_btn_tw.

Traynor, I. (2015a) 'Paris attacks: European leaders link terror threats to immigration', *The Guardian* [Online]. 14 November. Available at: www.theguardian.com/world/2015/nov/14/paris-attacks-european-leaders-link-terror-threats-to-immigration.

Traynor, I. (2015b) 'Migrant crisis: EU plan to strike Libya networks could include ground forces', *The Guardian* [Online]. 13 May. Available at: www.theguardian.com/world/2015/may/13/migrant-crisis-eu-plan-to-strike-libya-networks-could-include-ground-forces.

Treacher, A. (2007) 'The future is not there for the making: enduring colonialism, shame and silence', in 6, P., Radstone, S., Squire, C. and Treacher, A. *Public emotions*. Basingstoke: Palgrave, pp. 231-246.

Trilling, D. (2016) 'British hospitality', *LRB blog* [Online]. 19 October. Available at: www.lrb.co.uk/blog/2016/10/19/daniel-trilling/british-hospitality/.

Tronto, J. (1995) 'Caring as the basis for radical political judgments', *Hypatia* 10(2): 141-149.

Trump. D. (2015) 'Remarks announcing candidacy for president in New York City', *The American Presidency Project*. 16 June. [Online]. Available at: www.presidency.ucsb.edu/ws/?pid=110306.

Trump, D. (2016a) 'Immigration reform that will make America great again'. *Trump and Pence make America great again 2016* [Online]. 1 September. Available at: www.donaldjtrump.com/positions/immigrationreform.

Trump, D. (2016b) 'Donald Trump's full immigration speech', *Los Angeles Times* [Online] 31 August 2016. Available at: www.latimes.com/politics/la-na-pol-donald-trump-immigration-speech-transcript-20160831-snap-htmlstory.html.

Tuckman, J. (2015) 'Mexico's migration crackdown escalates dangers for Central Americans', *The Guardian* [Online]. 13 October. Available at: www.theguardian.com/world/2015/oct/13/mexico-central-american-migrants-journey-crackdown.

Tufft, B. (2015) 'Migrant crisis: Greek soldier saved 20 people singlehandedly off Rhodes beach', *Independent* [Online]. 26 April. Available at, www.independent.co.uk/news/world/europe/migrant-crisis-greek-soldier-saved-20-people-singlehandedly-off-rhodes-beach-10205175.html.

Twells, A. (2009) *The civilising mission and the English middle class, 1792-1850: the 'heathen' at home and overseas*, Basingstoke: Palgrave Macmillan.

Tyler, I. (2013) *Revolting subjects: social abjection and resistance in neoliberal Britain*. London: Zed Books.

UCLA Labor Centre (2008) *Underground undergrads*. Los Angeles: UCLA.

Ulloa, J. (2017) 'What you need to know about California's 'sanctuary state' bill and how it would work', *Los Angeles Times* [Online]. 13 April. Available at: www.latimes.com/politics/la-pol-sac-sanctuary-state-bill-explained-20170413-htmlstory.html.

United Nations (UN) (2016) *Summit for Refugees and Migrants – 19 September 2016*. Available at: refugeesmigrants.un.org/summit.

UNHCR (2015a) *Global trends: forced displacement in 2015*. Available at: www.unhcr.org/statistics/unhcrstats/576408cd7/unhcr-global-trends-2015.html.

UNHCR (2015b) *Joint statement on Mediterranean crossings*. Available at: www.unhcr.org/5538d9079.html.

UNHCR (2016) *Submission by the Office of the United Nations High Commissioner for Refugees on the inquiry into the serious allegations of abuse, self-harm and neglect of asylum seekers in relation to the Nauru regional processing centre, and any like allegations in relation to the Manus regional processing centre referred to the senate legal and constitutional affairs committee*. Available at: www.unhcr.org/58362da34.pdf.

UNHCR (2017) *Desperate Journeys: refugees and migrants entering and crossing Europe via the Mediterranean and Western Balkans routes*. Available at: www.unhcr.org/58b449f54.

Unzueta Carrasco, T. and Seif, H. (2014) 'Disrupting the dream: undocumented youth reframe citizenship and deportability through anti-deportation activism', *Latino Studies,* 12(2): 279-299.

US Customs and Border Patrol (CBP) (2014a) *The danger awareness campaign*. Available at: www.dvidshub.net/feature/dangerscampaign#.U76mQ41dXri.

US Customs and Border Patrol (CBP) (2014b) *CBP addresses humanitarian challenges of unaccompanied child migrants*. Available at: www.cbp.gov/border-security/humanitarian-challenges.

Vickers, J. and Isaac, A. (2012) *The politics of race: Canada, United States and Australia*, Toronto: University of Toronto Press.

Virdee, S. (2014) *Racism, class and the racialised outsider*. Basingstoke: Palgrave Macmillan.

Wade, J., Sirriyeh, A., Kohli, R. and Simmonds, J. (2012) *Fostering Unaccompanied Refugee and Asylum Seeking Young People: Creating family life across a 'world of difference'*. London: BAAF.

Waite, L., Valentine, G. and Lewis, H. (2014) Multiply vulnerable populations: mobilising a politics of compassion from the 'capacity to hurt', *Social and Cultural Geography*, 15(3): 313-333.

Walsh, C. (2017) 'White backlash, the 'taxpaying' public, and educational citizenship', *Critical Sociology*, 43(2): 237-247.

Warner, J. (2015) *The emotional politics of social work and child protection*. Bristol: Policy Press.

Watkins, J. (2017) 'Australia's irregular migration information campaigns: border externalization, spatial imaginaries, and extraterritorial subjugation', *Territory, Politics, Governance*, 5(3): 282-303.

Wazana, R. (2004) 'Fear and loathing down under: Australian refugee policy and the national imagination', *Refuge*, 22(1): 83-95.

Weaver, M. (2016) 'Give child refugees dental tests to verify age, says David Davies', *The Guardian*, [Online]. 19 October. Available at: www.theguardian.com/world/2016/oct/19/child-refugees-dental-tests-verify-age-david-davies.

Webb, D. (2016) 'Let them stay campaign a success', *Law Institute Journal*, [Online]. 2 May. Available at: www.liv.asn.au/Staying-Informed/LIJ/LIJ/May-2016/Let-Them-Stay-campaign-a-success.

Werber-Shirk, J. (2015) 'Deviant citizenship: DREAMer activism in the United States and transnational belonging', *Social Sciences*, 4(3): 582-597.

Wetherell, M. (2012) *Affect and emotion: a new social science understanding*. London: Sage.

Whitlock, G. L. (2007) *Soft weapons: autobiography in transit*. Chicago.: The University of Chicago Press.

Wintour, P. (2017) 'Italy considers closing its ports to boats carrying migrants', *The Guardian*, [Online]. 28 June. Available at: www.theguardian.com/world/2017/jun/28/italy-considers-closing-its-ports-to-ships-from-libya.

Withnall, A. (2015) 'Refugees welcome: 100,000 sign Independent petition calling for Britain to 'take its fair share'', *Independent*, [Online]. 3 September. Available at: www.independent.co.uk/news/uk/home-news/refugees-welcome-100000-sign-independent-petition-calling-for-britain-to-take-its-fair-share-10484931.html.

Woolley, A. (2016) 'Narrating the "asylum story": between literary and legal storytelling', *Interventions*, 19(3): 376-394.

Woodward, K. (2004) 'Calculating Compassion' in L. Berlant (ed) *Compassion: the culture and politics of an emotion,* New York: Routledge, pp. 59-86.

Wright, M. (2009) 'Justice and geographies of moral protest: reflections from Mexico', *Environment and Planning D: Society and Space,* 27(2): 216-233.

Zatz, M. and Rodriguez, N. (2015) *Dreams and nightmares: immigration policy, youth and families.* University of California Press.

Index

Note: Page numbers followed by an "n" indicate end-of-chapter notes.

Numbers

9/11 terrorist attack 110

A

AB540 154, 159n
Abbott, Tony 47–48, 81, 83
abolition movement 42
abuse 119–120, 122, 126
Achilli, L. 92
activism 127–136, 136–137
  see also undocumented youth
    movement
affect 22, 26
affective practice 22
affective turn 20–21
agency 31, 104, 105, 109
Agoustinos, M. 70
Ahmed, S. 34, 164
Aliens Act 1905, UK 2, 43
Altsultany, E. 70–71
America
  colonialism 39, 40
  see also United States (US)
Amin, A. 93
Amini, Abas 126–127
analytical approach 14–15
Anderson, Bridget 80
Arendt, H. 26, 29–30
Aristotle 29
art 161
  see also Center for Political
    Beauty; performance activism

assemblage metaphor 8–9
asylum regimes 136
asylum seekers 19, 102–103
  agency 104–105
  Australia 12–13, 126.
  see also irregular maritime arrivals
    (IMAs)
  criminalisation of 107
  Germany 56
  United Kingdom (UK) 12,
    48–49, 56
Australia
  Border Force Act 2015 122
  colonialism 39, 40, 41–42, 63
  criminalisation of migration
    47–48
  historic immigration policy 43,
    44–45
  national identity 70
  offshore detention centres 12, 47,
    48, 81, 162
  resistance 4–5, 14, 107–109,
    123–125, 126, 127–136
  testimonies 59, 118–122
  Operation Sovereign Borders
    (OSB) 12–13, 13–14, 48,
    92–93, 125–126
  Pacific Solution 12, 48, 78, 80,
    105, 121–122, 163–164
  people smugglers 80, 81, 83, 84,
    88–93, 107
  Ration Challenge 69

Syrian and Iraqi Humanitarian Programme 105–109
undesirable immigrants 2, 43, 44

B

babies 123, 124
Banks, Joseph 39
Bassel, L. 140
Bauman, Zygmunt 110
benevolent colonialism 40–42
Berati, Reza 119
biolegitimacy 103
boat people 47
  see also irregular maritime arrivals (IMAs)
Boltanski, L. 31, 55, 66, 164
Boochani, Behrouz 118, 119, 136
border enforcement 78–79, 80, 120
  see also offshore detention centres; Operation Sovereign Borders (OSB), Australia; people smugglers
Border Force Act 2015, Australia 122
Border Grannies 133
Brent, Linda 35
"Bring Them Here" protest 14, 124–125, 132
British colonialism 38–42, 63
Brokenshire, James 82
Brown, K. 103, 165
Burkitt, I. 22
Bush, George H.W. 28
Butler, J. 130

C

Cameron, David 4, 57, 72, 73, 97
care, feminist ethics of 34, 130–136, 158
Center for Political Beauty 5–6
children
  abuse 119
  children overboard incident 48
  colonialism 41–42, 63, 64
  compassion for 53, 57
  Dubs programme 58, 73–74, 161

Grandmothers Against Detention of Refugee Children 130, 131, 133, 134, 135
"Let Them Stay" campaign 123
see also Kurdi, Alan; unaccompanied minors; undocumented youth movement
Chinese immigrants 43–44
Christmas Island 91
civilisation 39
civilising process 39–42
Clinton, Bill 28
"Close The Camp" protest 14, 124–125, 127–128, 135
Cohen, S. 30–31, 162
collectivisation 153–154
colonialism 37, 64, 136–137
  early colonialism 38–40
  second empire and benevolent colonialism 40–42
coloniality of power 10–11
compassion 2–3
  assemblage metaphor 8–9
  as a basic social emotion 9–11
  and colonialism 39–42
  definitions 26, 28–30, 38, 66, 99, 110, 166
  DREAM Act, US 5
  Europe 4, 5–6
  and outrage 79
  politics of 27–28, 30–34
  and resistance 52–53
  resistance to 2
  as solidarity 34–35, 166–167
  and vulnerability 165–166
compassion fatigue 32
compassionate conservatism 28, 33–34
compassionate refusal 2, 34, 98–99
compassionate resistance 2
compassionate violence 78–81
Cook, James 39, 41
criminalisation
  of asylum seekers 107
  of migration 45–49, 147, 151, 156–157
  of solidarity 93–94
criminality 114
crisis discourse 3

Customs and Border Patrol (CBP), US 87–88

D

Daily Mail 68–69
Danewid, I. 136
Danger Awareness Campaign, US 86–88
data 15–16
Davies, David 61
decision-making 22
Deferred Action for Childhood Arrivals (DACA), US 5, 141, 145, 146–147, 151
Deferred Action for Parents of Americans and Lawful Permanent Residents (DAPA), US 151
democratisation 43–44
denial 30–31, 119–120
Denmark 94
Derrida, J. 163
deservingness 31, 48–49, 142
detention centres
  Australia 12, 47, 48, 81, 162
  resistance 4–5, 14, 107–109, 123–125, 126, 127–136
  testimonies 59, 118–122
  United Kingdom (UK) 49
  United States (US) 155
discourse analysis 14–15
discrimination, reverse 111–116
discursive turn 20
diversity patriotism 70–71
Douzinas, Costas 80
DREAM Act, US 5, 14, 141
  DREAM Act campaign 142–152
Dreamer narrative 156
Dublin Regulation 72
Dubs programme 58, 73–74, 161
Duncan Smith, Ian 27, 28
Durbin, Richard 145
Dutton, Peter 92, 93, 106, 108–109, 119

E

Eastern European immigrants 49
Eaten Fish 118–119, 126

Emotional Politics of Race, The (Ioanide, 2015) 25
emotionalisation 23, 27–28
emotions 7–8, 16, 64, 143, 162–163
  definition 22
  hostile emotions 24–26
  humanising emotions 8, 26, 28
  political emotions 23–24
  and racism 111
  and resistance 52–53
  and social relations 20–22
  see also compassion; hostility
empathy 26, 69, 135
ethical theorising 136
ethnicity 67
eudaimonistic judgement 29, 64–65, 110
Europe
  criminalisation of solidarity 93–94
  people smugglers 81–83
  perceived superiority 37, 39
  response to refugee crisis 3–4, 5–6, 110, 136, 161–162
European Commission 82
Evans, B. 33, 59–60
Every, D. 70
experiential-based campaigns 69
Express 69–70
eyewitnessing 54

F

facts 52, 53, 111
Fasenfest, D. 111
Fassin, D. 32–33, 102, 103
feelings 22
  see also emotions
feminist ethics of care 34, 130–136, 158
France 32–33
Freedland, J. 59
Friends, Families and Feminists Against Detention 135

G

Garber, M. 29
gender 42, 84
  see also feminist ethics of care

Germany 4, 56, 72
Gill, N. 166
Gillard, Julia 91
Giroux, H. 93, 94
Grandmothers Against Detention of Refugee Children 130, 131, 133, 134, 135
grief-activism 130
Guardian 59, 67, 72, 119, 125

H

Hochschild, A. 110, 115
Hoggett, P. 20–21, 31, 32
hostility 7, 24–26, 34
Howard, John 47, 163–164
Human Rights Law Centre (HRLC) 123
human rights regime 80
human trafficking 94
    see also people smugglers
humanising emotions 8, 26, 28
    see also compassion
humanitarianism 79–80, 93–94, 97, 102–103
humanity 80
hunger strike 126

I

identity 130, 154
ideological dilemmas 15
Illegal Immigration Reform and Immigrant Responsibility Act 1996, US 46
illegal migrants 45–49, 105–106, 115
    see also irregular maritime arrivals (IMAs); undocumented immigrants
Immigrant Youth Justice League (IYJL), US 149
immigrants 45–46, 49
    see also illegal migrants; undesirable immigrants; undocumented immigrants
Immigration Act 1971, UK 45
Immigration and Nationality Act 1965, US 44, 46
immigration policy
    1890s to 200s 42–49

and emotions 23–26
Immigration Reform and Control Act 1986, US 46
implicatory denial 119–120
Incidents in the Life of a Slave Girl (Jacobs, 1861) 35
Independent 57, 72
Inflatable Refugee 161
International Development Committee (IDC) 58
interpretive repertoires 15
Ioanide, P. 25, 163
Irish immigrants 43
irregular maritime arrivals (IMAs) 81, 106–109, 121
Isaac, A. 43

J

Jacobs, Harriet 35
Jewish immigrants 43
Johnson, J. 133, 164
Johnson-Reed Act 1924, US 44

K

Kahazai, Hamid 119
Kindertransport 73, 74–75
Kurasawa, F. 53, 54
Kurdi, Alan 13, 51, 53, 55–56, 144
    eudaimonistic judgement 65
    media coverage 55, 59, 60–64, 65–68, 69–70, 72
    visual testimony 59–60

L

Latinx immigration 45–46
Lauby, F. 143
Leggeri, Fabrice 94
"Let Them Stay" campaign 5, 14, 123–124
Levinas, E. 30
liberal terror 33
listening 140
Lowe, L. 39

M

majority world 18n
Manifest Destiny 39

Manus Island detention centre 5,
    12, 47, 121, 162
  resistance 125
  testimonies 118–122
Manzo, K. 64
Marcus, G. 23–24
Masoumali, Omid 108, 125
Massoumi, N. 84
maternal activism 130–136
May, Theresa 100–101, 104, 107
McMahon, S. 15
media coverage 58
  Alan Kurdi 55, 59, 60–64, 65–68,
    69–70, 72
  maternal activism 133
  see also specific newspapers
medical conditions 102
Mercer, Johnny 77
Merkel, Angela 4, 56, 72
Mestrovic, S. 31
Mexican immigrants 45–46
migrant sea crossings 3
migrants see immigrants
military intervention 33
minority world 2, 18n
Mirror 61–62
modernity 39
moral reform 41
moral spectatorship 55
Morrison, Scott 83, 84, 90, 107,
    119
Mortensen, M. 55
Mums4Refugees 129, 131, 133,
    134–135, 135–136

N

national identity 70
Nauru detention centre see
    resistance 12, 47, 121
  abuse 119–120
  resistance 5, 14, 108–109,
    123–125, 127–129
negative emotions see hostility
neoliberalism 31
Nicholls, W. 143, 153
"No to people smuggling," Australia
    88–89, 90–92
Nussbaum, M.
  compassion 29, 30, 110, 143

eudaimonistic judgement 64, 65
political emotions 23, 24,
    162–163

O

Obama, Barack
  Deferred Action for Childhood
    Arrivals (DACA) 5, 140–141,
    145, 146–147
  Deferred Action for Parents
    of Americans and Lawful
    Permanent Residents (DAPA)
    151
  deportation 97
  UN Summit for Refugees and
    Migrants 2016 161
  unaccompannied minors 85–86
offshore detention centres 12, 47,
    48, 81, 162
  resistance 4–5, 14, 107–109,
    123–125, 126, 127–136
  testimonies 118–122
  visual testimony 59
Oliver, Kelly 54
Operation Sophia 82
Operation Sovereign Borders
    (OSB), Australia 12–13, 13–14,
    48, 92–93, 125–126
outrage 79
overseas public information
    campaigns (OPICs) 85
  Australia 88–92
  United States (US) 86–88

P

Pacific Solution, Australia 12, 48,
    78, 80, 105, 121–122, 163–164
pain 32, 34, 154–155
people smugglers 79
  Australian response to 80, 81, 83,
    84, 88–93, 107
  European response to 81–83
  United Kingdom response to
    81–82
  United States response to 80,
    85–88
performance activism 129–130
  see also Center for Political Beauty
Perkowski, N. 79–80

Peterie, M. 164
Phillips, Alison 61–63
philosophy 22
pity 29, 30, 31–32
political cultural scripts 11
political emotions 23–24
political listening 140
politics of compassion 27–28,
    30–34
Porter Novelli 89
post-emotional era 31–32
post-truth world 20
power, coloniality of 10–11
protests *see* activism; resistance
proxy bodies 127–130
public information campaigns *see*
    overseas public information
    campaigns (OPICs)

R

race 25
  reverse discrimination 111–116
racism 43–45, 111
Ration Challenge 69
reason 21–22
reasoning 30
refugee crisis 3–4, 5–6, 110, 136,
    161–162
refugee sea crossings 3
Refugee Week 2017 161
refugees 48–49, 101–103, 161–164
  see also irregular maritime arrivals
    (IMAs); undesirable immigrants
"Refugees Welcome" movement
    57
religion 39
resistance 11
  and emotion 52–53
  offshore detention centres 4–5,
    14, 107–109, 123–125, 126,
    127–136
  United Kingdom (UK) 126–127
  United States (US) 127
resistance to compassion 2
responsibilisation 86, 107–108
reverse discrimination 111–116
Richards, B. 23
Rudd, Kevin 48, 81

S

Sanchez, G. 90, 92
sea crossings 3
Second World War 73, 74–75
shame 71
slavery 35, 38, 42
social media 55, 59, 65, 67
social relations 20–22
sociality of pain 34
sociology 21
solidarity 34–35, 93–94, 158,
    166–167
Spellman, E. 35
States of Denial (Cohen, 2001)
    30–31
Stierl, M. 129, 130
storytelling 141–142, 142–143,
    153–154, 156–158
subject positions 15
Sun 55, 65–66, 67–68, 77
Swerts, T. 153
Syrian and Iraqi Humanitarian
    Programme, Australia 105–109
Syrian Vulnerable Persons
    Resettlement Programme
    (SVPRP), UK 57, 73, 99–105

T

Tampa Affair 47
Tea Party 115
teenagers 61
  see also undocumented young
    people; undocumented youth
    movement
terrorist attacks 110
testimony 53, 54–55, 66–67, 69
  offshore detention centres 118–
    122
  suffering body as 125–127
  undocumented young people
    140, 143–145, 145–146, 147–
    149, 151–152, 153, 154–158
  visual testimony 59–60
  see also storytelling; witness
    bearing
Thomas, N. 41
Thompson, S. 20–21
Ticktin, M. 102, 103
trafficking 94

see also people smugglers
Trez, H.J. 55
Tronto, J. 134
Trudeau, Justin 27
Trump, Donald 110–116
Turnbull, Malcolm 27, 97
Twitter 67
Tyler, I. 126–127

U

UN High Commissioner for
  Refugees (UNHCR) 82,
  99–100, 125
unaccompanied minors 58, 61,
  73–74, 85
undesirable immigrants 2, 6–7,
  43–44, 82
undocumented immigrants 13, 19,
  46, 103, 140
undocumented young people
  140–141
undocumented youth movement 5,
  16, 139, 140, 141–142, 152–159
  DREAM Act campaign 142–146,
  147, 148–152
United Kingdom (UK)
  asylum seekers 12, 48–49, 56
  colonialism 38–42, 63
  detention centres 49
  historic immigration policy 43,
    45
  Kindertransport 74–75
  people smugglers 81–82
  pro-asylum discourse 70–71
  refugee crisis 13, 55–58
  resistance 126–127
  Syrian Vulnerable Persons
    Resettlement Programme
    (SVPRP) 57, 73, 99–105
  unaccompanied minors 58, 61,
    73–74
  undesirable immigrants 43
United Nations (UN)
  1951 Refugee Convention 106
  Summit for Refugees and
    Migrants 2016 19
United States (US)
  abolition movement 42

criminalisation of migration
  45–47, 147, 151, 156–157
Deferred Action for Childhood
  Arrivals (DACA) 5, 141, 145,
  146–147, 151
Deferred Action for Parents
  of Americans and Lawful
  Permanent Residents (DAPA)
  151
DREAM Act 5, 14, 141
  DREAM Act campaign 142–
    152
people smugglers 80, 85–88
presidential election 2016 110–
  111
  Trump campaign 111–116
resistance 127
undesirable immigrants 2, 42–44
undocumented immigrants 13,
  19, 46, 140
undocumented young people
  140–141
undocumented youth movement
  5, 16, 139, 140, 141–142,
  152–159
  DREAM Act campaign 142–
    146, 147, 148–152
see also America

V

Vickers, J. 43
victimization 110–116
vigils 129
violence 33
violent humanitarianism 80
visual testimony 59–60
voter behaviour 23–24
vulnerability 101–105, 165–166
Vulnerable Person Relocation
  Scheme see Syrian Vulnerable
  Persons Resettlement
  Programme (SVPRP), UK

W

Waite, L. 26, 31, 115
war story 84
Wetherell, M. 22
whistle-blowers 122

Whistleblowers, Activists and
    Citizens Alliance (WACA),
    Australia 128
Whitlock, G.L. 54
witness bearing 34–35, 53–55, 69,
    120, 154–155
  see also testimony
women 42
Woodward, K. 27–28
Woolley, A. 53
World War II 73, 74–75
Wright, M. 133–134, 135

Y

Yasin, Hodan 108
young people 61
  see also undocumented young
    people; undocumented youth
    movement